Wise and Foolish Virgins

Wise and Foolish Virgins

*White Women at Work in the Feminized
World of Primary School Teaching*

Sally Campbell Galman

LEXINGTON BOOKS
Lanham • Boulder • New York • Toronto • Plymouth, UK

Published by Lexington Books
A wholly owned subsidiary of The Rowman & Littlefield Publishing Group, Inc.
4501 Forbes Boulevard, Suite 200, Lanham, Maryland 20706
www.lexingtonbooks.com

10 Thornbury Road, Plymouth PL6 7PP, United Kingdom

British Library Cataloguing in Publication Information Available

Library of Congress Cataloging-in-Publication Data

Galman, Sally Campbell.
  Wise and foolish virgins : white women at work in the feminized world of primary
school teaching / Sally Galman.
     p. cm.
  Summary: "Wise and Foolish Virgins: White Women at Work in the Feminized World
of Primary School Teaching by Sally Campbell Galman asks the question, what does
it mean for an entire profession to be numerically dominated by white women, and
what is the relationship between teacher preparation and professional feminization?
Galman provides a sharp, unflinching look at the landscape of a profession on the verge
of transformation and offers a frank assessment of where teacher education must go in
order to maintain its relevance in the new economy." — Provided by publisher.
  ISBN 978-0-7391-4771-9 (hardback) — ISBN 978-0-7391-4773-3 (electronic)
  1. Women teachers—Professional relationships—United States. 2. Primary school
teachers—Professional relationships—United States. 3. Sex differences in education—
United States. 4. Feminism and education—United States. I. Title.
  LB2837.G35 2012
  371.10082—dc23   2011049544

Printed in the United States of America

Contents

~

Introduction

Young wives are the leading asset of corporate power. They want the suburbs, a house, a settled life, and respectability. They want society to see that they have exchanged themselves for something of value.

—Nader, 2009

Women are the only exploited group in history to have been idealized into powerlessness.

—Jong, 2003, p. 21

At midnight, there was a cry, "Behold, the bridegroom! Come out to meet him!" Then all those virgins got up and trimmed their lamps.

—Book of Matthew, 5:6–7

During a recent visit to Spain I had the opportunity to tour a village church and its eleventh-century cloister. Each of the twinned pillars that lined the cloister walk was adorned with intricate carvings of young women, some obviously self-satisfied, others in equally obvious distress. A guide explained to me that these were an illustration of the story of the Wise and Foolish Virgins, retold by St. Matthew in the Christian bible as a teaching story, or parable. To quickly sum up: ten virgins attend a wedding, and each brings with her a lit oil lamp to greet the bridegroom and usher him into the wedding celebration. Half of the virgins have the presence of mind to bring extra oil with them, while the other half light their lamps and assume the oil they have will last them until the bridegroom's arrival. To their great disappointment, the bridegroom is late, and the "Wise" virgins have more oil to keep their lamps burning while the "Foolish" ones do not. Like so many contemporary squabbling preteen girls whose bullying behaviors have a distinct relationship to their nascent understandings of gender and power, the Wise Virgins refuse to share, so the Foolish ones are sent to the shops to buy more and are subsequently absent when the bridegroom does arrive. He is met only by the Wise Virgins and their still-glowing lamps. The wedding party moves inside and bars its doors, and the Foolish Virgins, upon their return, are left outside, in darkness, to wail and weep at the fruit of their folly for all time. At one point they knock on the door and the bridegroom appears at the battlements above, shouting out, "I do not know you." He does not let them in. They were, after all, unprepared for his arrival and end up locked out of the ultimate party.

I was struck by the many possible interpretations of this teaching story, but one in particular stayed with me: goodness and badness, or wiseness and foolishness, are rigid categorizations that tend to stick—or, as Goffman (1963) would say, they are permanent valued or stigmatized identities, respectively. Drawing upon Goffman's work on identity, which is explained in further detail in chapter 1, I think of individual identity as performative; I thought about how young women in contemporary girl culture fret over appearances and the identity performance, per se. Perhaps they are aware that a poor performance of valued gender identity results in being "locked out" of both a valued identity and, in the end, the desired moral career. I looked sympathetically on the Foolish Virgins. Maybe they stepped out beyond the expected performance of a valued feminine gender identity and were punished for it, and I certainly identified with them more than I did the Wise, who assured themselves a place at the wedding party by playing to patriarchy and forsaking their fellows. The Wise Virgin plans ahead, expertly performs the valued feminine gender identity, and reaps the rewards—in part by shunning those other women who erred, who stepped out of line, who thought perhaps of their own convenience before that of the imagined, ever-anticipated and perseverated-upon bridegroom. I was also left wondering if the storyteller, and artist, took some degree of dramatic license in their portrayal of the Foolish Virgins—maybe missing the party wasn't the tragedy it seemed.

Elementary and early childhood teaching are "feminized"—meaning, that this is a profession where there tends to be large numbers of female workers, with recent estimates indicating that approximately 90 percent or greater of all P–6 teachers are female. This book presents one story of the gendered work and worlds of the white, middle-class females who dominate contemporary U.S. elementary-level teaching and teacher preparation contexts and their vision of becoming teachers as the work of care. It also examines how one kind of girl culture, emphasizing the anticipatory socialization of the iconic wife and mother, is both critiqued and reinforced in schools of education through the relationship between young, white women who will become teachers; the popular cultural and academic environment; and the perspectives of some of the women who teach them. How do preservice teachers navigate learning to do something they see as biologically based and "natural" while also enacting a valued self? To that end, this book will seek to:

- Describe the experience of doing historical "women's work" in the contemporary popular cultural context.
- Explore preservice teachers' stories of engaging with gendered work and (re)constructing identity in the midst of both hegemonically masculine and radically feminized school and schooling contexts.
- Disrupt the established scripts for gender, self, vocation and expectation, asking, what are the experiences of young, white women becoming teachers? What are the spaces that separate and connect these experiences?
- Offer pragmatic suggestions for teacher educators seeking to trouble dichotomies and support transgressive trajectories.

Background: Nice Girls and Women's Work

The vast majority of new elementary level preservice and novice teachers in the United States are young, white women from middle-class socioeconomic backgrounds (Cornbleth, 2008; Hollins & Guzman, 2005; Suarez-Orozco, 2000; Zumwalt & Craig, 2005). Many are attracted to the K–6 classroom because, in the popular US sociocultural context, it is a setting that can reward compliance and conformity (deMarrais & LeCompte, 1998; Dworkin, 1987) and emphasize adherence to valued female identity implied in dominant-culture, white, middle-class Western feminine norms. Many female preservice teachers can exhibit some of the same behaviors Holland and Eisenhart (1992) saw in their white, female participants: a marked need to please, to conform, and to be seen as "good girls" to the exclusion of conflict, critique, or political stances and activities (Campbell, 2005; Galman, 2006). This often resulted in these young women appearing to be socially conservative (Ginsburg, 1995) and to resist identification with the feminist movement or critical analyses of gender, irrespective of their actual beliefs and experiences (Hall & Rodriguez, 2003; McCabe, 2005). Jeopardizing their status as "good girls" would effectively lock them out of the proverbial "wedding party" or, as Goffman (1959) would suggest, prevent their attainment and maintenance of valued social identity forcing them to instead accept stigmatized, or undesirably, social or personal identity. For many participants in my research in this arena, one of the greatest penalties associated with a stigmatized identity is being excluded from the metaphorical "wedding party" or similar perceived affective and material rewards for performing the valued identity over time, the work of maintaining a "moral career" (Goffman, 1963).

Teacher education, meanwhile, has long aimed to challenge preservice teachers' prior knowledge, beliefs, and experiences about children and schools, privilege and oppression, and even social identity and teachers' work (Hollins & Guzman, 2005). The call for teacher education programs to explicitly address the challenge of preparing a predominantly white, middle class and female teaching force to work effectively with an increasingly diverse population of students is resounding, as is the call to diversify the teaching force itself (Darling-Hammond et al., 2002, 2006; Ladson-Billings, 1989; Sleeter, 2008). With regard to the former, the important work is complicated by teacher educators' own positionalities and work worlds: the majority of teacher educators are white, middle class women (Grant & Gillette, 1987; Tokarczyk, 1988) from a similar demographic as their preservice students. It is possible that many of them could be participating in socializing girls and women rather than in challenging valued identities and interrogating preservice women's reluctance to politicize their work, critically examine their gendered, raced, and classed habitus and transgress "niceness." In other words, we as teacher educators may be protective of and intent upon managing and preserving our enactments of valued identities (and subsequent moral careers). This could be one means by which we perpetuate a rigid system of stigmatized and valued identities for preservice women despite our insistence and good-faith belief that we are critical teacher educators whose students just "aren't getting it" year after year. We typically attribute this to their recalcitrance, or disinterest, or stupidity, or all of the above when in fact we cocreate that world with them and may be complicit (Galman, Pica-Smith, & Rosenberger, 2009).

Compounding this, teacher educators' work worlds further complicate their relationships with their students and the academy; as Liston (1995) suggests, faculty who work in preservice teacher preparation in particular engage in a "low-status, messy, student-centered, and labor-intensive endeavor" even within the low-status world of education that is the academic equivalent of women's unremunerated domestic labor when compared with the high-status, high-reward, public work of individuals who position them-selves as primarily writers and researchers (pp. 91–93). Liston's metaphor is apt: the majority of teacher educators working in the elementary licensure areas are women (deMarrais & LeCompte, 1998; Grant & Gillette, 1987), and their work, with its close proximity to and connection with young chil-dren, families, and care creates an even messier, more low-status and some would argue, more profound locus of historical powerlessness than is found at secondary levels, where a focus on subject matter—literature, science, mathematics, or history—carries with it some of the prestige of academia and less of the stigma of childcare, the domestic sphere and with that, "women's work" (Hoffman, 2003).

Data Sources

This analysis is the product of several connected qualitative studies seeking to understand women's experiences in teacher education and teacher educa-tors' experiences as women. The observations herein are a result of my on-going work as principal investigator in these studies, which span from 2002 to the present. The participants whose data are included in these analyses are all white, female preservice teachers in primary-grade teacher educa-tion programs at two large public universities in Northeastern and Western states and one small, private Midwestern college respectively.[1] While the teacher education programs involved enthusiastically embraced a critical and intellectual approach to teacher education and development, they also experienced varying degrees of friction between faculty and students. These were alternately blamed upon the perceived disconnect between theory and practice, poor student aptitude, faculty disconnectedness, or any number of other possible explanations, all of which varied wildly in student and faculty experiences.

In exploring preservice teacher experience (and, by extension, the expe-riences of teacher education faculty), I had to position myself as a research participant to some degree. This meant expanding data collection to include ethnography (examining preservice teachers and, tangentially, other teacher educators) and a small amount of self-study (my own practice as a teacher educator). That said, as I worked in teacher education while doing the data collection and analyses, I continually felt as though I was in the unenviable position of being what Whitehead calls "a living contradiction" (1993). Ja-nus-like, I talked about equity and critical awareness while at the same time having an inkling that my actions as a teacher educator told a different story than reinforced the very performances I was trying to interrogate. Getting to

the bottom of my own practice from a critical perspective required me to enter into an unfamiliar juxtaposition between the researcher and researched.
As Pinnegar (1998) writes,

> While the methods and methodologies of self-study are not much different
> from the other research methods, self-study is methodologically unique . . .
> although participant observation, ethnographic, grounded theory or statistical
> methods might be used in any single study, self-study involves a different philo-
> sophical and political stance . . . researchers who embrace self-study through
> the simple act of choosing to study their own practice, present an alternative
> relationship to the researcher and the researched. (p. 31)

To this end I employed a combination of ethnographic and self-study data
collection methods further augmented by a quantitative measure. In this way,
(1) my experience of the context becomes a focus of inquiry to further define
context by "make[ing] the researcher's own experience a topic of investiga-
tion in its own right" (Ellis & Bochner, 2000, pp. 733); and (2) program
practices, policies, and interactions are simultaneously captured using the
"wide net" of ethnographic data collection methods including interviews,
artifact collection, and observation. Recursive analysis, like the data collection process, was guided by the operationalization of concepts and close
auditing of an evolving conceptual framework. Overarching grounded theory
(Strauss & Corbin, 1990) analyses focused on themes derived from analyses
of field notes, transcripts, and other data texts. While concepts of validity
and reliability may be inappropriate in this context, standards of rigor were
addressed by an attention to "trustworthiness" as defined by Mishler (1990).
To that end, primary texts are included to the greatest degree possible in the
analyses and presentation of data and data collection and analysis methodologies are presented in great detail and their relationship to interpretation
made transparent.

The quantitative measure that was a supplement to one of the qualitative
data sources was the CFNI, or *Conformity to Feminine Norms Index*, developed
by Mahalik et al. (2005) to measure adherence to Western feminine norms.
While I was not able to administer the multiple choice index to all of the research participants with whom I have worked since 2002, the 100 plus white,
middle class, female preservice teachers whose results I do have showed
some interesting patterns. Adherence to "Western feminine norms" constitutes a great deal of the "readiness" required of the Wise Virgin. Isolated
by Mahalik et al. (2005) in his work to develop an inventory of conformity
to these norms, they consist of items that related to areas like "niceness,"

"focus on appearance," "interest in children," "sexual fidelity" (implicit in this heterosexuality and femininity), "modesty," "thinness," and "involvement in romantic relationships," "investment in appearance," and "focus on domesticity." It is not surprising here, and in the qualitative data, that the appearance of goodness and niceness was of great importance—but that it was more important than "interest in children" was surprising. When I first became aware of this trend, and when it became a central, pivotal point in the data analysis, was when I began to see that appearance of niceness, goodness, and attractiveness were the primary indicators of being a "good teacher" and, more importantly, constituted the valued identity of contemporary white, middle-class femininity. These two appeared to be one in the same.

Wise and Foolish

While there were many degrees of complexity in individual data, the story of being and becoming a primary-level teacher fell into two distinct groups of experiences. Rather like the introductory parable, the study participants were either engaged in what Goffman (1963) calls "role-making" or "role-taking"—the former being much more about creating a role in one's own image, and taking the risks to established valued identity that go with potential disobedience to the tropes of girl culture. The latter, meanwhile, is a pragmatic, safer choice, by which established, safer roles are taken up and individuals made to fit those parameters, rather than the other way around. It could be said that the latter focuses her energy on impression management, on the appearance of ideal and the enactment of the valued identity and established role. This is difficult work, as it is much more laborious to be at all times producing visible evidence of one's idealized femininity and self as object than to be simply an authentic subject living day to day life. It also implies a good bit of eager anticipatory socialization for the established role, which more often than not included preparation for marriage and motherhood—the Wise Virgin engaged in literal "readiness" for the bridegroom's gaze. This focus on the appearance of readiness is also deeply inscribed in girl culture:

- Be a feminine heterosexual and adheres to most, if not all, the Western feminine norms (Mahalik et al., 2005).
- Construct self as an object, resulting in a focus on the primary work of vigilant impression management most clearly visible in a focus on

niceness and appearance, political conservatism, and distancing self from critical, feminist stances.

- Have as her primary motivation to be a teacher an affective orientation: caring and loving, and being loved in return by children.
- Believe that teachers are born, not made, and women make better teachers of children than men most of the time. The central qualification for elementary teaching is to love the children.
- Have a general expectation that teaching is a means by which a successful moral career can begin, rather like an entry-level position with an eye on being well-prepared, for marriage and motherhood. In this way, patriarchy is generally not seen as a problem for many preservice teachers.

Meiners's (2002) description of a student fits the bill perfectly:

> On the first day of class, I routinely ask everyone to "briefly introduce yourself and to tell the class a little something about why you are here"—an exercise I always found so painful yet I now replicate, for convention. Invariably, the majority of the female students in my classes begin to evoke the same figure. This lady—the future elementary teacher—has always loved children. Her mother, her husband or boyfriend (even strangers in the streets) have remarked upon her natural aptitude with children and small animals. She is gracious, nurturing, often soft-spoken, and is usually married (or engaged). The words money, career, union, labor, or even job are rarely mentioned—leaving listeners with the impression that she does not need to rely solely on her income as a teacher to survive. For her, teaching is a calling or a vocation, and she has always known that she wanted to be a (elementary school) teacher. Often, despite a chaotic schedule, she volunteers through her church with special needs children in her spare time. Sometimes, a redemptive narrative circulates: she has always had a desire to save underprivileged children. (p. 89)

Meiners conceptualizes this as the legacy of "Lady Bountiful"—a white, middle or upper class woman doing the semimissionary "good work" of civilizing the "native" (p. 87). She suggests that one of many problems with Lady Bountiful is that her influence is as the fore of a racist, heterosexist, classist endeavor to regulate which bodies make acceptable teachers and which do not. White women, Meiners suggests, were historically used as colonizing and control agents through the call to teach, a call that emphasized the moral career embodied by the "Lady Bountiful" ideal. This may be one of the pernicious barriers to the diversification of the teaching force, as will be discussed in subsequent chapters. However, it is the performance of self and the vigilance enacted by this Wise Virgin that suggests it is practiced and iconic, not just in the popular girl culture but also within the walls of the school of education.

The other trend toward role-making, what I might call the pattern among the fewer, more diverse "Foolish Virgins" embodies risk. While other participants were ever-ready and always performing, the Foolish Virgin may have taken time off from school, been directionless, be unsure of her life trajectory, or aspire to arenas that are decidedly outside the comfort zone of the vocational sure thing. They may be older than most preservice teachers. Instead of college→teacher education program→classroom→marriage→ motherhood, other trajectories may be less targeted at specific moral careers (here the moral career of the wife and mother). They may construct teaching as work independent of love. They may not "love" children. They may complain about the low status of teaching, about gendered work, about pay without giving the typical moral nod to "love" making it all "worth it" despite financial and social insult. They may not be conscious of themselves as object performances. For the Foolish Virgin, teachers are made, not born and the work of the teacher can be comprised as a body of skills that can be taught and operationalized. In sum, their deviance creates third spaces, new options, exceptions to rules and a host of problems for the pat and formulaic.

Teacher educators, especially white, middle-class, female teacher educators, may share an experience of white girl culture with their students regardless of obvious generational differences. And, like many classroom teachers, they often conflate performed valued identity with content mastery (deMarrais & LeCompte, 1998; Galman, 2009a). In this case, some teacher educators see some preservice teachers' performances of desirable, valued identity—loving children, niceness, attractiveness, and so on—as one in the same with being a "good teacher." Just as popular film and literature affirm that goodness is equated with physical attractiveness, so also good teachers are attractive ones, while bad teachers are ugly (Bauer, 1998). Those who have learned impression management are "good students" and good prospective teachers. Teacher education is partly the work of, as Meiners (2002) suggests, regulating which bodies make acceptable teachers in the image of "Lady Bountiful" (p. 87). Sensitive to the risks of transgression themselves, and all too aware of their own status in the academy and their own schools of education (Liston, 1995), many teacher educators do not want to make anyone feel too uncomfortable.

By not questioning the popular cultural interpretation of teachers and teaching, including the popular narrative of teaching as the work of love, the teacher educator (and teacher education programs) may find themselves in a bind. For many, to do the critical work, reflective work of high quality teacher education programs must ask her students to critique, even abandon, the moral career of the wife and mother. So, the question for teacher educators is between the bad and worse: receiving bad evaluations for failure to "deliver" the grade, the "correct" experience, the suburban placement; failure to get tenure or to generate credit hours via low enrollments; being "difficult," and therefore constructed as a "bad colleague," a "bad professor," or a "bad teacher"—and nobody likes that no matter how tough, how Wise or how Foolish they think they are.

Reader's Guide

As per the stated goals of the text, the following eight chapters are grouped into three sections, each addressing one particular area of interest. Part I, "Care and Reason," provides the theoretical and empirical background for contextualizing the raced, classed, and gendered experience of doing "women's work" in girl culture. Chapter 1, "The Windy Side of Care: Doing the Work of Love" introduces the theoretical framework that will be used to shape data analysis. It incorporates Goffman's (1963) identity theories with Etzioni's (1969) and Griffiths's (2006) theories of work, self, and gender and other theories of love and care. Chapter 2, "No Other but a Woman's Reason: Notes on the Feminized Profession," continues with an in-depth review of the relevant research literature, especially as it relates to contemporary and historical characterizations of teaching as a "feminized" profession and how that may play out in popular media-saturated contemporary girl culture, teacher preparation, and the "domestic ideologies" (Drudy, Martin, Woods, & O'Flynn, 2005) of the public sphere.

Part II, "Learning to Work in the Shadow of Iconic Girlhood," delves into the data sets, with detailed analyses of narratives of the young women involved in the studies, examining individual participant experiences with identity, work, and the popular cultural milieu. Chapter 3 presents a short overview of study methods, while chapters 4 through 6 present the stories of participants from the three research sites, Mountain University, Valley University, and Prairie College. Individual cases from across the data sets illustrate the themes that emerged from data analysis, building upon the theoretical model presented in chapter 1.

Part III, "New Stories of Love and Transgression," interprets and builds upon the stories presented in part II by chapter 7. "For Goodness Sake, Consider What You Do: Teacher Educators and Preparation for Literal and Moral Careers," presents some stories and data on teacher educators who worked with the young women at each site, including some self-study of my own practices as a teacher educator. Taking a cue from McWilliam (1996) their experiences represent mostly iconic transgression from the valued feminine identity performed by the majority of participants in the form of the school-marm and the seductress, two failed moral careers. This chapter also provides some analysis of institutional and policy-level factors that impact individual experiences in preprofessional teacher education settings. Finally, chapter 8, "Sweet Are the Uses of Adversity: Wise fools, Radical Love, and Resistance" attempts to radically reconstruct each in the context of teacher education as a possible experience in subversion. As Griffiths (2006) suggests, it may be that feminization of the teaching profession is not a problem—but rather a solution to the problem of hegemonic masculinity (Connell, 1995). In this way, the book concludes by outlining a new theory of teacher education, one that provides practical action suggestions for teacher educators who want to trouble girl culture-driven moral careers and support transgressive trajectories, identities, and practices. Teacher educators are entreated to interrogate our own practice for impression management, interrogate the academy for benefiting from the structures of sex-segregated labor. A final conclusion brings the text to a close.

Once More into the Breach, Dear Friends[2]

Looking at white women, or at white women teachers, is well-traveled scholarly terrain (Case & Hemmings, 2005; Fine, Weis, Powell, & Wong 1997; Grumet, 1988; Ladson-Billings, 1989; Luttrell, 1993; Mazzei, 1997; Weis, 1988). The conversation around feminized and semiprofessions is an increasingly crusty, problematic, and unfulfilling one, dominated by pundits despite the conclusions drawn by excellent scholarship (Cortina & San Roman, 2006; Griffiths, 2006; Hoffman, 2003; Mills, Martino, & Lingard, 2004; Silver, 1988). However, an examination of what happens between women in the school of education and what kinds of hidden curricula are inscribed upon/by their interactions and experiences, represents a new wrinkle to the old conversation and perhaps a window into identity, belief teacher practice.

With regard to teacher efficacy, the connection between the image of the teacher and the preservice teachers' performance of the valued identity as a moral career may shed light on the nature of the connections among belief, identity, and practice. The relationship between preservice teacher identity and beliefs and eventual teaching practice is well-documented (Anderson & Piazza, 1996; Carpenter, 2000; Dunkin, Precians & Nettle, 1994; Kagan, 1990; Lortie, 1975, Pajares, 1992; Pohan, 1996). Meanwhile, popular cultural stories about teachers and teaching play a significant role in individual preservice teachers' vocational choices (Gates, 1989; McWilliam, 1996). However, the connections between these elements are not so well understood despite consensus that the relationship between teachers' stories and identity could be a fruitful direction for exploration (Beijaard et al., 2004). The literature also does not demonstrate how teachers reconcile the negative or stigmatized (Goffman, 1963) aspects of teacher portrayals with their own, often gendered, moral careers (Goffman, 1959). Meanwhile, the singularity of the work teachers do—which occupies a unique professional niche—and the teaching demographic—which is made up of mostly young, white middle class women—requires a consideration of the literature on adolescence and work. These variables are also not connected with identity development or the effect of story on that development.

It is important for teacher educators to understand social and popular-cultural stories about teachers and teacher education because individuals who decide to become teachers very often form their opinions about the profession with significant input from this narrative milieu (McWilliam, 1996). While the popular press and even the university itself alternately champions and disputes the story of teaching as semiprofessional work for the less intelligent (Etzioni, 1969) more interesting from the perspectives of preservice teachers, their families and their friends are images of teaching in the popular media. These images, whether in cinema, television, or prose, fail to overtly contradict the semiprofessional stereotype but nonetheless are embraced as positive images by the majority of preservice teachers (McWilliam, 1996). Finally, it is important to acknowledge that all of this affirms that the profession continues to be defined from the outside, and that "understanding how society views teachers through the prism of the cultural imagination can productively challenge the profession to create its own pedagogical images" (Bauer, 1998, p. 312).

Poet and journalist Marya Mannes wrote that "Nobody objects to a woman being a good writer or sculptor or geneticist as long as she manages also to be a good wife, mother, good-looking, good-tempered, well-dressed, well-groomed and unaggressive" (1964, p. 59). In other words, the rules of feminine performance as laid out in the dominant, raced, and classed girl culture are rigidly defined in terms of women's ability to prioritize performing the appearance of an idealized gendered self. To return to the introductory parable, ultimately, I'd like to think that the Foolish Virgins realized at some point that there was more to life than the wedding party, and that theirs may have been more of a liberation than a failure. Similarly, I'd like my teacher education students to be unafraid of making mistakes, taking risks, and toying with different selves—moving, perhaps, from an unquestioning take on caring and compliance to identities more radical, intellectual, and critical in flavor. I'd like them to be comfortable in different identities, without fear of their being locked out of the proverbial wedding party or perhaps more of a willingness to deviate from the trajectories associated with sanctioned performances. The same goes for teacher educators. For them, reflection might mean re-framing their own valued identities and moral careers, and at what cost they are insulated and held separate from professional life.

At the end of the day, my hope is this: that the Wise and Foolish alike question the "party" and see that there is work to be done in the dark, beyond the pale. As women, we must explore what constitutes bad behavior and ask, what if the "good" girls and Wise Virgins, who are comfortable with patriarchy and enact something like hegemonic femininity, do more than collude? The structures of racism, classism, and sexism rely on handmaidens in the form of well-intentioned new teachers, forever waiting for the bridegroom, eyes trained on the horizon while squalor grows unchecked at their very feet. Finally, I want to emphasize that despite initial appearances, this is not a facile dichotomized picture of "good and bad" but rather an attempt to turn St. Matthew's parable on its head and back again, and by doing so, recreate and then trouble how we think about gender, identity, and work. As Saffold and Longwell-Grice (2008) write, the young, middle class white women who fill teacher education programs are not a homogenous group, though they may be sculpted that way. The Wise may in fact be Foolish, and the Foolish very Wise, but everyone inscribes each act with real meanings, and defensible reasons for the pragmatic choices they make in everything they do, believe and say. I seek to honor them all.

Notes

1. Detailed discussion of research contexts will be provided in chapters 4, 5, and 6.
2. This from William Shakespeare's *Henry V*, Act X, Scene X.

PART I

~

CARE AND REASON

~

CHAPTER ONE

The Windy Side of Care

Doing the Work of Love

Don Pedro: In faith, lady, you have a merry heart.
Beatrice: Yea, my lord, I thank it, poor fool, it keeps on the windy
side of care.

—*Much Ado About Nothing*, Act II, Scene I, 308–15

In Shakespeare's *Much Ado About Nothing*, Don Pedro, Prince of Aragon spars briefly with Beatrice, a woman whose orientation toward love and marriage has a decidedly witty, combative quality. Like many of Shakespeare's heroines, Beatrice refuses to marry until she can find a partner who is her intellectual equal, and perhaps seeing this as a pragmatic impossibility, trumpets disparaging views of love and romance. It may be a stretch to say that Beatrice is holding out for egalitarian marriage, but her refusal to be subjugated is at the root of her cynicism. However, when a cousin finds love, she is happy for the couple—and Don Pedro notes, with amusement, that she does seem to have a "merry heart" after all. She adds, rather cryptically, that her heart, foolish as it is, keeps "on the windy side of care." Thus the phrase "windy side" is interpreted here as meaning that through the heart's natural, baser, more thoughtless tendencies, it cannot help but be happy and put itself in danger of falling in love. Beatrice is professing to her heart's (the "poor fool") doing what comes naturally to avoid the unhappiness that comes with perpetually going against the grain: it celebrates and ultimately seeks romantic love.

This represents a unique moment of transparency for a Shakespearean heroine; in my reading, it is reminiscent of the preservice primary teacher whose motives for becoming a teacher focus on the affective rather than purely instructive: that she wants to do the work of love, work that comes "naturally" to her because she has "always liked kids" or because she is more interested, and personally, emotionally, even biologically apt, in nurturing small children. These motivations are oftentimes more compelling than the desire to pursue other professional aspirations that may be more perceived as more difficult or more of a social or personal uphill climb. For example, one Mountain University participant began college dreaming of being a physical therapist, but the "physio and math courses, they were just too much . . . I was struggling to make a C . . . maybe it wasn't for me . . . then I thought about how much I loved babysitting, how everyone said I was a natural, and how much I love kids, and I was, like, I can teach!" She, like so many, wants to do the work of love, to do what comes "naturally," and to stay on the "windy side of care" as pragmatic self-preservation. As one other young woman in the same cohort disclosed with a shrug, "Why would I want to torture myself with all the politics, the misery [and] the long hours when I could just go to work every day and love the little kids?"[1]

I interpret these choices as turning to the "windy side" of care; further-more, they are made in multiple, often contradictory ways. The women's actions can represent problematic reductionism that should be aggressively and critically examined—any time young women talk about how caring for children is biologically more "natural" for women is potentially problematic. However, I can also see how their choices represent a transformative and agentive re-imagining of the work of teaching and a sensible option, both in the job markets of 2003–2007, when the majority of participants were speaking with me, as well as the post-recession and recovery environment of contemporary times. It is important to note that I, too, am a white woman, in my late twenties and early thirties when this research was being done, and a former elementary school teacher (now teacher educator) myself. In these ways, my twin interpretations of their experience are colored by my own, something that will be explored at greater length in later chapters. Regard-less, both interpretations, and the gray area in between, are located against the backdrop of a feminized profession dominated by young, white women whose experiences with contemporary popular and girl culture leave them wandering a difficult terrain of work, identity, care, and love. These terms and others will be defined in the following paragraphs.

The Moral Career

To begin to frame what it means for young, white women to choose teaching in the first place, and to frame that as the "natural" work of love, this chapter sketches out a theoretical landscape that draws from Goffman's (1959; 1963) theory of the "moral career" with Etzioni's (1969) and Griffiths's (2006) theories of gendered work. Discussion begins with an overview of the theory of moral career, normative role enactment, valued identity, and the place of the reference group(s) and imagery frameworks. The theoretical model is illustrated in figure 1.1, which illustrates how participants navigated the process.

The central arrow in figure 1.1 represents the individual participant's "moral career" (Goffman, 1963). While the common definition of the word "career" implies a wide variety of work-related successes and failures, the "career" to which Goffman refers is a "moral career" (1963, p. 119), which is defined as the series of predictable and normative steps and processes that are affiliated with the various social roles which individuals inhabit. Within any given career—which is to say, process of role enact-

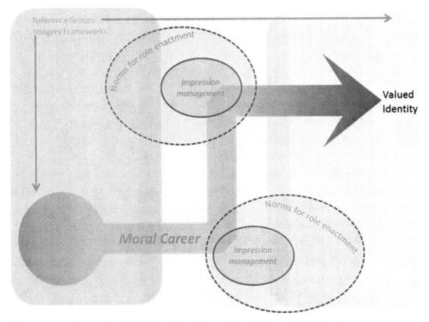

Figure 1.1. Theoretical Model of Participant Moral Career Trajectories

ment—there are changes and alterations that are expected as part of the "typical" story of being: the individual is acting in conformity with the set of norms that govern how one "ought to" or "must" behave in negotiation with how one personally enacts a given social role. Some social roles can include what it means to be a teacher, a woman, or a mother in a given social milieu. Again, this negotiation can be thought of as the work of "impression management"—something which requires constant vigilance to make the correct adjustments and stay on course. The "moral" component of the career pertains not just to the career of typical experiences and changes associated with belonging to one social category or another, but rather to the process by which an individual maintains the *integrity* of her performance of that role (read: the normative ideal of that role as assigned by the audience or, in the case of teachers, society, communities, children, parents, teacher educators, and the body of professional teachers, to name a few) during important happenings or turning points along this career.[2] Studies have documented the stages of moral careers where individuals are in the process of identity reconciliation and shift, from self-saving spousal abuse victims (Chang, 1989) to gay Christians (Yip, 1997). While the stages are relatively uniform and represent key negotiations in the individuals' careers as such, preservice teachers' moral careers *as* preservice teachers are much more idiosyncratic. For one, their moral careers as young women in a given sociocultural and historical location drive a great deal of the periodic adjustment in their moral careers as teachers. As illustrated in figure 1.2, Model of Identity Development (from Galman, 2009a) the pre-service teachers' moral career is demarcated by two stages: (1) entering the school of education or other teacher preparatory experience, and (2) reconciling the associated reference groups and imagery frameworks into her established performance. As Goffman writes, this constitutes "the regular sequence of changes that career entails in the person's self and in his framework of imagery for judging himself and others" (1963, p. 28). One desired outcome of a successful moral career is the enactment and relative ownership of a valued identity.

The "valued identity" is a concept dependent upon the sociocultural assumption that all identities are not valued equally in a given context; some are highly valued-meaning that they are favorable—while others are stigmatized, meaning that they are negatively associated (Goffman, 1959, 1963) regardless of who possesses them. According to Goffman, a stigmatized identity will always be stigmatized: one can only seek to manage, disguise, or reinterpret the negative aspects of the stigma, but the stigma cannot be erased or transformed. Good things are expected from individuals with valued identities and generally unpleasant things are expected from those with stigmatized ones. The availability of valued identities is also an issue; in some contexts, the available valued identities may be limited, or constraining. As Neuhouser (1998) found in examining groups of women involved in collective housing action in a Brazilian shantytown, many women were driven to collectivize and act because the only available valued identity for them was motherhood, and the promise of a valued identity was enough for the women to make choices that confound. As Neuhouser asks, "What is rational about women struggling to keep their families together when this commits them to lives of hard work and grinding poverty? Why would poor women with few resources risk confrontation with a military dictatorship?" (p. 332). He continues,

> in the context of extreme poverty, "mother" was the primary positive identity available to women. To be mothers, however, required having a house in which to care for children. Women with precarious access to housing had to choose between the risks of activism and the risk of losing their identity. For men, poverty and high unemployment also made the father role of household-provider difficult to sustain, but other, less costly identities were available (work, sex, soccer), making a material interest in housing an insufficient incentive to participate. The combination of commitment to the mother identity and women's inability to access the resources necessary to be mothers linked motherhood to mobilization. (p. 333)

Several of the young women whose stories are told in this book had friends who effectively asked them about the rationality of choosing teaching, which is hard work, with long hours, slight autonomy, low status, and scanty remuneration, when other options are open to educated women in the contemporary world of work? For whatever reason, the young, white females becoming elementary or early childhood teachers, "teacher" is the primary "valued identity" (Goffman, 1959) available to them. In conversations with participants, teacher educators and others it seemed like there were other valued, neutral, or even stigmatized identities available, but still other young women insisted that the identity of teacher was the only one that would be suitable for her constraints, which included balancing economic and domestic needs, such as being independent, but able to adjust career aspirations to become a wife and mother. These became part of the long-term trajectory of the teacher as valued identity, and which would not have been attainable otherwise.

The expectations we hold about the kinds of identity other persons have "allow us to deal with anticipated others without special attention or thought . . . we lean on these anticipations that we have, transforming them into

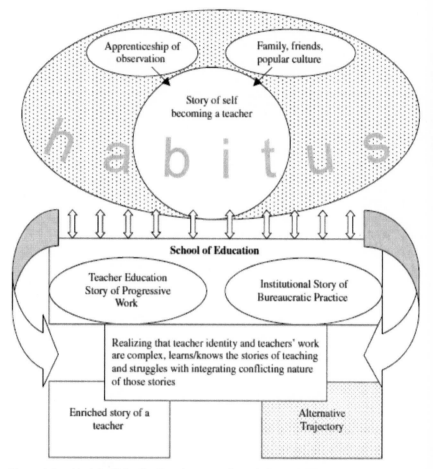

Figure 1.2.   Model of Identity Development (from Galman, 2009)

normative expectations" (Goffman, 1963, p. 2). The expectations, in turn, constitute a set of obligations regarding appropriate behavior and belief on the part of others. These obligations constitute the structural aspects of one's self and they make life more or less predictable. Thus, the construction of identity is in large part the construction of a normalized, "acceptable" identity, and ultimately a successful moral career.

Reference Groups and Imagery Frameworks

The arrow in figure 1.1 moves through different rectangular shades which represent different reference groups and imagery frameworks. Reference groups exist within every field. Mead (1934) defines these as groups of others to which one does not belong but to which one might be interested in belonging. For preservice teachers, these others are usually other teachers—either those practicing around them, or, more likely, the ones they remember from their own apprenticeship of observation (Lortie, 1975) or from the pervasive popular media. Reference groups help us to determine who we might be interested in becoming as well as set parameters for what kinds of behaviors and actions are appropriate and inappropriate across different settings. They are the groups that, as the name suggests, we *refer* to in determining how to act and fundamentally how to begin shaping the moral career. They are our social touchstones. One might even imagine belonging to a reference group and focusing on initial strides toward identifying with them. However, one's possible imaginings or identifications depend upon the reference groups that are available in a particular field. In other words, the boundaries of that which we might become are in some ways dependent upon the reference groups available to us; concepts of self hinge upon the modeled possibilities around us in the form of these reference groups. The introduction of a new reference group might have a significant impact upon the individual's concept of self, as prior to the introduction individuals will most likely identify only with those reference groups commonly present in their particular milieu. For example, Deborah Holloway (2000) writes that participation in the arts served to introduce new reference groups to the young women and girls involved in a mentoring and art program. The new reference group, in this case, was a community of artists; not only did the introduction of the new reference group have a significant impact upon the girls, but continued interaction with the artists' community helped the girls maintain the shift from old concepts of self to new ones. For preservice teachers, being exposed to a new reference group can be a significant event in the formation of their teacher identity; being exposed to "real, live teachers" can be a desirable introduction or, as in the case of some individuals who leave teacher preparation, a reference group that they ultimately reject. Part of the typical story of any given career is derived from said "framework of imagery" provided by reference groups, including one's own teachers and the cache of desirable popular culture images of teachers and women to which one aspires. In the US contexts, the valued identity, and the successful moral career, of any teacher of young children, depends largely upon producing a series of complex, even contradictory, performances of femininity as reflected in such frameworks. These might include archetypal images that are culturally and historically specific, such as the spinster schoolmarm; the frontier schoolmistress; the Catholic school teacher brandishing her ruler;

the no-nonsense, tough-loving inner city teacher who reaches even the most marginalized students; the pretty, young kindergarten teacher with an apple on her desk; and so on. These image frameworks will be discussed in detail in chapters 4, 5, and 6.

Roles and Performances

The individual strives to give an impression that is desirable to themselves and creates the desired effect upon others, the overall pattern of which may be thought of as the shape of the central arrow in figure 1.1. It bends and twists, and rapidly adjusts to the reference groups and frameworks of imagery, to normative expectation for how given roles are appropriately enacted in the face of audience response.

The skillful navigatrix, in this case, engages in appropriate impression management at just the right times to maintain the integrity of her performance. Goffman (1963) wrote about theories of moral career, valued identity and the effects of normative expectations through dramaturgical analysis: examining how individuals manage themselves, just as an actor would manage and perform a role on stage. Using the metaphor of the theatrical stage, Goffman sees the interactions that define self as a performance of specific roles in which the performer engages in a kind of interaction with the "audience"; this is because the performance is crafted in such a way that the impressions given are in keeping with the goals of the actor and those of the audience. Both the audience expectations and the consciousness of the actor with regard to whether he is "fully taken in by his own act" (1959, p. 17) contribute to this reciprocal interaction. The individual actor develops an identity as a result, taking cues from the audience as a way to keep restructuring and refining the performance of the role. It is important to note that in this performance, the actor and the audience do not exist in a vacuum. The role itself, the actor's interpretation of it, and the audience's expectations are all socially constructed and historically situated. In this way, the very aspect of the performance is in some way connected to a historical and social niche and cannot be examined in isolation. "Role-taking" (1963) occurs when the individual puts themselves in the role of the teacher, making themselves "fit" into that role as best they can and engaging in occupying that role as it is externally and generally defined. Meanwhile, "role-making" (Goffman, 1963) is the process by which the individual makes that perhaps awkward initial fit more comfortable by bringing her own interpretation to the performance. So, while a preservice teacher may engage in role-taking by putting herself into the "role" of teacher (thinking about and incorporating the social definition of that role, even to the tune of sacrificing parts of herself for the "fit") she will be role-making when she brings herself back into the role and imbues that performance with her own interpretation. As an individual monitors her moral career, paying attention to the reference groups and imagery frameworks in a given milieu, the performance of the role may change—depending on audience feedback, and the individual's satisfaction with their interpretation of the role, and the role's level of concordance with the individual's sense of the way things ought to be. As the role is performed more often, the performance changes in small ways so as to manage audience impression.

Part of a good performance involves interpreting and performing roles in such a way that the interpretation is aligned with expectations both of one's current position and also of one's immediate audience. Bruner (1993) describes this process as "self-making," or choosing and enacting roles that satisfy self and others. The performed self in these roles "turns out on close inspection to be highly negotiable, highly sensitive to bidding on the not-so-open market of one's own reference group." Of course, as Goffman has suggested, impression management in performance accounts for the constant process of adjusting and refining one's interpretation of role with regard to audience expectation and agreement.

To put this another way, while the actor is undeniably a distinct individual, she is playing a role with prescribed dimensions that have been socially constructed and are historically situated. The performance itself, while open to some degree of personalization and individualized interpretation, must adhere to those prescribed dimensions, just as an actor must adhere to the general script when playing a part. These dimensions are the structural or normative (Guba, 1981) component of self and identity. If the actor does not adhere to these socially constructed and agreed-upon parameters, then it is possible that the audience will not recognize the role and the actor risks, at least metaphorically speaking, being "booed off the stage." For example, Shakespearian actor and scholar Derek Jacobi is well known for having offered one of the most popular and well-executed performances of the role of Shakespeare's *Hamlet* (BBC Film, 1980). However, even though elements of this role are prescribed and the role has been played by countless others, Jacobi is nonetheless recognizable and distinct from other actors as himself while playing the role. The way Jacobi performs Hamlet adheres to the socially agreed-upon boundaries and specifications of the role itself, but within those boundaries, he is able to add something of himself to show through the structured persona of Hamlet as the eyes and other features would show through a mask, thus making his rendering of Hamlet unique—*but still Hamlet*. This uniqueness constitutes the individual, idiopathic (Guba, 1981) or agentive aspect of identity or self. However, if Jacobi were to take off the metaphorical mask altogether, or to change the role of Hamlet beyond what is recognizable by the audience (Hamlet kills himself in the first act, Hamlet and Ophelia live happily ever after, Hamlet breaks into song, and so forth) then his rendering would cease to be the correct role and the performance would be a failure. For preservice teachers, the "role" at stake is that of teacher, but it is entwined with other roles for which there are specific gendered and social expectations, not all of which are congruent with all interpretations of the teacher role. They must learn how to perform all of these roles in a way that is not only aligned with the moral career but also recognizable to an audience and themselves. To more deeply understand the complexities of such navigation, it is important to situate the individual and her moral career in the unique landscape of a feminized profession and the work of care.

The Semiprofessional Work of Love and Care

Teaching is a "feminized" profession, or field in which disproportionately large numbers of women work. It is frequently constructed as the work of love, meaning that as affective work it is neither intellectual nor professional. Instead, this construction suggests that teachers' work comes "naturally" to women, who are biologically more apt for nurturing. Etzioni's classic 1969 work, *The Semi-Professions and Their Organizations* opens by acknowledging that teaching belongs in the category of the "semi-professions" whose "claim to the status of doctors and lawyers is neither fully established nor fully desired" (p. v). Teaching, like nursing and social work, is marked by shorter training and a smaller body of acknowledged specialized professional knowledge, lack of legal protections vis-à-vis privileged communications, and less autonomy. Of course, we know that teachers, nurses, and others have extremely specialized professional knowledge, however, the conflation of the work of love with a biological aptitude for care—in other words, that the professional knowledge associated with teaching is primarily instinctive female knowledge—the drive to see teaching as specialized, highly skilled work deserving of autonomy and special protections rapidly evaporates. The principal and administration in elementary schools may occupy structural positions of apparent total authority, but teachers know that these administrators cannot know their individual teaching and content area as well as they do; thus teachers are left to accept the authority and direction of someone, usually male, who is simultaneously more powerful and less specifically knowledgeable than they are. This "variable zoning" (deMarrais & LeCompte, 1998; Lortie, 1975) is a source of conflicting messages about teachers' autonomy, but very clear messages about who is more apt for which task. The very traits that so many preservice teachers shared with me as their primary motivations for seeing themselves as teachers—ability to care, innate connection with children, interest in nurturing children, and so forth—contribute to the discourse of biological determinism that is at the core of semiprofessional status and harem-like power structure.

But this isn't the end of the conversation about the work of care. Etzioni calls teaching one example of low status, meagerly compensated "female employment." While few dispute the fact that elementary and early childhood teachers are overwhelmingly female, and white, there are others who insist that a feminized profession—perhaps historically dominated by women, but contemporarily dominated by the antecedents of feminine practice—can be a site of empowerment and resistance. For example, Griffiths's (2006) theory of teaching as a "feminized" terrain in which both women and men work is defined by practices of care and love that have nothing to do with biological aptitude, but everything to do with resistance hegemonic masculinity, and its attendant forms of racism, sexism, classism, and homophobia (Connell, 1987; Griffiths, 2006; Liston & Garrison, 2004; Noddings, 1984).

Feminized Practices

As Simpson and Simpson (1969) described how the very presence of women degraded the nursing, teaching and social work to semiprofessional status, Bennett and Hokenstad (1975) suggest that these indictments rested on "psychological inventories of college students and workers show[ing] that women attracted to the semi-professions possess such damning characteristics as altruistic motivations, desires for pleasant social relationships with colleagues and a preference to work with people rather than things" (p. 125). Simpson and Simpson equate these tendencies with women's inability to gain intellectual mastery, lack of ambition to achieve, and the absence of professional commitment. While the Simpsons' analysis and Bennett and Hokenstad's rebuttal are both almost four decades old, the interpretation of behaviors and attributes associated with the feminine remains relevant today. "There is a hegemonic form of masculinity," writes Griffiths (2006), "which can affect schools in which there may be few males, let alone females, who identify with that form of masculinity," the culture of which is independent of the number of women in the school itself (p. 388). Initially coined by Connell (1987, 1995) and reformulated in light of contemporary critiques in Connell and Messerschmidt (2005), the term "hegemonic masculinity" emphasizes individualism, aggressiveness, competition, ambition, compulsory heterosexuality, violence, and adherence to rigid social hierarchies. It may be self-reproducing in schools and schooling practices. While influenced by femininities and subordinate masculinities, it is nonetheless dominant and active in the continued subordination of both. As Connell and Messerschmidt (2005) write of the original construct,

> Hegemonic masculinity was understood as the pattern of practice (i.e., things done, not just a set of role expectations or an identity) that allowed men's dominance over women to continue. Hegemonic masculinity was distinguished from other masculinities, especially subordinated masculinities. Hegemonic masculinity was not assumed to be normal in the statistical sense; only a minority of men might enact it. But it was certainly normative. It embodied the currently most honored way of being a man, it required all other men to position themselves in relation to it, and it ideologically legitimated the global subordination of women to men. Men who received the benefits of patriarchy without enacting a strong version of masculine dominance could be regarded as showing a complicit masculinity. (p. 832)

As schools can be a vehicle for the reproduction of hegemonic practice, it is apparent that, as Smith, Hardman, and Higgins (2007) write, "teachers need support to achieve a greater awareness of the implicit processes which can lead to imbalance in the classroom" (p. 467). While boys have been shown to dominate classroom behavior and teacher attention with an overwhelmingly negative effect on female students (Sadker & Sadker, 1994; Smith, Hardman, & Higgins, 2007), an analysis incorporating the machinations of hegemonic masculinity in schools might include the damaging and truncated way in which boys are socialized to monolithic masculinity as the only way to enact maleness and the valued identity. It has been suggested that hegemonic masculinity and the ways in which it complicates boys' orientation toward schooling may be connected to boys' academic underachievement by causing them to associate academic success with masculine failure (Reynolds, 2001; Skelton, 1997).

So, Feminization Is Not the Problem

The trend of women's numerical dominance in the primary teaching force has been theorized as a function of everything from the sweeping changes of the civil rights and labor movements, and persistence despite the effects of the Women's Movement amidst the economic necessities created by compulsory schooling (deMarrais & LeCompte, 1998), to teaching as a profession feminized from its inception as a function of political and social discourse designed to ensure an inexpensive, reliable labor force (Cortina & San Roman, 2006) to women's biological or natural predisposition in these fields and their subsequent inability to achieve in other, more professional arenas (Simpson & Simpson, 1969). The boy-crisis discourse positions the phenomena as not merely a numeric trend but rather an alarming female[3] invasion that unfairly emphasizes and over-values the "feminine," resulting in wholesale failure for boys. The simplistic conflation of sex and gender expression aside, these discourses are not unrelated to the accountability and scripting trends in public education, both of which are significant sources of de-skilling, surveillance, and control of primary level teachers. These teachers, it implies, must be watched, and their practices monitored, lest our young men be feminized and outnumbered, and our universities overrun with hordes of women as the "War Against Boys" (Hoff-Sommers, 2000) continues. Such is the spurious and reactionary "general 'blaming' discourse directed at girls and women teachers" (Reynolds, 2001, p. 370) that has characterized much of the facile accounting around boys' underachievement and the boy crisis argument to date.

It should be hardly surprising, then, that if "feminization" is positioned as the problem, that "masculinization" is considered as one proposed solution; this strategy includes hiring more male teachers as well as developing curricular and pedagogical approaches aimed at accommodating for alleged biological and developmental "differences" in how boys learn (Okopny, 2008). Targeted male recruitment and matching of pupil and teacher genders has been shown to have varied results, and individual teachers and pupils respond in idiosyncratic ways—both positive and negative—to teachers of the same of different genders, despite individual teachers' suggestions that there are real benefits for male students in the presence of male teachers (Carrington & McPhee, 2008). Such meat-fisted attempts at solving the "problem" of feminization also fail to address how feminized practices may be beneficial to all genders in creating a space to resist the hegemonic. Just as having a variety of male and female role models and interactions may potentially benefit all children, so also hegemonic masculinity serves to detract from the educational experiences of all children, most of whom choose to embrace femininities and non-hegemonic masculinities and find themselves both subtly and overtly marginalized as a result. As Reynolds (2001) suggests, "the conflation of non-hegemonic forms of masculinity, femininity and 'studiousness' not only makes academic study problematic for all boys, but particularly difficult for boys (high and low achievers) who would like to, or chose to, invest in and take-up alternative masculinities" (p. 382). Similarly, a larger social and governmental structure that fails to make "children, childcare and child protection . . . at the centre of state policy" reinforces monolithic, hegemonic masculinity to the exclusion of "alternative domestic ideologies which emphasize caring as a core human value" and thus elevate the cultural, social, and popular professional status of teaching as work (Drudy, Martin, Woods, & O'Flynn, 2005, p. 155).

Feminized Practices as Resistance

The feminization of teaching, per se, is not the problem in schools, whether related to girls' or boys' patterns of achievement and/or attrition. Implicit in the pathologized feminization discourse is the "achievement" of a post-feminist ideal, which is to say that girls have achieved "success" while boys are now at risk from female achievement in general. Girls' success, meanwhile, is cast as the herald of a postfeminist age in which gender inequality in schools is "no longer a problem" (Ringrose, 2007). However, as Ringrose (2007) writes, "The reactive 'feminization of education' thesis mobilized in the educational debate" ignores, in its facile interpretation of both gender identity and achievement, "that measures of so-called gender equity in academic achievement do not necessarily translate into ideals of wider social equity inside or outside of schools" (p. 485). Meanwhile, Griffiths's (2006) theory suggests that feminization is not only the problem, but rather it presents a solution: "the feminization of teaching, insofar as it exists, is to be welcomed because it provides a space for resisting hegemonic masculinity" (p. 387) and possibly disrupting its self-reproduction. It affirms that "any practice is properly seen as fluid, leaky and viscous: different practices seep out into each other as a result of the embodiment of their individual members" (p. 387). Whereas hegemonic masculinity emphasizes individualism and competition within a rigid hierarchy, feminized practices represent the inverse: embodiment, diversity, and a nonhierarchical, democratic distribution of and relationship to power. This analysis seeks to frame new teachers' work as a body of feminized practices that are "leaky" and "viscous."

In the watery metaphors of this theory of embodied practice, leakiness is a function of fluid practices which

> leak into each other . . . Their boundaries are permeable. Being a woman teacher also means being seen by students and colleagues as—and perhaps seeing herself as—a daughter, auntie, mother, nanny. . . . Equivalently, for a man it means being seen as a son, uncle, father, breadwinner, doing something important elsewhere. The practice of teaching leaks into the practices of mothering, fathering, managing, facilitating, counseling and philosophizing, and vice versa. (p. 396)

Considering that one common critique of shifts in the nature of teachers' work intensification is its expanding job description (wherein teachers had to be not only "teacher" but also, for example, mother, nurse, and social worker as well) the strength of "leakiness" as a marker of fluidity and heterogeneity in feminized practices is of particular interest. Griffiths writes: "practices associated with women leak into women's practices of teaching, and similarly for men" (p. 403). Similarly, "viscosity," described as the slow, sticky flow of practices as they respond "to internal and external changes" in a way that makes these practices not only more flexible and non-hierarchical but also more receptive to change and diversity in such a way that it attempts to meet the needs of and be inclusive of many, excluding none, and incorporating the divergent practices of many. This serves to create communities of practice in classrooms that are "more like the Himalayas and less like the single peak of Kilimanjaro" (p. 396) and may in fact be sites of resistance to the often overwhelming force of hegemonic masculinity as the force of dominant school and teaching practice. At the center of this is the issue of what defines love and care in the classroom, and what that means for preservice teachers when love becomes work, and vice versa. One of the central goals of this work hinges on what it means when individuals become conscious and self-aware vis-à-vis the way "love" plays out in the feminized classroom.

Love, Caring, and Callings

It has long been asserted that teaching is the work of love; it *is* emotional in nature and its eventual product should be children and young people who experience love and care and teachers who find themselves deeply fulfilled by the act of caring and relating to others. Writing in this area recognizes that this is asking a lot of teachers, but in no way questions that this is what the job is really about (Fried, 2001; Intrator, 2000; Palmer, 1996). Furthermore, definitions of love itself are widely divergent, and not all of them benign.

Spurned Lovers and Romanticized Others:
Primary Teaching and Love
Despite recent scholarly attention to emotions in education (Boler, 1999; hooks, 1994; Liston, 2000; Liston & Garrison, 2004), the craggy contours of "love" remain treacherous. As Dale (2004) reminds us, love is at odds with the dangerous, business-like pragmatics of the contemporary educational landscape—but this does not always make it a "good" in and of itself. As Liston and Garrison (2004) suggest, love must be retrieved from the "ontological basement" (p. 5) and part of that retrieval is its critical use—holding

it up to the light. The concept has been defined and redefined multiple times, and referred to alternately as both "love" and "care." Four of the most frequently cited conceptualizations of love at its best and also its worst are Liston's "Enlarged Love," Duncan-Andrade and Valenzuela's critical love, or "cariño," and hooks's "ethic of love."

Liston (2000) describes two distinct kinds of love at work in teachers' experience: a "spurned, romantic love" and a "transformative enlarged love" (p. 83). He continues,

> Good teaching entails a kind of romantic love of the learning enterprise; it is motivated by and infuses others with a love of inquiry. Teaching in and with this love is a vulnerable undertaking, one that leaves the teacher open to pain and rejection. When a teacher's love of learning has been scorned she may find herself in despair. This despair afflicts the teacher's soul. An enlarged, transformative love is one way to come to terms with this despair; to live with and perhaps transform the night in our days; to inform the quiet heroism that teaching must become. An enlarged love entails a diminished sense of self (or more accurately ego) in the teaching enterprise, an attentive gaze outward toward the other, and an accompanying search for the "good." If guided by an enlarged love teaching can become an ongoing struggle that nourishes our students' and our own souls. (p. 83)

So, not unlike other conceptualizations of love, good teaching (a) requires love as an ingredient and (b) must be transformed from the work of personal fulfillment into a more self-less focus outward, on the other. It is only by focusing on the other, on the search for the good, can the teacher diminish the despair that comes with having that first blush of love—for teaching, for learning, for the small students themselves—fall short. "To love teaching is to be enamored of the attempt to share the attraction and hold the world has on us," Liston continues, "to love teaching is to give of yourself in a way that can be so tenderly vulnerable" (p. 92). Liston is careful to note that seeking an enlarged love cannot "wipe the slate clean" of personal and professional failures—instead, it is a way of "resuscitating lives and loves" (p. 95) by offering a greater love, one that drowns out "the unnecessary noise of the teacher's self" (p. 97).

Like Liston's "enlarged love," "cariño" (Duncan-Andrade, 2006; Valenzuela, 1997) is a sense of authentic, critical caring that is reciprocal, instilling "a sense of hope and promise, one that is directly tied to individuals' sense of themselves as capable change agents" (Duncan-Andrade, 2006, p. 455). Duncan-Andrade (2006) writes,

Cariño is often translated as caring, affection or love, but most is lost in this translation . . . Cariño is more a concept than a word. It is the foundation of relationships among the poor and working classes—often the only thing left to give, in families raising children on substandard wages . . . schools serving poor and working-class Latino/-a children often fail to develop reciprocal relationships whereby children are authentically cared for, and in turn open themselves up to care about school. (p. 451)

The concept of "cariño" is a kind of critical care, or "authentic caring" as opposed to "aesthetic caring." The latter is a juxtaposition developed by Valenzuela to describe the difference between reciprocal caring relationships and pro-forma exercises in "caring" which do not take into account the perspective of the cared-*for* but only the idea and actions of "care" as an aesthetic. She writes, "schools are structured around an aesthetic caring whose essence lies in an attention to things and ideas" rather than authentic relationships and reciprocity between people (Valenzuela, 1999, p. 22). As illustrated by Monzo and Rueda's (2001) study of Latina paraprofessionals and teachers in relation to students, cariño was part of many paraprofessionals' family-like orientation to children and a mark of quality that separated relationship from being "only a teacher." As one of Monzo and Rueda's participants illustrated,

The role of the teacher is to be a teacher and a parent at the same time because if she/he is only a teacher, cold, then they don't . . . show them cariño [a relational expression of caring characterized through gentle smiles, light touching, and calling students mija/mijo (my child)] maybe if they have a problem, they can tell you about it. (p. 450–51)

This interpretation, as well as others (Hill, 1998; Montero-Sieburth & Perez, 1987), emphasizes that critical love profoundly relational in orientation, and revolves around comforting and building a relationship above and beyond that of teacher, to "be a teacher and a parent at the same time" (Monzo & Rueda, 2001, p. 450). So, while Liston's "love" is an enlarged love, rather like a higher purpose that can drag the spurned romantic from the depths of his "falling out of love" with teaching and focus on the work and the greater good, Duncan-Andrade and Valenzuela theorize an act of reciprocal, critical caring. The difference between a love and the act of caring is that the latter is active, while the former is an inducement, a concept.

For Duncan-Andrade and Valenzuela, caring is good and bad—cariño is positioned as the alternative to "aesthetic caring," which is, effectively, a culture of "false caring, one where the most powerful members of the relationship define themselves as caring despite the fact the recipients of their so-called caring do not perceive it as such" (Duncan-Andrade, 2006, p. 451). Aesthetic caring is about the salvation of the person who is doing the caring. In other words, the person who is doing the "caring" is doing so primarily for the advancement of their own social or more value; they may not take into account the perspective of the cared-for but only the actions of the carer as morally/socially valuable. Equally disturbing is the fact that the cared-for may be othered in the process—essentialized, romanticized, and exoticized while the carer enacts his own performance of valued identity. This takes on a semicolonialist tinge in cases where white teachers may be working with children of color and allow themselves to be seduced by the messianic, racist narratives of the special value of caring for children in urban settings (Galman, 2007).

Finally, hooks (1994) asserts that an ethic of love as the "practice of freedom" (p. 290) is the first and best alternative to the historically monolithic "ethic of domination." Like Gandhi and King, she asserts that love, frequently overlooked by progressive politics and change movements, is an essential part of doing battle with oppression. hooks's theory is fundamentally about addressing the interconnectedness of oppression and seeking liberation for everyone, not just each of us from within our own self-centered silos of experience. This insistence on connectedness and moving beyond the primacy of personal experience and interest is profoundly subversive and strikes at the heart of hegemonic masculinity. She writes,

> A culture of domination is anti-love. It requires violence to sustain itself. To choose love is to go against the prevailing values of the culture. Many people feel unable to love either themselves or others because they do not know what love is. Contemporary songs like Tina Turner's "What's Love Got To Do With It" advocate a system of exchange around desire, mirroring the economics of capitalism: the idea that love is important is mocked. In his essay "Love and Need: Is Love a Package or a Message?" Thomas Merton argues that we are taught within the framework of competitive consumer capitalism to see love as a business deal: "This concept of love assumes that the machinery of buying and selling of needs is what makes everything run. It regards life as a market and love as a variation on free enterprise." Though many folks recognize and critique the commercialization of love, they see no alternative. Not knowing how to love or even what love is, many people feel emotionally lost; others search for definitions, for ways to sustain a love ethic in a culture that negates human value and valorizes materialism. (p. 293)

The crux of hooks's argument is that love, as a practice of freedom, isn't something that a person "has" or "falls into" but rather something he or she chooses, and that act of choosing to love and to extend oneself for the benefit of another, that makes love a practice, not a static concept. And by framing love as something a person chooses to do every day, love is freed, somewhat, from its conflation with female biology—which is to say that women are somehow better equipped to love and nurture children. If love is a practice, we might say that the only way to become adept is to practice; being able to love is learned, therefore, and not inborn in one sex or the other.

Vocation

An additional aspect of love/care discourse is that teaching is framed not as "work" but rather as "vocation" or "calling," most often in the form of being "called" by one's love of children. This is problematic. The religious community has long defined "vocation" as the work to which a person is "called" by some higher power to perform as part of a larger theological design. What's more, success in one's chosen vocation was a sign not only of divine grace but also that one had chosen well and correctly—proof positive of a healthy moral career. Writers on teaching-as-vocation, in particular, have long used the language of the "calling" or the "gifts" of innate ability to distinguish vocation from work (Palmer, 1996). It is also important to note that the word "vocation" has long been used to describe the unremunerated work of low-status members of society, including but not limited to women in general and teachers specifically. The logic here is that because the work is imbued with meaning—and, in some contexts, spiritual meaning—it needn't be as well-compensated as less "meaningful" occupations. The subtext here is also that "vocation" or meaningful work is somehow less demanding than other work, less "hard," or deserving of remuneration. This has long been the story of women's unpaid labor, and of the low wages in many of the feminized professions, such as nursing, child care, domestic labor, secretarial work, and teaching.

Meanwhile, work—which Csikszentmihalyi and Schneider (2000) discuss in the context of the Protestant Work Ethic (work = salvation/self-worth)—is a source of tremendous meaning and identity, and even work that the participants would not call "vocation" (i.e., a "calling" from which identity is partially if not wholly derived) is a central concern in the lives of most people. Young people in Csikszentmihalyi and Schneider's early 1990s study were less able to develop a solid work-identity because they did not have early access to the inner workings of occupations in which they might have interest (Asakawa, Hektner, & Schmidt, 2000). Contrast this with the eighteenth century farmer's son, who not only had a near-absolute guarantee of his line of work but also an intimate knowledge of what the farmer *does* and who the farmer *is*. Add to this the fact that the cultural picture of work has changed:

> However, the reasons that people value work seem to have changed considerably in the past few decades. Whereas the early Puritans may have seen work's dividends as a sign of divine goodwill, by World War II most people saw work almost exclusively as a means of material advancement and security. It was not until the [affluent] 1960s that young people began to think of work as a way to achieve personal fulfillment . . . recently, material concerns have become more salient again, with an added twist: Young people value work because it provides the means to indulge in expensive leisure and consumption habits. (p. 8)

And one might venture to say that while all of those historical motivations are present among the contemporary post-adolescent generation, the motivation for personal fulfillment is most interesting in the case of young women who have chosen to become elementary and early childhood teachers. This is because of the language preservice teachers use in talking about teachers and teaching; it is not always the language of practicality, and certainly not of compensation, but rather of affective fulfillment and the embodiment of what Goffman (1959) would term a valued gendered identity through doing the work of love. The moral career is about enacting love and care, simply put. Teaching may be the vehicle, the means by which one remains on the windy side of care, certain at risk for falling in love, but safeguarded against the greater risks of a spoiled identity and derailed moral career.

Conclusion

Questions remain about what will happen when these optimistic young women find themselves disappointed by, for example, how the work of love does not necessarily include elementary age students guaranteed to love their teacher, or their school, or learning, in return. What one does about work as unrequited love is, according to Liston (2000), to seek an enlarged sense of purpose, or love, for others. Alternatively, love becomes subversive when framed as a practice of freedom, and a stand against hegemony (hooks, 1994). Still, the impact that might have on the valued identity and the moral career is unclear. Subversion is tantamount to going against the grain, a potentially stigmatizing and therefore risky activity, even in the name of love. The aspiring teacher may find herself willing to do anything to feel secure in the impending love of her students, and their love of the material she brings to them—but this spurned romantic cannot persevere. Meanwhile, the teacher who finds herself unable, or uninterested, in the work of love, may be similarly derailed, accepting her stigmatized identity and a failed moral career—as both a teacher, and a "social mother" (Cortina & San Roman, 2006)—despite being an excellent pedagogue with strong pedagogical and content knowledge. Either way, it seems, you cannot win at the work of love. The "windy side of care" may be more elusive, and less natural, than we are initially led to believe.

It is possible, then, to have a successful literal career and a failed moral one. However, few of the young women in this book worry about an inability to love and be loved. They are mostly banking on this as coming naturally: they feel confident in having chosen the windy side of care, though they will still need to pay attention to and manage their performance throughout. It is much more likely, in the reference groups and imagery frameworks available to the young women in teacher education, to experience a failed moral career, and a stigmatized identity, by struggling, like Beatrice initially does, to swim upstream in the pursuit of a different, attractive but practically unobtainable moral career. As that same Mountain University student continues, "I mean, I know I can do [a degree in physical therapy] but what if I spend all that time in school, trying and trying, and I miss out on so much? With teaching I can do something I love, and still, you know, be me." Who that "me" turns out to be is heavily dependent upon the reference groups and imagery frameworks at work.

Notes

1. Interview with preservice elementary teacher, 2003.

2. It is important to note here that when talking about normative ideals or beliefs, the "normative" implies a set of expectations from the audience, which, in turn, are experienced as obligations—even moral ones—by the performer.

3. This brings to mind images from the 1958 Nathan Juran science fiction film, *Attack of the 50 Foot Woman*—not surprisingly since this film, released at a time of women's nascent but palpable increase in public influence, banked on the general US panic that women, given any modicum of real power (in this case from aliens) would wreck social havoc.

CHAPTER TWO

~

No Other but a Woman's Reason

Teaching, Work, Girls, and Girl Culture

I have no other but a woman's reason:
I think him so, because I think him so.

—*The Two Gentlemen of Verona*, Act I, Scene II

Julia, another plucky Shakespearean heroine, must decide between suitors. She asks her trusty lady-in-waiting, Lucetta, for advice: should she choose a brave knight, a wealthy merchant nobleman or Proteus, one of the two gentlemen of Verona (and not what we might call an advantageous choice). Even so, Lucetta recommends Proteus, because she has the secret knowledge that he loves her mistress best and that this is an important ingredient for a happy marriage. When Julia presses her for a tangible, practical reason behind her recommendation, Lucetta shrugs and says, cryptically, "I have no other but a woman's reason: I think him so, because I think him so." Her response could mean she has inferior reasoning abilities, only a "woman's reason," which is no reason at all. Or, it may be more than that—she has "but a woman's reason"—meaning, she has insider knowledge, and must protect it and herself by hiding its true value and feigning ignorance. So also, the world of "women's work" or the "feminized professions" is much more complex than it might initially appear, though practitioners and others may camouflage this and other truths against hegemonic discourses that cast historical women's work as semiprofessional. That said, preservice teachers, influenced heavily by popular and "girl culture" (Greenfield,

2005) might act upon misunderstood and conflicting messages about what it means to do this work.

Elementary and early childhood teaching are "feminized"—meaning, that this is a profession where there tends to be large numbers of female workers, with recent estimates indicating that approximately 90 percent or greater of all P–6 teachers are female. The reasons for feminization vary. As explained in the introduction, the trend of women's numerical dominance in the primary teaching force has been theorized as a function of everything from the sweeping changes of the civil rights and labor movements, and persistence despite the effects of the women's movement amidst the economic necessities created by compulsory schooling (deMarrais & LeCompte, 1998), to teaching as a profession feminized from its inception as a function of political and social discourse designed to ensure a reliable labor force (Cortina & San Roman, 2006), to women's biological or natural predisposition in these fields and their subsequent inability to achieve in other, more professional arenas (Simpson & Simpson, 1969). It has rarely been constructed as benign in either historical accounts or the discourse of the contemporary "boy crisis" (Acker, 1995; Okopny, 2008).

However, as Acker (1995) so deftly sets out, "my problem is not how to professionalize teaching or to reverse trends toward feminization . . . [but to] argue that serious study of teachers' work needs to take serious account of gender, but not in the commonsensical and frequently sexist way" as is often the case (p. 100). This chapter seeks to do so by beginning to sketch out the contradictory and complex terrain of gendered life and work facing new teachers. It builds upon the framework outlined in chapter 1 with a review of the literature relating to contemporary and historical characterizations of teaching as a feminized profession, the discourses that perpetuate semiprofessionalism and the practices that orchestrate those same discourses in resistance to hegemony. Of particular interest is how the feminized profession is played out in (1) popular culture, (2) teacher preparation, and (3) the "domestic ideologies" (Drudy, Martin, Woods, & O'Flynn, 2005) of the public sphere. In each context it is possible to interpret having "no other but a woman's reason" either way: as the internalized sexism of the self-titled "postfeminist" generation (Kleinman, Copp, & Sandstrom, 2006), or as a pragmatic strategy for subversion and survival in the midst of hegemonic masculinity.

Feminized Work in Popular and Girl Culture

Judge (1995) suggests that there is a relationship between the iconic teacher in American culture and the unique purposes and structures of schooling in the United States. He notes that for most of its history the United States has always privileged localized, rather than centralized, schooling structures, and as a collective culture the United States became inured to the ebb and flow of change, with schools remaining flexible, temporarily bowing and readjusting as the pendulum swings. In addition, the US school has been historically shaped by the influx of immigrants, "On a scale that is simply inconceivable anywhere else in the world, requir[ing] the school to be the one agent of assimilation" (p. 262). The teacher, then, must be such an agent, and "the image of the teacher must be everywhere and always be amiable and welcoming and typically also female:

> The teacher is always a "she." The persistent image of the teacher in such a world is, therefore, of the individualist preparing children for lives in a competitive world, but a world in which it is possible for the talented citizen to progress in one generation from the log cabin to the White House. Such a teacher must, in principle, welcome all pupils, whatever their social or ethnic origins, and be prepared to offer them what will suit them best. The teacher must ensure that the pupil is, to use a distinctively American expression, "comfortable." (p. 252)

So, it is possible that a major part of the work of the teacher is affective in nature, such as the task of making students comfortable by being a welcoming, kind and friendly agent of assimilation. This also entails the work of impression management (Goffman, 1959). As detailed in chapter 1, Goffman's dramaturgical conceptualization of impression management is fundamentally about constant consciousness of others' responses, and adjusting one's performance of a given role (teacher, woman, mother, etc.) in accordance with these and general social agreements on what constitutes a valued identity. So, the teacher must maintain the valued identity of the sweet, encouraging welcomer in her performance of self, while also being conscious of the weight of her social charges. It is possible that this leaves precious little time for instructional objectives for any but the most skilled performer.

However, if the work of impression management, and therefore the maintenance of the moral career, was not an intensification of the teachers' already busy day but instead simply part of "natural" womanhood and femininity, matters could be streamlined. Teaching younger children is often constructed as an extension of the "natural" work of mothering (and in so professional aptitude becomes conflated with biology). In this way of thinking, teaching is being a "natural woman"; men who teach young children, they must learn to do what women already inherently know—and it therefore no surprise that they do not typically remain in the classroom (moving instead to administration), or accept a stigmatized masculine identity (de-Marrais & LeCompte, 1998). Meanwhile, a woman who does not naturally "know" how to welcome and comfort children (or who insists that teaching is anything else, including intellectual or political, rather than affective care-work) must accept a stigmatized identity, a derailed moral career and possibly failure both professionally and personally. There is not typically an administrative rung for her to climb to, so the stakes for success are actually quite high.

Generational Factors

Images of teaching at the primary level are fraught with contradiction: they emphasize the work as heroic, but not professional; as labor for the complacent and unintelligent, but also for the intellectual and critical—even revolutionary. Teaching is constructed as the holy vocation of loving and caring, but also asserts that working with children is low status drudgery. Work for those who "can't do," it is also heralded as the creator of all professions. Shiva-like, these stories build up with one hand what they destroy with the other. While several studies have examined the gendered image as a propulsive factor in the cycle of elevation and denigration of teaching (Borman, 1991; Etzioni, 1969; Lortie, 1975) the contours of contemporary experience suggest that the current cadre of preservice and novice teachers may be generationally different from the participants in many important mid-to-late-twentieth century research studies. For example, considering that most new preservice teachers are white, middle class and under the age of twenty-five (Zumwalt & Craig, 2005), the experience of having themselves graduated from a school system saturated by No Child Left Behind reforms has certainly had an impact, as has this generation's significantly amplified experience with the multisensory assault of technologically enhanced popular culture.

For many who enter teacher preparation either during their final undergraduate years, or as part of an intensive fifth-year model, the time in which they are becoming teachers is, not unlike the young women of Kathy Borman's (1991) "postponed generation," arguably an extension of adolescence fraught with the anxieties of a demographically unique historical moment. Their ambivalence for women's career development and seeming acceptance of a non-permeable, totally masculinized corporate culture and ladder (as opposed to previous generations that celebrated women's involvement in the workplace as a victory) and wholesale rejection of feminism (Aronson, 2003; Hall & Rodriguez, 2003; Kleinman, Copp, & Sandstrom, 2006) marks these women's experiences as fundamentally different from other contemporary generations. These young women also came of age in the midst of a raced, classed, conservative Christian renaissance of the early 2000s (Magolda & Ebben, 2007; Nail & McGregor, 2009). This was marked by a rise in white student political and religious conservatism on college and university campuses. This period, which continues although less fervently today, included the blacklisting of faculty for "liberal bias" by Republican and other right-wing student organizations, requiring faculty to sign "loyalty oaths" and governing boards of many universities' endowing of chairs in "conservative studies" and similar in a misguided attempt at appeasing these groups by establishing political and ideological "balance"[1] (Jacobson, 2004; Shrecker, 2006; Surber, 2010). This was the case in at least one of the data collection sites discussed in this book.

The political tone then, and reverberating still today, was also evident in the gender and sexuality expressions of young, middle class, white women. For example, a large number of the preservice teachers participating in the research project at one site in particular wore purity rings, and had attended purity balls, having pledged virginity and purity to their fathers as preadolescents. In the world of Christian Purity Balls, girls make this promise both to their fathers and in the context of their religious beliefs, and while rooted in developing strong and healthy relationships between daughters and fathers, the combative language and discourse of masculine custodianship—fathers are "warriors" for and guardians of their daughters' physical and emotional purity until they marry—is not unproblematic (Banerjee, 2008; Baumgartener, 2007; Gibbs, 2007). Fueled by abstinence organizations and young celebrity endorsements,[2] virginity and abstinence became a fashion statement—even if contemporary research suggested that, in reality, those who pledged their virginity were as a whole only slightly less likely to engage in sexual activity before marriage, and were significantly more likely to do so without contraceptive protection when compared with nonpledgers (Bearman & Bruckner, 2001; Beggs, 2005). Many also planned their schooling and career expectations around a common discourse of biological destiny for marriage and motherhood and driven by conservative normative expectations for performing a female-valued identity, compulsory heterosexuality, and a particular moral career.

Even participants who were not members of evangelical Christian groups and did not necessarily subscribe to similar views about biology, destiny, and virginity participated in a popular cultural diet that emphasized same in contradictory, confusing ways that require constant impression management for participating girls and women. While I acknowledge that popular girl culture in the US context is diverse, rich, and by no means wholly oppressive, current trends in both popular culture writ large, and girls' cultures, as Joan Brumberg writes in her introduction to Lauren Greenfield's disquieting visual spectacle, *Girl Culture* (2002), reflect a trend toward controlling bodies and aspirations in specifically raced and classed ways. She writes, "American popular culture is especially dangerous for girls . . . everywhere we see girls and women looking in mirrors, nervously checking who they are" (pp. 88–89). So, for all the collective attention to impression management, contemporary girl culture does not produce terribly reflective or self-aware girls and women capable of internal self-definition. Instead, we collectively encourage girls and women to focus on, as Mahalik et al. (2005) defines as one of the quintessential Western feminine norms, a nearly obsessive interest in "appearances"—of niceness, of love, of idealized self. This perpetual performance for the mirror, for the other, is problematic. As Brumberg suggests, dominant white, middle class girl culture in the United States has shifted radically over the last century from an internal focus in which girls learned "critical skills from older women" and endeavored to become women of substance to an obsessively appearance-oriented "toxic culture" in which "as the twentieth century progressed, more and more young women grew up believing that good looks rather than good works were the highest form of female perfection" (p. 5). It goes without saying that such appearances imply not only compulsory heterosexuality but also a raced and classed standard for both "goodness" and beauty.

For example, as a group, girls and young women voraciously read the *Twilight* novels by Stephenie Meyer (2006). This popular vampire saga essentially builds upon the themes of the sociopolitical conservative renaissance and its image of what constitutes a valued feminine identity through seemingly innocuous, pop entertainment. The valued female identity is that of the passive, obedient, sexualized child; in the narratives, girls and women surrender to their need for total masculine control over their minds and bodies in the name of protection—from the implicit violence of men—as well as from experience, from biblical "sin" and from themselves. The storylines glorify voyeurism, stalking, and abusive, controlling relationships where partners withhold physical affection to get what they want and require total obedience in the name of keeping their women "safe"—and where women are nothing without their men. These books construct the female as selectively powerful: her empowerment comes only in the context of what she is or is not willing to do for a man, and men are constructed as violent, even dangerous, and constantly struggling with animalistic appetites. That these themes create popular reading for girls and women is not surprising. The general thrust of the era's popular cultural signposts emphasizes the value of girls' virginity, obedience to male authority, choosing motherhood and/or the caring professions over careerist orientation and removing themselves from the politicized sphere and intellectual visibility (Banerjee, 2008; Bersamin et al., 2005; Gibbs, 2008; Krasnow, 1998; Meyers, 2001). Unlike the preceding generation, who reacquainted themselves with the urgency of Feminism with Faludi's (1992) and others' work, this generation could be described as "post-Backlash," and for the most part fundamentally wishes to distance itself from association with feminism, the ultimate F-word. This may be in part because they do not see patriarchy as particularly threatening to their moral careers and valued identities as women, or possibly because their conceptualization of the feminist woman is not compatible with the valued identities (read: appearances) they must perform in their respective milieu. As Hall and Rodriguez (2003) found, the archetypal feminist is a truly stigmatized identity, depicted by students, girl culture, and the popular media alike as simplistic, "negative portrayals: women's lib, man hater, bra burner, unfeminine, lesbian and/or sexually deviant, feminazi (ugly, unable to catch a man, dyke), and whining victims" (p. 880). This was further expanded upon by Kleinman, Copp, and Sandstrom (2006), who found that "the vilification and trivialization of feminism in the mass media is long-standing, shifting over time only in rhetorical content." They continue, illustrating that in "the last several years, we have heard students inside and outside our classrooms use violent terms like 'male-basher' and 'feminazi,' without irony, to describe feminists . . . [we] have noticed students' patterned resistance to the idea that sexism persists and is a pervasive feature of U.S. society" (p. 126–27).

Representations of the Iconic Teacher

Just as the new cadre of primary preservice teachers is overwhelmingly made up of white, middle class, heterosexual females (Hollins & Guzman, 1995; Zumwalt & Craig, 2005), so also are the images that dominate popular representations of the iconic teacher of white, middle class, heterosexual women. As illustrated by Meiners (2002), is possible to "sort" these representations into gendered tropes: the schoolmarm, seductress, and my own additon, schoolmistress. The differentiated value between these three hinge upon the woman's skill at impression management and her well-navigated moral career and valued feminine identity. All three archetypes tacitly communicate what kinds of identities are valued and which are stigmatized by how each is punished or rewarded in the narratives they occupy. The sexualized elements of each are as taboo as they are tired, archaic, and mundane; as Bauer (1998) writes, "Hollywood eventually misrepresents all professions, and all vocations are ultimately sexualized . . . perhaps the [teaching] profession is too bankrupt to invent other models for itself than these hopelessly idealized or eroticized ones" (p. 301–12). This extends beyond contemporary Hollywood creations and includes the newly reimagined and reproduced fairy tale, the princess narrative that so many young women and girls find attractive, despite troubling story lines. After all, as Lewis (1993) suggests, "today's most popular fairy tales subtly reinforce erroneous or limited views of women inherent in the Freudian outlook: Snow White and Cinderella win their princes through a combination of good looks, extraordinary housekeeping, and modesty; the punishment for Bluebeard's wife's curiosity—a symbolic sexual transgression—is death" (p. 404).

Schoolmarms

The schoolmarm is a spinster. She is neither attractive, nor necessarily invested in the appearance of "niceness," nor successful in marrying and leaving the classroom to care for her own, biological children (an achievement typically pitched as one very significant leg of a successful moral career). While images of the schoolmarm might be occasionally heartwarming, such as Normal Rockwell's "Schoolteacher" (1956), in which a middle-aged, prim schoolmarm stands in front of a chalkboard decorated with children's birthday wishes, darker images of the stigmatized identity and derailed moral career dominate the US pop culture context, especially images contemporary with the present generation of new and preservice teachers. Roald Dahl's novel, *Matilda* (1988) was made into a feature film in 1996 in which the featured schoolmarm, Miss Trunchbull, is nothing short of a frustrated sadist who genuinely dislikes children. She not only fails to embody the valued feminine identity, she is a hypermasculine caricature intended to activate the heterosexist lesbian gym teacher stereotype-as-stigmatized-identity. As Griffin (1998) writes, "the image of 'a lesbian boogeywoman' haunts all women, scaring young women and their parents, discouraging solidarity among women in sport, and keeping women's sport advocates on the defensive" (p. 53). It also reinforces the feminine norm of sexual and physical passivity by masculinizing and pathologizing physicality and, at its core, pleasure in the physical.

Similarly, the bounds of racially and culturally specific standards for physical attractiveness come into play: just as Miss Trunchbull violates all of the Western feminine norms (Mahalik et al., 2005) associated with valued identity and successful moral careers among young, white women, this and other images suggests that bad teachers are ugly while good teachers are attractive (Bauer, 1998). This can be hardly surprising as the steady diet of books and movies most girls and women are exposed to from birth through adolescence affirm that ugliness in a woman is the ultimate physical and moral stigma from which there can be no recovery and for which no sympathy. From early Disney princesses and their respective ugly stepsisters, wicked witches, or stepmothers to contemporary reality television exploits, girls and women are told that being physically unattractive is a moral failing in itself, and evidence of internal ugliness as well. It also goes without saying that these media communicate a Eurocentric standard for beauty. Just as the wicked witch is almost always a dark, shrill, or accented and hook-nosed anti-Semitic caricature, the heroine is almost always white, blonde, and Western European in appearance. Even recent animated portrayals of girls and women of color as heroines, while representative of a great stride forward in children's entertainment, is still really more of the same. The girls and women, despite being shaded with a different brush, are really still Eurocentric in form, voice, and shape. As Seyaki (2003) observes, popular representations of beauty are always white:

> When Black women were (and are) presented, they typically met (meet) Eurocentric ideals in terms of body type, skin color, and hair texture. Actress Halle Berry and singer/performers Lena Home and Dorothy Dandridge, for example, have light skin, slim bodies, and straight hair. There are exceptions made for "exotic" trends such as dark skin, larger lips, and naturally coarse hair. For example, Alek Wek of the Sudan graces the covers of fashion magazines. Ms. Wek is dark-skinned with large lips, but is as thin as any White model. (p. 469)

To sum up, as a rule: schoolmarms are constructed as ugly, barren, unkind sticks-in-the-mud who are obsessed with rules, grammar, and obedience, and who do not like children, have failed to attract and to marry men, are probably lesbians, and an example for all girls of something to be avoided at all costs. Norman Rockwell aside, these generally stigmatized female and teacher identities.[3]

Seductresses

The seductress is another example of a stigmatized identity and cautionary tale. A dangerous and sexually predatory older female whose age, failure to secure a heterosexual marriage, she is portrayed as unwilling to display selfless love for and devotion to her pupils, opting instead to focus on her own pleasure. This makes her not only a threat to men but also an example of a failed feminine and teacherly moral career. It is important to note that sexual availability is part of the feminine valued identity only in terms of passive heterosexual attractiveness and availability, not sexual aggression, initiation or active pleasure. As Henry Giroux writes of the 1977 film, *Looking for Mr. Goodbar*, the choices available to the young teacher protagonist are essentially between repression and death—not unlike Bluebeard's wife in Lewis's (1993) analysis quoted at the beginning of this section. She is effectively "punished" for deviating from her role as gentle teacher of deaf children and seeking out her own pleasure and sexual adventure. Similar punishments are meted out to other teachers, notably in Hellman's *The Children's Hour* where lesbianism, and heterosexual failure, is the offence at hand (Titus, 2000). The seductress is not, as primary teachers are popularly constructed to be, appropriate "managers of virtue" (Tyack & Hansot, 1988) and perhaps the most iconic image of this kind of transgression and punishment is Muriel Sparks's 1961 novel and Ronald Neame's 1969 film, *The Prime of Miss Jean Brodie*. Farber's (1969) contemporary review of the film describes the protagonist, Brodie, in harsh but revealing terms:

> Jean Brodie is not the noble, self-sacrificing heroine we expect; there's something frightening about the influence she wants—and gets—over her girls' lives. She goes so far as to scheme to involve one of her girls with her own former lover (a sort of sexual intercourse by proxy). . . . A Svengali of the boarding-school, Miss Brodie is a strange mixture of idealistic aesthete and fascist, sexual libertarian and fierce authoritarian. . . . Though Miss Brodie is a monster, she is appealing too, for her desires are only more extreme forms of desires we all have. She refuses marriage because she will not accept a subservient role in her society; she insists on creating a meaningful life that is hers alone. Her dedication to teaching is ultimately selfish—she wants dominion, power to control other destinies, the satisfaction of molding human lives in her own image. (p. 63)

The good teacher, then, is constructed as noble and self-sacrificing whereas a bad teacher, in the guise of seductress, has selfish, base desires—"desires we all have"—but which are inappropriate for a teacher. For the teacher, these desires are wrong for being both sexual and selfish. In the end of both the book and the film, Brodie, like so many other seductresses, is punished with betrayal and death to make that final, instructional point.

Schoolmistresses

Finally, the schoolmistress is no less sexually available than the seductress, nor less single as the spinster schoolmarm, but she typically does a much better job of impression management. If she has "desires" they are passive ones; we certainly never know about it. She is single, but she is also young, pretty and nice, is focused on loving and caring for children, and is unconscious of her own sexuality and void of desire. She waits rather passively in the class-room for marriage and family of her own. Also significantly, she is without the stigma of age and failure to secure a husband that ruins the schoolmarm, or the threat to masculinity and aggressiveness that blight the seductress. It is clear that the schoolmistress is the "correct" performance of the feminine valued identity, while the schoolmarm and seductress are stigmatized identities and to be avoided. The grade school teacher, Miss Marquez, played by Jennifer Lopez in the 1996 film, *Jack*, is attractive and kind (and rarely seen teaching) and spends the entire film ministering to the emotional needs of her students. To return to the Dahl's *Matilda* of film (1996) and novel (1988), the character performing the obvious valued identity, Miss Honey, is kind and attractive, sexually unconscious, with the innocence (and, one should note, the powerlessness) of a child. In this way she is, ostensibly, more able to minister to the needs of children, being herself almost a child.

These themes are certainly in step with research on preservice and novice teachers' beliefs about what constitutes a "good" teacher. The good teacher, in their eyes, is obviously within the schoolmistress trope, and her perfor-mance is irrevocably tied to a successful feminine and teacherly moral career. As Weinstein (1989) found, when preservice teachers are asked to describe a "good" teacher, the top five categories of consensus echo Mahalik et al.'s (2005) top Western feminine norms: being caring, understanding, warm, friendly, and relating to or liking children. Intelligence, pedagogical knowl-edge or abilities, political acumen, and similar did not appear in Weinstein's top categories. This certainly corresponds with many of my preservice study participants' beliefs that while teacher education programs can teach almost anyone to write a lesson plan, good teachers are in fact born, not made. The vast majority asserted that good teachers' most important skills are innate and gendered: they had to love their students and be able to attend to the children's affective needs in a sweet, caring way, and that these skills came most easily to women—though they are certainly within the realm of the possible for men as well.

Teacher educators also acknowledge the dominance of the schoolmistress archetype as the valued identity for their students (though, as will be dis-cussed later, they also participate in reinforcing that dominance). As Mein-ers (2002) writes, the persistence of images of "Lady Bountiful"—a white, middle or upper class, heterosexual woman doing the semimissionary "good work" of civilizing the "native" (p. 87)—is one face of such a valued identity. Meiners suggests that one of many problems with Lady Bountiful is that her influence is at the fore of a racist, heterosexist, classist endeavor to regulate which bodies make acceptable teachers (and, ultimately, good students) and which do not. White women, Meiners suggests, were historically used as colonizing and control agents through the call to teach, a call that emphasized the moral career embodied by the "Lady Bountiful"—a schoolmistress—ideal. Meiners writes of one such successful embodiment of the trope:

> On the first day of class, I routinely ask everyone to "briefly introduce yourself and to tell the class a little something about why you are here"—an exercise I always found so painful yet I now replicate, for convention. Invariably, the majority of the female students in my classes begin to evoke the same figure. This lady—the future elementary teacher—has always loved children. Her mother, her husband or boyfriend (even strangers in the streets) have remarked upon her natural aptitude with children and small animals. She is gracious, nurturing, often soft-spoken, and is usually married (or engaged). The words money, career, union, labor, or even job are rarely mentioned—leaving listeners with the impression that she does not need to rely solely on her income as a teacher to survive. For her, teaching is a calling or a vocation, and she has always known that she wanted to be a (elementary school) teacher. Often, despite a chaotic schedule, she volunteers through her church with special needs children in her spare time. Sometimes, a redemptive narrative circulates: she has always had a desire to save underprivileged children. (p. 89)

This figure is well known to most teacher educators. Even the iconoclastic Jane Eyre or Anne Shirley must mellow from willful girlhood into a more docile form to become teachers of children, and it is becoming a teacher that acts as their initiation into adulthood and "appropriate" femininity (Gates, 2004). The few deviations from this valued identity come from comic attempts at cross-occupying the masculine. These are usually, if not always, white women for whom comic cross-dressing is loathingly, reluctantly attempted in a "desperate" situation (Goldie Hawn as the white, female football coach [*Wildcats*, 1986]; Michele Pfeiffer as a former Marine-turned-teacher [*Dangerous Minds*, 1993]) for which their delicate femininities and biological aptitudes for care and love are ill-suited. For these situations, with "difficult" (read: urban, black, or Latina/o) schools and pupils, they must become masculinized, "save" their students from themselves and their communities, but at the same time be able to reveal their inner valor and vulnerability to appropriate masculine figures, such as would-be suitors. As odious as this seeming modern-day resurrection of Kipling's "white man's burden" (1999) may be, equally retrograde is that the only other stereotype that represents alternatives to the moral career of the iconic schoolmistress is the aforementioned lesbian physical education teacher. However, this is a null choice; the lesbian is always a stigmatized identity in the popular culture and certainly for the feminine and teacherly moral career (McCullick, Belcher, Hardin, & Hardin, 2003).

The Feminized Profession in Teacher Preparation

Pop cultural imagery and the tropes of the feminization are well-represented in the teacher education setting. While girls and women themselves experience most of their gender socialization in the popular cultural milieu, I suggest that one powerful mechanism for solidifying that socialization and connecting the beliefs, practices, and cultural patterns associated with feminization and feminized work with teaching is located in the practices and relationships in schools of education. This occurs between girls and women, between preservice teachers and their professors or mentors, and between the individual and the institutional discourses in play.

Teacher Educators

Just as the overwhelming majority of preservice and new primary teachers are white, middle class women, so also are most of the teacher educators who work with them (Cole, 1999; Fuller, 1992; Grant & Gillette, 1987).[4] The pattern is even more concentrated among the nontenured and clinical faculty, both of whom are more likely to do the lower-status work of teacher licensure than are tenured, older, white male colleagues (Cole, 1999; deMarrais & LeCompte, 1998; Suarez-Orozco, 2000; Vare, 1996). Lanier and Little (1986), Judge (1982), and Ducharme and Agne (1982) described a teacher education professoriate in the 1980s as suffering from a collective identity crisis: torn between being seen as anti-intellectual, plebian, and excessively pragmatic by university colleagues in other departments and as out-of-touch, excessively intellectual residents of the ivory tower by teachers in the field.[5]

While this identity crisis is still very much in play in the contemporary context, more contemporary studies have focused on the differences in individual careers, lives, and trajectories (Cole, 1999). Apart from generational differences, teacher educators at work in the late 1990s and first decade of the 2000s have a culturally and politically distinct existence from those described in the Lanier and Little review. For example, their work was and is more heavily surveilled through accountability procedures. Similarly, attacks on teacher education have increased in frequency and venom; teacher educators have become scapegoats, with schools of education characterized both pits of ineptitude and dens of left-wing brainwashing (Berliner, 2000; Duncan, 2009). While this is part of larger, complex cultural and political phenomena, attacks on the academic preparation of teachers still speak to the general trend of de-skilling the work of the teacher by asserting that it is neither (a) intellectual work requiring a grasp of abstract theoretical concepts wedded with practice, nor (b) professional work that requires specialized training beyond pure apprenticeship. Furthermore, these trends are more pronounced at the elementary level, where schools are more likely to be scripted or otherwise externally controlled. In these contexts and others, teacher educators are constructed as out-of-touch with the practical realities of teachers, preaching for an ideal world, and so on. They are characterized as obsolete, and their accountability surveillance—already highly unusual in higher education—continues. And for the most part it is tolerated, at least by some teacher educators, especially those in untenured positions, who must acknowledge their relative powerlessness in the face of lessened autonomy as a function of state and federal mandate. As Cole (1999) found in her study of teacher educators, the choice to work in teacher education often meant taking a drastic step down: a choice to take a lower salary, with little status, little support, and no voice in the institutional hierarchy. However, as one of her participants said, "I gave up money. I gave up status. I gave up all my security . . . but you see, I love the work. I love teaching. I love writing. I love the flexibility" (p. 283). Love, it seems, makes what sounds like a generally miserable experience worthwhile, or at least endurable. It is no wonder that most preservice teachers also firmly believe that they can tolerate a host of ills as long as love is there to sustain them.

Love and Control

As Liston (1995) discusses, schools of education are often seen as the academic equivalent of women's unremunerated domestic labor when compared with the high-status, high-reward, public work of individuals who position themselves as primarily writers and researchers and within that, the faculty who do the work of elementary preservice teacher preparation engage in an even lower-status, "messy, student-centered and labor-intensive endeavor" (pp. 91–93). But, as Cole (1999) found, this experience is mediated by love. As the work of teachers and teacher educators is gendered work, teacher educators and preservice teachers alike may construct valued feminine and teacherly identity with ideas of obedience, goodness, niceness, self-sacrifice, and filial piety—emphasizing and valorizing a moral career that may not favor critical examinations of the structural factors contributing to inequitable conditions in higher education (deMarrais & LeCompte, 1998). Similarly, the seemingly innocent discourses of love and vocation can become mechanisms for reinforcing the status quo in teacher education work. In particular, discourses around "vocation" have long been used to describe the unremunerated work of low-status members of society, including but not limited to women in general and teachers and teacher educators specifically. The logic here is that because the work is imbued with meaning—and, in some contexts, meanings associated with activism and social change—it needn't be as well-compensated as less "meaningful" occupations, such as the high-status research work of the academy where one is not expected to receive nonmaterial rewards, such as the love of one's students, in return. As Brannon (1993) writes of teaching among women in the composition field of higher education, the iconic schoolmistress

> offers service, dedication, patience, and love as the dominant trope for teaching, making teaching fully women's work, work that needs no financial compensation or reduced loads for the time that is spent. To ask for money or fewer students or "a life" only evokes the crass masculinist values of power and self-interestedness. The nurturer, then, must remain silent and thereby deny the contributions of and reinscribe the invisibility of women's work. (p. 460)

The "silent nurturer" who works as a teacher educator may add to this invisibility of her work as a relative plebe in the research institution, and add this to a ventriloquated rationale for her low status. The subtext here is also that such meaningful work is somehow less intellectually rigorous than other work, and therefore less deserving of appropriate remuneration. This has long been the story of women's unpaid labor, and of the low wages in many of the so-called service vocations and certainly in the feminized professions such as teaching and caring for children, but when combined with the abstract reward of love, the pattern of control and exploitation becomes almost impossible to see.

While most teacher educators, and many preservice teachers, are drawn to their work out of a deep desire to affect social justice, change, and reform, the accompanying discourses of love and vocation can still be problematic from a gendered perspective. One of the many contradictions inherent in teacher education is that while these discourses ensure continued compliance beyond the reasonable and remunerated parameters, often to the detriment of individual scholarly work, these discourses are also part of the discourses of accountability and accreditation. So, teacher educators may work even longer days at their chosen vocation to meet the expectations for valued identity. In this way, love and vocation become mechanisms for controlling teacher educators, and as part of an institutional discourse eventually ventriloquated by its familiars, the preservice teachers with whom they work. In this way love and vocation in their less critical forms become part of a performance of valued identity in teacher education that is replicated by preservice, and later novice, teachers as a means of controlling their own students, and so on.

Gee, Hull, and Lankshear (1997) define this as "pastoral control"—a post-modern process by which "workers are asked to invest their hearts, minds, and bodies fully in their work. They are asked to think and act critically, reflectively, and creatively" (p. 7) and to consider power and responsibility as shared. Unlike disciplinary control, which is brutal, physical, demeaning, and obvious, pastoral control conscripts the worker into collusion with authority, distributing the source of authoritarian control and rendering any definable locus of oppression as invisible. As Schutz (2004) writes,

> Unlike traditional settings that tend to sanction divergences from a static norm, then, pastoral settings foster particular forms of creativity, often harnessing them to serve the (loosely coupled) systems in which participants are enmeshed. And because control in progressive [setting] is distributed throughout the environment instead of located in (apparently) identifiable figures or systems, it is extremely difficult for participants to detect or resist. (p. 15)

The patterns of pastoral control that keep teacher educators working in the trenches of "domestic labor" are the same mechanisms they will employ to mobilize their preservice students, and subsequently, they their young pupils. Co-opting desires to be loved, to have a true vocation, or "calling," and to work toward an often ill-defined ideal of social justice (North, 2010) are all noble-enough sounding aspirations; however in a pastoral control economy, these can become systems of intensification, de-skilling, and control. Such mechanisms also feed upon individuals' drive toward impression management—the schoolmarm and seductress, while simple archetypes, nonetheless constitute a powerful threat—so much so that the individual motivation for establishing a valued identity and maintaining the moral career can be easily manipulated. Teacher educators are certainly aware of these dynamics, however consciously they manage their own identities and often encourage critical thinking and reflection while at the same time unconsciously conscripting preservice teachers' desires for love and vocation to serve their own needs.

However, this does not mean that we should make love taboo in teacher education, as the concept is as complex as Lucetta's reason; instead, we must examine and critique what "love" is and name its relationship to gendered work and "vocation" in teaching. It is only disrupted when the value of love and vocation are taken down from the pedestal, questioned, and, as Liston (2000) would suggest, teachers are permitted to fall out of romantic, idealized love with their work, name the limits of care, and begin looking for more edifying forms of love to drive a professional life.

The Feminized Profession and Domestic Ideologies

As discussed in chapter 1, Griffiths (2006) suggests that the so-called feminization of the elementary classroom is not the problem it is made out to be, despite contemporary panics over boys' achievement, classic arguments around semiprofessionalism and perpetual realities of low status and remuneration in feminized professions across most Western contexts (Acker, 1995; deMarrais & LeCompte, 1998; Etzioni, 1969; Galman, 2006; Gordon, 1992; Okopny, 2008). Instead, rather than focusing on the "problem" of feminization, it might be productive to instead examine the domestic ideologies that pervade a culture and define what constitutes valued masculine and feminine identity in a given context. For example, it has been suggested that fewer men become elementary educators because masculinity is constructed as incompatible with caring and nurturing children (Drudy, Martin, Woods, & O'Flynn, 2005). Connell and Messerschmidt (2005) frame this as one face of an encompassing "hegemonic masculinity" that emphasizes individualism, aggressiveness, competition, ambition, compulsory heterosexuality, violence, and rigid social hierarchies. It may be self-reproducing in schools and schooling practice because, even though schools are influenced by femininities and subordinate masculinities, hegemonic forms of masculinity are nonetheless dominant and active in the continued subordination of all other forms both inside and outside of the schoolhouse walls. Domestic ideologies like these operate at the national priority level as well: Elementary and early childhood teachers who do the caring work of educating children are typically among the lowest paid, lowest status professionals in most Western industrialized nations. Caring for and teaching children, as something frequently constructed as the natural, biological purpose of women, is not constructed as true work, and simply not prioritized in remunerative terms, resulting in the further deprofessionalization.

Given the biological arguments implicit in some domestic ideologies, it is important to note that while the archetype of teacher-as-mother[6] is absent from the schoolmarm/seductress/schoolmistress triad, it is no less significant. While not necessarily representative of an immediate valued or stigmatized identity and subsequent moral career for the postadolescent preservice teacher, the trope of teacher as "social mother" (Cortina & San Roman, 2006) drives much domestic ideology in Western contexts. As Cortina and San Roman found in their historical analysis of teaching as gendered work in Catholic contexts, what began with a demand for female workers—in schools for girls, in institutions of teacher training, as low-cost labor compatible with child-rearing—resulted in discourses to ensure a reliable labor force, convinced of its innate biological aptitude for mothering children. They found that domestic ideology is also driven by strategy and economic necessity:

> the role that women traditionally occupied in the domestic space began to extend itself into the public sphere [and] the demand for women did not occur because of requirements for professionalization; on the contrary, their entrance into teaching should be understood as a result of the glorification of the so-called feminine nature that made a woman a suitable candidate to be put in charge of young children in her role as social mother. (p. 5)

Even outside explicitly Catholic historical and social contexts, the discourse of the "social mother" can be a central part of the domestic ideologies driving feminization of P–6 teaching. In Britain and the United States, for example, women have long been conscripted as social mothers, beginning, as noted earlier as "welcomers" and handmaidens for cultural and linguistic assimilation. Meiners's (2002) "Lady Bountiful" also performs these duties. But, as Acker (1995) notes in her review of the research on teaching and gender, this social mother is markedly different from literal mothers in that she is an idealized, generalized, distillation of a cultural icon of motherhood; she is always nurturing, always kind, and the valued teacherly identity, in this case, combines the discourses of love and vocation with self-sacrifice, poor boundaries and the relentlessness of socially expected "nurturant labor" (Grumet, 1988, 87).

It is interesting, then, that so much of the recent panic over the feminization of teaching has created tacit policies of amelioration-by-masculinization. Despite research suggesting that the gender of the teacher is not a significant factor in boys' or girls' social, emotional, or academic development, some schools in the United States and European Union have employed targeted male recruitment and incentive structures as an effort to increase boys' achievement by adding male teachers, with unclear results (Carrington & McPhee, 2008; Martino, Mills, & Lingard, 2004). Similarly, US government programs attempt to do the same by providing fast civilian employment in teaching for returning soldiers and laid-off business workers, most of them men and nearly all without experience in education. They are "fast-tracked" to licensure so they can begin teaching immediately in high-need schools (Becker, 2009; Chandler, 2009). This sends a powerful message about the value of professional preparation and the knowledge necessary for high quality care work. Meanwhile, reports suggest that educated women, driven back to the workforce to compensate for the effects of the recession, are having difficulty securing jobs in teaching and other forms of care work, once plentiful (Greenhouse, 2009). Interestingly, the combined effects of scarcity and masculinization have not had a professionalizing or otherwise positive effect on care work: instead, these trends are seen as early "proof" that teaching as care work requires little training and is instead a transition point profession designed as a stepping stone to higher status employment.

Whether directly or indirectly, all masculinization interventions suggest that maleness is an improvement upon women's performance as workers thus far, and the recession has provided a crop of men ready to work in the feminized professions—for the time being. As Ringrose (2007) writes, such strategies ignore "that measures of so-called gender equity in academic achievement do not necessarily translate into ideals of wider social equity inside or outside of schools" (p. 485). However, in the wake of the devastating global recession of 2008–2009 and subsequent state efforts at economic recovery, more men are choosing—and being actively incentivized—to work in the feminized professions, often in large numbers and at speeds that do not necessarily allow for adjusted local or national domestic ideologies. As this trend continues, the previously protected niche of the feminized care work professions may be radically affected: what were once pockets of women's financial autonomy, sites of quiet resistance to hegemony and sources of informal social support for working women and their families are beginning to change. Documenting and understanding this radical interruption, and possible reversal, of a well-established recent historical trend toward feminization of teaching is crucial as Western nations in particular seek to reinvent work, and themselves, in a new economy. This reinvention has advantages and marked disadvantages for working women and their families. It is possible that in the midst of the emotionally exploitative domestic ideologies driving the expectations for teachers to be "social mothers," the feminized professions have offered women and some men from a wide range of socioeconomic brackets opportunities for relative financial autonomy, flexibility for child and family care, and informal social support networks, especially for working mothers and their families. Furthermore care-based work has been shown to afford women enhanced educational and professional opportunities, especially when social and economic restrictions may also be present (Trotman, 2008).

Conclusion

In their study of men as temporary clerical workers, Henson and Rogers (2001) found that the men "did masculinity" in such a way that the performance was "shaped by the gendered expectations of their agencies, their clients and even themselves to reassert the feminine identification of the job while at the same time rejecting its application to them." They continue,

> Paradoxically, rather than disrupting the gender order, the gender strategies used by these male clerical temporaries help to reproduce and naturalize the gendered organization of work and reinvigorate hegemonic masculinity and its domination over women and subaltern men. (p 218)

In other words, rather than becoming "feminized" by a feminized profession and work environment (meaning, one in which there are and have been large numbers of female workers, not that these female workers hold considerable power in the face of hegemony or domination of the work site) as posited by "boy crisis" proponents, these men's performances had an opposite effect: the work site became even more feminized, and they, as men, more aligned with hegemonic forms of masculinity. As Goffman (1959) suggested, understanding the typical begins with a thorough exploration of the atypical, and to see what is considered "normal" one must first look at the transgressive, and stigmatized. Considering that a "normal" work world in the US context, at least, is one that is effectively masculinized (meaning that there are both large numbers of male workers, and that they hold positions of power and domination over women and subaltern men), a deeper understanding of the workplace as a site of challenge to hegemonic masculinity might entail understanding the feminized professions and how they operate. However, as Henson and Rogers (2001), Griffiths (2006), Connell (1995), and others have illustrated, feminized professions, while illuminative as cases, are not exempt from the dominance of hegemonic masculinity. Still, as in Henson and Rogers's work, the feminized profession does create a unique backdrop against which the mechanisms of hegemony masculinity are thrown into rather sharp relief. Additionally, as Griffiths (2006) suggests, just because teaching, as a feminized profession, may be pervaded by hegemonic masculinity, it does not preclude transgression on the part of the workers, especially those who engage in subversive, resistant practices. These practices have the potential to transform feminization, and the popular-cultural genealogy of the iconic girl-teacher, on its head.

For a profession that has historically enacted control by selecting for conformity and obedience in its workers (deMarrais & LeCompte, 1998; Dworkin, 1987), many of these workers' practices and beliefs "contradict the commonsense notion that women teachers are spineless conformists who do not stand up for their rights" (Acker, 1995, p. 177). Similarly, examining the "feminized profession" as (1) problematic sites of deprofessionalization, insufficient remuneration, pastoral control, and sex-segregation, or (2) potential pockets of women's autonomy, sites of quiet resistance to hegemony and sources of informal social support for women and subaltern men may not be as contradictory as it might first appear. Rather like Lucetta's claim that she has "no other but a woman's reason"—it is possible that a deeper understanding of the feminized professions begins with becoming comfortable with contradiction, and locating within it possibilities for subversion. A "woman's reason," then, can be a valuable thing indeed.

Notes

1. It has since been argued that there are other reasons for the seeming preponderance of liberal faculty in higher education in general and the liberal arts and social sciences in specific, including that, like teaching, working in academe self-selects for a certain demographic (Surber, 2010).

2. Virginity and its surrender were used as marketing devices for Jessica Simpson's albums and image, beginning with the live broadcast of singer's 2002 wedding and frank discussion of her virginity. The wedding special was followed by the MTV series, *Newlyweds: Nick and Jessica* (2002–2005) which portrayed Jessica as the archetypal "dumb blonde," whose stupidity was employed as the sitcom's primary comic focus.

3. Karl Rove demonstrated his dislike for Supreme Court nominee Sonia Sotomayor by claiming that she offended him by correcting grammar, saying she is "sort of a schoolmarm" and not his equal in that regard (Fox News, May 26, 2009).

4. This could not be more different from patterns in the rest of higher education, which is dominated by white males. This is true to such an extent that many female undergraduates either do not apply to graduate school, or, for those who do, drop out because of feelings of isolation, alienation, and silent sexism (Sadker & Sadker, 1994). Whether or not women flock to teacher education because of the perceived relative safety of a feminized environment, or because of schools of education courses' notorious, and mostly untrue, "easy A" status, is unclear (Campbell, 2005).

5. This is also a contemporary issue: recently I participated in an interdisciplinary series on campus in which I was the only participant from education. After I gave

my presentation, a colleague from the humanities noted, innocently but with amazement, "I didn't know you did research *over there*."

6. It is important to make the distinction between this predominantly white ideology and the mothering discourses found among black teachers, which are completely different and focus not on self-sacrifice, romantic self-abnegation, and a raced and classed domestic ideology, but rather a cariño-like focus on unsentimental capacity building, critical care, and motivating and empowering black children (Acker, 1995).

PART II

~

LEARNING TO
WORK IN THE SHADOW
OF ICONIC GIRLHOOD

CHAPTER THREE

~

Seeking to Understand

Methods of Inquiry

Qualitative research is the wide-ranging term, used to cover interviewing with open-ended questions, life history interviews, oral histories, studying personal constructs and mental maps and observational studies whether the observer is a participant or non-participant. Ethnography, my preferred term, can be used to mean most of the above, but here is used to cover observational research. Participant observation is used interchangeably with ethnography . . . both these terms imply that the researcher values the views, perspectives, opinions, prejudices and beliefs of the informants, actors or respondents she is studying and is going to take them seriously . . . your job is to find out how the people you are researching understand their world.

—Delamont, 2002, pp. 6–7

In this chapter, I will describe the methods I used in my personal quest to understand the phenomena discussed in the previous two chapters. This means that I will start out by describing the research contexts and give some specific information about the research contexts as well as how I collected data in these sites and analyzed those data. As noted in chapter 1, I will also spend some time talking about my own role as a researcher in the different research sites, as well as some of the limitations of my study design.

However, let me begin by privileging, as Delamont (2002) suggests above, how the people I am researching understand their world. This means seeking out their stories. The stories individual participants told about how they understood themselves becoming teachers, working with teachers, and doing the gendered work of teaching were the focus of my study. I hesitate to some degree to call this a true ethnography because my immersion in the culture of each site was hardly participatory—indeed, I was not a teacher licensure student, nor did I play the part of one, at either site. That said, my interpretation of ethnographic practice is rooted in examining not only what is immediately occurring but also what might be possible. As LeCompte (2002) writes, a current trend in thinking about ethnography points toward focusing on the individual in terms of a longer-term trajectory of possibility—"of what they are producing, including identities, aspirations and possible futures"—rather than descriptive elements of the static immediate present. The subversive roots in ethnography (LeCompte, 2002) make it an ideal choice for projects whose agendas include uncovering marginalized or traditionally silenced voices—in this case, preservice teachers and teacher educators doing the isolated, low-status work of the feminized semiprofessions, and their stories. My methods were designed to foster relationships with research participants and present an emic interpretation of the data. Both researcher stance and data collection strategies were rooted in an interpretivist perspective (Lincoln & Guba, 1985; Wolcott, 1994), sampling was purposive/theoretical rather than random or representative, and the primary data-collection mechanism was the researcher herself (Lincoln & Guba, 1985). It was not expected that findings could be easily generalized to other settings. Data collection was recursive and emergent in nature. In this case, data were triangulated between method (Delamont, 2002) (using more than one method to get at the same questions, such as collecting information on one issue using observation and interviews) as well as within method (getting data of multiple types within one method, such as asking a variety of questions in the interview).

Research Contexts

This research was conducted in multiple sites over the course of seven years, spanning roughly from 2003 to 2009, and in some respects ongoing. While I interpret the corpus of data discussed in this volume as the products of connected, ongoing study, the sites of study from which data are drawn are all teacher education contexts, where preservice teachers and teacher educators were the primary actors. These were three separate, though comparable, contexts, given the intentionally plain pseudonyms, Mountain University (MU), Prairie College, and Valley University. Data were collected at Mountain University from late 2002 through 2004, at Prairie College in 2003, and at Valley University from fall 2006 through spring 2008. In-depth discussion of each appears in chapters 4, 5, and 6.

Mountain University

Mountain University is a large, public research-1 university in an affluent suburban community in the Western United States. The total student population at Mountain at the time of data collection approached 28,000 students (47 percent female, 53 percent male), with nearly 24,000 undergraduate students and about 5,000 graduate students in 150 areas of study taking part in the 3,400 courses offered each semester. Sixty-six percent of these were in-state residents, 34 percent were nonresidents, including 4 percent international students (University Website, 2004). In-state and out-of-state students alike paid one of the highest public university tuition rates in the nation ($1,388 for residents and $9,060 for nonresidents per semester, excluding room and board) and were among the most affluent and least civically engaged and socially responsible of their age group, according to 2002 data from the National Survey of Student Engagement (University Website; NSSE study).

At MU, the school of education was its own community within the larger university. It had its own dean and facilities and even its own admissions and graduation requirements, as did the other professional schools on campus that provided undergraduate preprofessional programs. Founded in the late 1800s along with the rest of the university, the School of Education followed the standard "normal school" model of teacher preparation until in the early 1980s when MU became the first institution in the state to abandon the bachelor's degree in education in favor of requiring all preservice teachers to obtain a bachelor of arts degree in a separate field of study *in addition to education coursework* (MU School of Education website, 2004). The School of Education offered a variety of MA and PhD programs in education, and many of the undergraduate and post–BA licensure courses were taught by doctoral students. Students interested in becoming teachers were required to apply to the school for admission one of three routes: (1) undergraduate licensure, (2) post-BA licensure, or (3) graduate-level licensure concurrent with a master's degree. The variety of licensure programs and the flexible course offerings attracted nontraditional and second-career students to the programs. The majority of the tenured faculty was heavily involved in research and many taught upper-level graduate courses in addition to managing a demanding schedule of research and service. The undergraduate teacher education courses were taught by some tenure-line faculty, several advanced, qualified doctoral students, and a large pool of clinical and adjunct faculty.

Preservice Participants at Mountain

Study participants at Mountain (N = 17) came from the elementary un-dergraduate and post–BA licensure pools. These groups received the same instructional treatment—they were in classes together, were advised by the same faculty, and had identical routes to licensure. All seventeen partici-pants self-identified as white. All preservice participants were between the ages of nineteen and twenty-four, with the vast majority under the age of twenty-one. While the post-BA program typically has students who are not in that age range—and indeed, the students who were on the older end of the age spectrum did come from the post-BA program, during the time frame of this data collection, no older students were observed as part of the cohort. While the post-BA program typically has students who are not in that age range—and indeed, the students who were on the older end of the age spec-trum did come from the post-BA program—during the time frame of this data collection, no older students were observed as part of the cohort. The overwhelming majority of post-BA students at the time of data collection were students who had graduated from MU the previous semester and were continuing on to pursue licensure.

Faculty Participants at Mountain

Faculty participants (N = 6) included not only formal, tenure line, or oth-erwise appointed faculty but also the doctoral students and supervisors who taught in the teacher education programs. Of these, participants included four women and two men, three of whom were tenure line faculty members while the rest were doctoral student or clinical instructors.

Valley University

Valley University is a large, public land-grant research-1 university in a small college town in the Northeastern United States. As of 2009, there were a total of 19,600 undergraduate students, and 4,100 graduate students enrolled at Valley University (Valley University Website, 2010). The overwhelm-ing majority (more than 80 percent) of undergraduate students were Mas-sachusetts state residents, while 30 percent of graduate students hailed from Massachusetts. Roughly 80 percent of both undergraduates and graduate students self-identified as students of color, with the largest reported per-centage at both levels identifying as Asian/Pacific Islander. The majority of all undergraduate students were between eighteen and twenty-one years of age, and graduate students between twenty-six and thirty years of age. While slightly higher numbers (less than 10 percent) of female students than male students enroll as first year undergraduates, more male students complete the undergraduate programs. Graduate programs begin with the same subtle skew but finish with much higher levels of female attrition. Tuition for in-state undergraduates was roughly $20,000 per year including all expenses. Graduate students, who do not pay room and board, pay an in-state tuition rate of roughly $11,000. Out-of-state students pay around $10,000 more in each instance. Forth-seven percent of all undergraduates receive financial aid of some kind. To provide some context for these tuition rates, a recent national survey proclaimed Valley University to be a "best buy" among public colleges and universities.

The School of Education at Valley, recently ranked among the top fifty in the United States, grants doctoral and master's degrees in education, offers an undergraduate minor in education, and provides teacher licensure at the elementary level primarily through its Teacher Education Partnership Program (TEPP).[1] Like Mountain, Valley University was state-mandated to offer licensure at the master's level, and even then only recognizing a handful of undergraduate majors as relevant to teacher preparation—there was not at the time of data collection, nor had there been for some time, a major in education.

The TEPP program is a nine-month, intensive MEd and licensure program in which preservice teachers must complete rigorous coursework while simultaneously completing two internship experiences in local rural, suburban, and urban school districts. In addition to meeting graduate school admissions requirements, the TEPP program requires applicants to successfully complete a significant number of prerequisite courses and pass the state-mandated teacher licensure examination prior to admission. The majority of TEPP students begin as Valley undergraduates completing the education minor. While there are typically one or two individuals who are not matriculating undergraduates from the education minor (such as graduating seniors from other institutions, or people who are second-career professionals) TEPP's major source of enrollment has been stable for some time, and the time of data collection was no exception.

It is important to note, however, that at the time of this writing, as will be reflected in the concluding chapters and discussion, enrollment in the TEPP program had been dramatically dwindling. For example, during the 2005–2006 academic year, the TEPP program (which at that time did not distinguish between elementary and early childhood tracks) had seventy preservice teachers enrolled. Many faculty were surprised to find the program attracting (and admitting) such numbers, and discussion about the value of a smaller program began cropping up at faculty meetings. However, the program continued to thrive with sixty-four of that number graduating from the program. In 2006–2007, only fifty-eight students enrolled and completed the program. By 2007–2008, when the program differentiated between elementary and early childhood, separating into two distinct cohorts, the elementary program admitted only twenty-five students. Data for 2008–2009 and 2009–2010 continued to hold at upwards of twenty-five to thirty admissions, with the prospective 2010–2011 pool being smaller still. While this trend is by no means unique to TEPP and Valley University, it was a significant elephant-in-the-room for many respondents. This represents a further rub considering that the TEPP tuition for 2010–2011 is much higher than the projected average graduate student tuition at Valley, at just over $16,000, not including books and computer software and data management fees. While this makes sense given overall tuition increases and the fact that TEPP students take more courses and receive more credits than individuals in less intensive programs, the impression of higher tuition still packs an emotional punch for many.

Preservice Participants at Valley

Preservice study participants (N = 25) in the TEPP Program at Valley differ significantly from those in the Mountain and Prairie samples in that they were not in the early coursework-only phase of teacher preparation. Instead, because they began field placement internship experiences immediately and concurrently with their coursework, there was no such period of "imaginative rehearsal" (Goffman, 1959) to capture. They were also not undergraduate level students. However, as many faculty and others would argue throughout data collection, the experiences of the TEPP students were unlike those of other graduate students: they did not have significant thesis projects or course autonomy, but were participating in a demanding, but tightly prescribed "plus-one" (to borrow Prairie College language) program not unlike an undergraduate teacher education experience. In all other respects, they were demographically very similar to the other samples: overwhelmingly white, female, middle class English speakers with an average age of twenty-two.[2]

While many more Valley preservice, education minor, and general undergraduate women participated in taking the Conformity to Feminine Norms Index (CFNI) measure, described in the next paragraphs, twenty-four preservice TEPP students participated as respondents in the ethnographic study at Valley. Of these, all twenty-four included in the analysis were white.[3] Seven were in a semisegregated early childhood track within TEPP, while the remaining nineteen were in the elementary track. As will be discussed in greater detail in following chapters, this was due in part to ethical demands of my role as an instructor in TEPP and the subsequent necessity to only recruit students not directly in my course. However, the twenty-five study participants can be considered demographically and otherwise representative of the total number of TEPP enrollees during the 2006–2007 and 2007–2008 academic years of data collection.

Faculty Participants at Valley

Program faculty as of 2007 (N = 15) were predominantly tenure-line faculty and lecturers, most of whom had affiliation in other subdepartments in the School of Education, but taught in TEPP as part of their professional load. Of these, the overwhelming majority were female (N = 12). Qualified graduate students, most of whom were also female, were involved as supervisors, overseeing student progress in the student teaching and early internship opportunities.

Prairie College

Prairie College is a small, liberal arts college in a relatively remote geographic corner of the Midwestern United States. At the time of data collection, the college did not have a formal school of education, and instead prepared prospective teachers by offering an undergraduate minor in education. Similarly, the college did not grant a formal teaching credential. Instead students took a variety of theoretical, discussion-based classes, most of which did not necessarily include a field placement, though some students did engage in an internship in schools before graduation with the minor in education. Founded in the mid-1800s by members of the Religious Society of Friends (Quakers), Prairie College was primarily an undergraduate liberal arts college community consisting of ninety-six full-time faculty and 1,170 students (56 percent female, 44 percent male), 7 percent of whom are international students. The college was nearly twice as ethnically diverse as Mountain University despite its size and relative geographic isolation, with 22 percent of students identifying as students of color. While statistics are not available on socioeconomic diversity at Prairie College, it was my observation during my time there that strides have been made on the part of recruitment, admissions, scholarships, and budgeting personnel to find ways to attract economic, ethnic, and cultural diversity to campus. Without scholarships or other enhancements, tuition was significantly higher than Mountain University at $25,364 per year, or $31,782 including room and board.

The education department at Prairie College had gone through many incarnations before assuming the form at work during the period of data collection. While at one time the college had both elementary and secondary licensure programs, eventually this dwindled to only a secondary program.

In 1994 the college decided that it would discontinue its secondary teacher education program. It was replaced with an education minor, and faculty encouraged students to get a master's degree or post-BA license elsewhere after their undergraduate degree at Prairie was completed. This was called "four-plus-one": four years at Prairie and one year somewhere else. At the time of data collection, a new, intensive in-house Master's in Teaching program had been instituted to provide the "plus-one" at Prairie. Though not a site for extensive data collection, this small program was innovative, successful, and a source of pride to the education faculty.

Preservice Participants at Prairie

Preservice study participants (N = 11) were all undergraduates under the age of twenty-one, all enrolled in the education minor. Again, this sample was much more diverse than the Mountain or Valley University samples, including two women of color and, most surprisingly, large numbers of men (N = 10; these were excluded from this study). While the presence of so many men in a teacher education pool is unusual, our collective astonishment must be mediated somewhat: (1) this was not a licensure program, (2) it did not distinguish between elementary and secondary (where there are typically larger numbers of male candidates), and (3) based on second-year follow-up emails, the overwhelming majority of these men did not, in fact, go on to become teachers, most opting for graduate school programs in other areas. Of the eleven females, meanwhile, only two indicated a possible interest in secondary education, and of these one ultimately decided on elementary level preparation.

Faculty Participants at Prairie

Faculty members at Prairie were not necessarily exclusive to teacher preparation; instead, theirs was an interdisciplinary identity. While they maintained their primary affiliation with their home department (English, history, biology, etc.) they taught courses as service to the education department. Faculty participants (N = 3) were two males and one female. The male participants were professors from other disciplines, while the female faculty member was attached to the education minor as a logistical and planning liaison and in a non-tenured capacity.

Data Collection Methods

At all sites, participant selection relied heavily on convenience sampling at the institutional level, and "snowball" sampling at the individual participant level (Lincoln & Guba, 1985). As this was an ethnographic study, methods of data collection cast a "wide net" and included interviews, nonparticipant observation, a wide range of artifact collection, and CNFI (Mahalik et al., 2005).

Interviews

With the research focus on participants' identities, stories, and meaning-making processes, in-depth, open-ended interviews were particularly important data sources. Interview questions for preservice and novice teachers fell into three categories of inquiry: (1) questions around the context of participant experiences, particularly participant's social and cultural backgrounds and stories about family, childhood, and beliefs; (2) questions about professional trajectory, motivations for choosing teaching, imagined classroom work and future selves, and stories about teaching and schooling; and (3) stories about the teacher preparation experience. Questions for teacher educators focused on the same themes but also probed for their experiences as teacher educators and their perceptions of teaching as a profession.

Interviews typically lasted between one and a half and two hours. All preservice and novice teaching participants at all sites were interviewed at least twice, if possible, with digital communication such as email or social networking/media websites facilitating follow-up both before and after my departure from a given site. Interviews with teacher educators varied, but typically involved one lengthy or two shorter interviews. Interviews were tape recorded and supplemented with my handwritten notes.

Observations

Observations were conducted using Wolcott's (1981) strategy for observation by "broad sweep" with more particular foci emerging from recursive data analyses. Regularly scheduled nonparticipant observations were conducted in teacher education course settings at all three institutions.

Artifacts

Artifacts included a wide variety of things that can be loosely grouped into two categories: (1) personal artifacts, and (2) program and institutional artifacts. All artifacts were treated as "field texts" (Clandinin & Connelly, 1996) and their analysis contributed significantly to start-lists of codes and recursive analytical processes while I was still in the field.

Personal Artifacts
These artifacts included student assignments, volunteered materials like photographs, journals, email correspondences, art projects, course syllabi, and other program materials. At both the Mountain and Prairie sites, participants volunteered and worked with me to create and discuss representational artwork related to their experience of adulthood, school, and work.

Program and Institutional Artifacts
These materials were typically teaching syllabi, texts, and other materials used in institutional practice for both teachers and teacher educators. Additionally, program or institutional documents—such as publicly available reports, websites, and memos—were made available to help me more clearly understand the research context.

The Conformity to Western Feminine Norms Index

While all other data was qualitative, the set incorporated one quantitative measure. The CFNI was developed by Mahalik, Morray, Coonerty-Femiano, Ludlow, Slattery, and Smiler (2005) to assess how and to what degree individuals conform to what are defined as "Western feminine norms" by having respondents rate their levels of agreement or disagreement with a series of statements corresponding to eight specific behavioral and attitudinal injunctions associated with Western feminine norms. Acknowledging that there are many more feminine "norms" and related injunctions present in contemporary US culture than may be represented in the CFNI, these eight injunctions, and the measure as a whole, was developed using careful procedures for reliability and validity with the hopes that further refinement and development might follow. The authors also strongly advocate for examination of "groups of women from diverse backgrounds in future research" as "the gender norms from the most powerful culture in a society affect the experiences of persons in that group, as well as persons in all other groups" such that members of historically marginalized groups are profoundly affected by the dominant group's "notions of femininity" and normalcy (p. 433). That said, the injunctions were developed using, in part, a series of focus groups of women that were demographically similar to the participant pool writ large. They were on average mostly white, mostly heterosexual and while a bit older than the preservice demographic, their average age of thirty-two accommodates for teacher educator participants in this study.

The CFNI was administered to all preservice and novice participants and to some teacher educator participants and several general undergradu-

**Table 3.1.   Valley University Preservice Scores on Eight
CFNI Injunctions (Mahalik et al., 2005)**

Feminine Injunction Definition (Mahalik et al, 2005, p.424)	Preservice Participant Mean Score
Niceness in Relationships	82%
"developing friendly and supportive relationships with others"	
Involvement with Children	85%
"taking care of and being with children"	
Investment in Appearance	71.5%
committing *"resources to maintaining and improving physical appearance"*	
Thinness	64%
"pursuing a thin body ideal"	
Sexual Fidelity	43%
"keeping sexual intimacy contained within one committed relationship"	
Modesty	36%
"refraining from calling attention to one's talents or abilities"	
Involvement in Romantic Relationships	41%
"investing self in romantic relationship"	
Domesticity	64%
desire for or practice of *"maintaining the home"*	

ate women at Valley University only, as the measure was not available at the time of data collection at the other sites. While specific scores will be explored and analyzed in subsequent chapters, table 3.1 illustrates the eight injunctions in the context of this study by providing the mean scores from the Valley University preservice participants.

The individual injunctions correlate with certain other behaviors and other indices; for example, scores on the CFNI have been positively correlated with high scores on eating disorders indices and negatively correlated with high scores on feminist identification indices. These and other trends will be discussed in the context of study participants in subsequent chapters.

Overview of Data Analysis Procedures

Creative descriptions of how researchers analyze data are numerous: "Raw" data are "cooked" (LeCompte & Schensul, 1999, p. 3); data are "crunched" (Goetz & LeCompte, 1978) and—my personal favorite—big piles of data are made into little piles of data (LeCompte & Schensul, 1999; Patton, 1987). There are really three stages: (1) getting that big pile of data into smaller logical and manageable smaller piles and sorting those piles and reassembling them; (2) creating an explanation of the phenomenon; and finally (3) linking the explanation to one's conceptual framework.

For all three steps, analytic procedures featured both "top-down" and "bottom-up" approaches to examining the data (LeCompte & Schensul, 1999), focusing on recursively evaluating and reevaluating the conceptual framework and theoretical model in light of the story the data told while simultaneously examining the data for emerging themes and comparing these with the evolving theoretical "hunch" that drove the initial framing of the study. Inspired by Glaser and Strauss's (1967) grounded theory data analytic processes, a kind of dialectical relationship was achieved as coding lists were derived from both the conceptual framework and the data itself in a mutually refining, recursive fashion. So, to make a long story short, the little piles were arranged in such a way as to speak to both the larger phenomena and the conceptual frame in play. To create these small piles, interview and observation transcripts, notes and other documents were used to create a start list of codes related to themes in the data. These codes were then used to analyze the data set as a whole. Constant Comparative Method (Glaser & Strauss, 1965) focused on themes derived from analyses of field notes, artifacts and interviews (Spradley, 1980; Strauss & Corbin, 1990). Data were triangulated between and within method using both multiple methods and collecting multiple kinds of data via each means of collection (Delamont, 2002).

In terms of the task of coding the data, the initial working codebook I constructed, i.e., the "start list" of codes (Miles & Huberman, 1994) was drawn from the analytic framework. Additional codes were added as data were collected and analysis progressed. In continuing to develop and use codes, I used an inductive approach, described by Strauss and Corbin (1990), in which I worked from my start list of codes with the data to generate categories or labels until my list grew. After data were coded using the start list, those subsets of coded data were evaluated to develop new, inductive codes. From the items isolated using the start list codes I was able to further analyze this smaller group of data into subcodes. Subcodes grew out of the start list to further analyze data into smaller and smaller subgroupings. What followed were lots and lots of very small piles, which were then put together—not unlike a child's "connect the dots" exercise—to string together an image, or story, of the phenomenon at hand.

Given the wide range of artifacts collected for this study, finding consistent methods of analyzing visual and other texts was essential. For this, I relied primarily on content analysis, drawn from the photographic analysis work of Chalfen (1998) that emphasizes frequency counts as a useful place to begin analyzing images in particular. While content analyses and frequency counts are useful, they are not completely harmless, as analyzing visual and other texts as part of an ethnographic data set presents unique challenges for misinterpretation (Galman, 2009b). As such, foregrounding the meanings participants assign to the texts is of paramount importance. For many image-based texts I have relied upon collaborative analysis, in which the participant or participants involved are asked to comment on the meaning of the text at hand. With regard to the sole quantitative measure, the CFNI, these themes served to additionally inform the development of the start list of codes, as well as to check, and eventually illustrate, the paramount trends in the other data.

Reliability and Validity

Applying positivistic standards for reliability and validity to ethnographic work is not an easy fit, but establishing guidelines for research quality demands some form of their application (LeCompte & Goetz, 1982; LeCompte & Preissle, 1993; Norris, 1997). LeCompte and Preissle (1993) interpret reliability in the ethnographic context as a matter of clarity and transparency in reporting, especially with regard to researcher positionality and stance,

Table 3.2. Reliability Canons

External Reliability	Internal Reliability
Reports should clearly describe and critically reflect upon the position/ social relationship of researcher and the impact of that position(s) on the study.	"Low-inference descriptors" (p. 338) and the presence of large amounts of the actual data allow others, including other researchers, to "judge for themselves" about what was seen.
Reports should go into detail about "the kinds of people who served as informants," how they were recruited and a specific picture of the contexts involved (LeCompte & Preissle, 1993, p. 335).	
Concepts and research thinking should be described clearly; "they should be intelligible to other researchers and, where appropriate, to the participants being investigated" (p. 336)	
Data collection and analysis should be described with precision and with sufficient detail (p. 337).	

representational issues and methodological specificity. Standards for validity were addressed on three points: (1) member checking with participants; (2) ensuring that data collection methods were effective and elicited the information desired by using a well-piloted interview instrument; and (3) providing detailed accounts of the context, participants, and findings in the research report.

For the purposes of this qualitative study, reliability is more than just determining whether or not a repeated study will get the same results. Interpreted as such, that is not a useful measure for ethnographic work because it occurs in naturalistic settings where exact replication is impossible to achieve. However, rather than give up completely, LeCompte and Preissle (1993) interpret external and internal reliability in the ethnographic context as a matter of the following measures of clarity. I have used the following aspects of their typology.

Validity in ethnographic research falls into four subcategories: procedural validity, construct validity, internal validity, and external validity. These measures of validity were addressed in the following ways throughout this study.

Table 3.3. Validity Measures

Procedural Validity: *Data collection procedures were effective and worked as intended.*	The data collection mechanisms were piloted well before the study began to assure procedural validity.
Construct Validity: *Interview questions elicited data that was understandable to participants, useful to the study, and interpretable by the researcher.*	Interview questions were open-ended and constructed to incorporate multiple prompts; tailored as per participant response, use of early, small-scale pilot study results and recursive analysis in the field to further refine constructs.
Internal Validity: *The story presented by the researcher is in agreement with the story presented by participants.*	Participants engaged in member-checking of transcripts, field notes, and talk-alouds with researcher regarding presentation of findings.
External Validity: *The story is understandable and relatable to others who are reading the work or attempting to replicate the measures in similar settings.*	While others have not attempted to apply results to similar groups, discussions, and sharing of drafts of the study findings with colleagues and others has yielded helpful conversation in this vein.

Source: Derived from LeCompte, 2005, personal communication and LeCompte & Schensul, 1999

Researcher Subjectivity and Role

Careful monitoring of researcher subjectivity and roles was a significant aspect of data collection throughout this study and its multiple parts.

Researcher Subjectivity

In examining both Peshkin (1988) and Heshusius (1993) with regard to steps taken to address, minimize or attempt to ameliorate the effects of researcher subjectivity, I ended up turning yet again to Delamont (2002), who is not in disagreement with either of them, but rather provides a happy medium. Peshkin suggests that we pay attention to our "cold spots," "hot spots," and "multiple I's," and Heshusius examines the possibility of refocusing the energy devoted to eliminating what cannot be eliminated: subjectivity writ large. By contrast, Delamont writes that the researcher "should not waste time trying to eliminate 'investigator effects.'" Instead she argues that one should concentrate on understanding those effects:

> data should be collected at different levels of reactivity, and theories made explicit. Finally, everything we develop to explore the world should also be used to expose the way in which we do that exploration. (p. 8)

I admit that there are subjectivities in my work. My means of exploring them do "double duty" by also reflecting on my own subjectivities and allowing what I think is a less mediated presentation of findings. Managing these subjectivities in data collection consisted mostly of keeping a researcher journal to encourage reflection as I collected and analyzed the data. This effort, while diligently followed, failed to become as resolute a habit as I had hoped; "reflexivity" not being as easily achieved as I assumed it would be. That said, my fieldwork sites were fraught with potential subjectivity in the form of hot and cold spots (Peshkin, 1988)—one because of the horrible isolation, terrible weather, and political upheaval unique to both that moment in US history and the setting, and the others because I was too close to them. I had been a teacher education instructor, student, and professor, respectively. The danger in the too-too-familiar sites was not in *going native* (of "losing the researcher's twin perspectives" [Delamont, 2002, p. 37] of researcher and researcher outlook) but rather in confusing what was, for the most part, a hindward glance to where I had been with what was there at the time of the study and separating out what the data confirmed and what my own, often distorted by time and exhaustion, professional impressions might have been. Considerable effort, plus my flawed but ultimately consistent use of the researcher journal, helped me to keep my multiple selves, roles, and

experiences distinct in my mind and thinking for the duration of the studies
and on into my writing and ongoing work.

Researcher Role

During the period of data collection at Prairie College, I was fortunate
enough to be allowed to serve as a visiting faculty member in sociology and
anthropology. As such, I taught a class in theory and practice in education
and despite the small number of excellent potential participants who were
in my class, I could not recruit them for participation in the study for ethical
reasons. At Mountain University I had been a teacher educator in semesters past, but did not teach during the semester of data collection, thereby
avoiding such ethical problems in that setting. During observations, I was a
nonparticipant observer. However, my role as visiting faculty at Prairie gave
me considerable access for participant recruitment via email, as I had access
to the email addresses of students who had become education minors. My
role as a senior graduate student and former teacher educator in the School
of Education of Mountain University gave me similar access advantages. At
Valley University I was a member of the teaching faculty and served briefly
as TEPP coordinator. Due to a parental leave, I was able to spend the one
of the semesters of the data collection period outside the program—and by
not teaching in it, I was able to recruit individuals to participate in my study
without risking coercion. Similarly, as TEPP coordinator, I served as a rather
distant administrator, and was not teaching in the program; so, I was able to
approach students more freely, though not without great consideration for
the ethical constraints of participant recruitment in a program of that size.

At all three institutions I developed close relationships with participants—indeed, at this writing I still hear from many of them. Given the
fact that they shared their personal stories with me as well as their personal
reflections on their ideas and feelings about themselves, it felt strange to
simply cut off the tape recorder, dismiss them from my office, pack up my
data, and leave town. Studs Terkel (1972)—a self-proclaimed journalist, not
researcher—said that this kind of data collection gave him a "thief in the
night feeling" (p. xviii). Terkel writes,

> I was no more than a wayfaring stranger, taking much and giving little. . . . I
> was the beneficiary of others' generosity. . . . My tape recorder, as ubiquitous
> as the carpenter's tool chest or the doctor's black satchel, carried away valu-
> ables beyond price. On occasions, overly committed, pressed by circumstance
> of my own thoughtless making, I found myself neglecting the amenities and
> graces that offer mutual pleasure to visitor and host. It was the Brooklyn fire-

man who astonished me into shame. After what I felt was an overwhelming experience—meeting him—he invited me to stay for supper. . . . I mumbled, "I'm supposed to see this hotel clerk on the other side of town." He said, "you runnin' off like that? Here we been talkin' all afternoon. It don't sound nice. This guy, Studs, comes to the house, gets my life on tape and says, 'I gotta go' . . . it was a memorable supper but looking back, how could I have been so insensitive?" (p. xvii)

There were times during this study that I was similarly insensitive, I am sure, as I tried to juggle the researcher role with my feelings of being a stranger and my need, in a strange place and in a familiar one, to keep myself somehow removed from the lives I was examining and the places we held in common. As LeCompte, Schensul, Weeks, and Singer (1999) write,

> Ethnographic research imposes many varied identities and special role relationships on researchers during the course of their investigations. Ethnographers not only occupy the normal roles people play in everyday life, but they also acquire additional roles that are specific to their activities in the field. (p. 6)

For me, my role as teacher educator, researcher, faceless administrator, and sometime friend represented opportunities as well as conflicts. For resolving this, I have no easy answers or suggestions, only that being researcher and trusted stranger in a strange place was a balancing act I have yet to perfect. I kept them at arms' length, partly because, as discussed previously, I once stood where they did not terribly long ago—and not altogether comfortably, either.

This is probably a good place to speak more concretely about my personal and cultural positionality, apart from my formal distinctions in each research site—as a teacher educator, a guest faculty member, a scholar interested in the nuances of method, etc. After all, in ethnography, the researcher herself is the instrument, the constructor of the research question and agenda, and I acknowledge who I am plays a huge part in how this project was conceptualized and carried out. When I say that I "stood where they did" I mean that I myself was an elementary teacher licensure student in a similar program roughly a decade before I began this project. I was young, freshly out of college myself, struggling with the choices associated with vocation, and the struggles of choosing what my own mother called, "women's work"—teaching, or care work. A white, middle class woman from a working class and military background, even though I attended an elite liberal arts undergraduate college and was groomed by my professors and peers toward medicine, the arts or law careers, my parents nonetheless emphasized the desirability of teaching. My mother was a teacher, and her mother before her, and they both praised teaching, not as a vocation, but rather as a good career "for a woman," as my mother would continue, "because then you are on the same schedule as your children, with summers off." She also told me that teaching "made sense" for women because it was not too political: "After all," she said, "if you are teaching about the alphabet, what's political there?" I remember sighing with relief—somewhat exhausted by years of political action, engagement, and thought. When I began teacher education, I rapidly realized that teaching and working with young people was perhaps among the most political activities conceivable in contemporary culture, but in the early days my vision of retiring to a career that was crafted for me as a waiting room for marriage and motherhood was attractive. It did not remain attractive for long as I tired of low pay, low status, and the constant, unrelenting expectation that my vocational interest would not outlive my inevitable heterosexual marriage and motherhood. On a selfish level, I also tired of sending students out the door to new and different things, while I believed I was expected to do the same thing, year after year, and to take joy only in the growth of my young charges. I was supposed to love the children, and love the work, but here, as in so many things, love was not enough. As a teacher educator I still do not have a good story to tell, or a convincing narrative to provide, when my preservice students ask why I am no longer in the elementary classroom. Perhaps I feel guilty, or lucky—either way I feel as though I am protecting a dark trade secret from their dewy, new eyes.

For all her praising the easy virtues of a life in the classroom, my mother also told stories about how, after years of watching her own mother grade papers well into the night, stay late for meetings, and supplement her meager income by selling encyclopedias door-to-door during her summers "off" she said, "one thing's sure, Mother, I'll never teach." And she didn't intend to. She chose to attend an elite women's college, she majored in English literature. She studied and thought and flirted with progressive politics and beatnik ideals. But in the end there were just not that many attractive choices: "I could be a shopgirl, a secretary, a nurse, or a teacher," she told me. And her mother had been a teacher, so, "better the devil you know." My mother also left teaching to stay at home with children, eventually becoming an administrator once my brother and I were grown, and in her words, never looking back. She and I were both "good girls" and we were both rewarded and punished for it.

Study Limitations, Thoughts on Method and Conclusions

Oh no! Not another learning experience!

—Bumper sticker observed in Dust Camp Trail parking lot,
Mountain City, January 2005

The limitations of this study are many, but all of them were significant in that I learned a great deal about methodology, design, data collection and, most of all, researcher subjectivity.

One important limitation of this study was that conceptual clarity was inhibited by my desire to cling to my own romantic story about teaching and teachers' stories, and my initial unwillingness to thoroughly and critically analyze participant and other stories as data. Also important was the fact that my studies were largely comprised of convenience samples. Seeking out a more diverse setting to obtain a larger and more diverse participant pool would be an excellent adjustment in any future work because then the data and subsequent findings would reflect a wider range of preservice teachers' experiences. Additionally, it would have been helpful to have included a fourth site: possibly an emergency licensure cohort, or *Teach for America* or *Americorps*-type cadre in an urban area would be a nice complement to the formal schools of education at MU and VU and the informal Prairie program. As will be discussed in concluding chapters, the current economic and political trends point to radical changes in the contours and content of teacher education,[4] and knowing more about how gender, care, and work intersect outside of the university setting could be crucial.

It is also worth noting that the contextual information I was able to glean and present about Prairie College was much "meatier" than what I have been able to present about Mountain University or Valley University. This is because, despite promises to the contrary, and what I considered at the time to be my own prowess at assessing and shelving my subjectivities, the substantial "cold spot" (Peshkin, 1988) hovering around the large university data shows in the flatness of the histories and contexts that I have been able to present. Part of this is that it lacked the exoticism of the strange, Quaker land I lived in while collecting the Prairie data—indeed, we never study the familiar with as much zeal as we do the strange, and my attempts to make strange the VU and MU research contexts failed rather miserably. I'll admit it—for much of the time I was bored stiff because I opted to study something so close to my own experience. This was also, of course, why I chose to study it. As Margaret LeCompte once wisely—and I think prophetically—told me, the areas of inquiry that most seductively compel us are always auto-biographical in some way and part of a process of working through our own identities, decisions, and life trajectories. As a woman, a former teacher, and—most importantly—a "good girl" and foolish virgin in my own right, this played an important role. That said, getting past my own expectations and elitist attitudes about what constitutes the "right" idea about vocation and work and teaching and learning was a huge step in limiting the impact of my biases upon the work, but the bias is by no means effectively resolved. In future work I will hopefully make use of any additional help from colleagues and others to go through over-familiar data, and also develop the presence of mind to select either (a) more unknown sites to examine, or (b) more direct comparisons to help "make strange" those familiar stomping grounds.

Notes

1. Pseudonym.

2. I also suspect that they were, like other samples, predominantly heterosexual, though no formal, program-wide survey on sexuality was implemented to solidify this suspicion. Further discussion of compulsory heterosexuality as a feminine norm will follow in subsequent chapters.

3. There were two preservice students of color included in the larger sample, but only one completed the full study participation and as an international student her experience with US gender norms was limited, and she was excluded from this analysis of white, female preservice teachers.

4. Thanks to Professor Celia Oyler for her astute observations on this topic.

~

CHAPTER FOUR

The Moral Careers of Wives, Mothers, and Others

Mountain University

I failed classes. I had careers that didn't work out. I left home and went out on my own and had to go back home after screwing up. I get funny looks because I dress like a dude. I want to go live in a tent in the woods and grow my own food . . . and that makes people [uncomfortable].

—Interview with Maya, research participant at Mountain University

As discussed in chapter 1, preservice teachers' ideas about work, gender identity, care, and love are complex. In this chapter I will present the case of Mountain University, its preservice teachers and their experiences becoming teachers. The cases of Kari and Maya, two preservice study participants at Mountain, serve to illustrate the general trends of that population: namely, that the moral careers of the elementary teacher may not necessarily be simple or straightforward (or even wholly about becoming a teacher). What is apparent is that their journey of becoming teachers is marked by consciousness of the gendered (and relational—as wives and mothers) nature of the work, and themselves. As Maya notes in the quote, above, her gendered presence makes people uncomfortable. This need to conform, or clash, with the gender identity expected of a teacher figures prominently in participant narratives, as will be discussed at length in both Kari and Maya's cases.

The contextual background for the time period I spent at Mountain, and its School of Education, begin the chapter. The chapter is concluded with initial analyses of the ethnographic cases provided and an overview of relevant themes.

Background and Context

Mountain University (MU) was founded in the late 1800s as part of a community initiative that hinged on donations of money and land from townspeople who often had to make personal sacrifices to contribute. Since then, the university has been active in the surrounding community and maintains its involvement in community life. A major research institution bringing in nearly $300 million dollars in research money each year at the time of data collection, MU is situated in an affluent, bustling-but-quaint town in the foothills of a major mountain range where the cost of living exceeds most other cities in the United States. The majority of the students at the university at the time of data collection were white (13 percent identify as ethnic minorities according to university data), and in the School of Education the overwhelming majority of the students were white females.

In-state and out-of-state MU students alike paid one of the highest public university tuition rates in the nation ($1,388 for residents and $9,060 for nonresidents per semester, excluding room and board) and were among the most affluent and least civically engaged and socially responsible of their age group, according to 2002 data from the National Survey of Student Engagement (university Website; NSSE study). At the time of this study, MU had recently obtained the grim distinction of being the "No. 1 Party School in America" after three semesters of drunken, couch-burning riots, and other civil disturbances. Shortly thereafter the university would be caught in a sexual assault and prostitution scandal involving its athletic department. When I left the field there had been few consequences and only one criminal charge related to the sex scandal, and while the school had happily lost its "No. 1 Party School" ranking, investigations were underway regarding the alcohol-related death of a first year student during a fraternity initiation. Meanwhile these scandals and others—including a rash of racist incidents on campus during the final month of data collection—pushed the president of the university to resign amid questions about why this top-tier institution cannot keep its presidents for more than a few years at a time.

Another issue in play during the data collection period was the alleged weakening of academic standards at MU. The headline of the December 9, 2004, *Mountain University Clarion* was, "Getting Tough: The Business School, College of Arts and Sciences Both Raising Standards Soon." Questions had been raised about the academic rigor in both the Business School and the College of Arts and Sciences following what was described as a "disconcerting" undergraduate student survey in the spring of 2003. According to the *Clarion*, students said that their freshmen year was "too easy" with limited faculty contact and community, leading them to be completely blindsided during the comparatively difficult junior and senior year curriculum in the two schools. The *Clarion* suggested that the subsequent 49–4 vote in favor of new curricula designed to promote rigor and connection with faculty was also a result of MU's reputation as a school with a significant alcohol problem.

The School of Education

The overwhelming majority of the instructors MU preservice teachers interacted with were enthusiastic about teaching and about students, both K–12 students and their preservice teachers. Many preservice teachers claimed that their education courses were their favorites because of the small size and individual attention; this was notable, as the standard MU classes range from 50 to 100 to even 1,000 or more in large lectures.

However, despite the many reports from pleased students who loved their education classes it was equally easy to find disgruntled teacher education students who disliked their School of Education coursework. They said they considered the work "an easy A," "a waste of time," or, more generously, a "ticket to punch" on the way to a job they may or may not stick with. The more vociferous of these students railed against the "incompetent" instructors[1] who teach "useless" classes or force them to endure endless, "horrible" practicum placements in local schools, which are designed to function as real-life experiences that complement course learning. By the time these less-happy students began their student teaching, they had often developed deep animosity toward the School of Education. The contradictions in these disparate responses—some students hate their coursework and others loved it—seem to be related to individual factors more than legitimate differences in quality of instruction.

Teacher Preparation Coursework

Study participants were enrolled in teacher education coursework through the Mountain University School of Education and were selected for participation in the study on the basis of two criteria indicating they were in the initial part of their teacher education experience: (1) they had formally enrolled in the institution's education licensure or similar degree program, and (2) they had not yet had their intensive student teaching internship experience but were still taking their content and pedagogy courses with limited or no field interactions. The participants in this study had taken no more than three total teacher education courses, including the sequence of social foundations courses as well as one subject-specific methods course. The rationale for this selection and recruitment strategy was that accessing participants at a time when they are still, to some degree, engaged in imaginative rehearsal of rather than concrete internship around teachers' classroom work. So, participant sampling was purposeful and theoretical rather than random or representative of all teacher education students at Mountain. Participants who were enrolled in intensive master's programs that offered simultaneous coursework and student teaching experiences were excluded from the potential participant pool. As a result, participants were drawn only from undergraduate and post–BA licensure programs at the elementary level.

Student participation in the teacher education program, usually began prior to formal admission to the School of Education, was called "Seminar One." This class attracted a wide variety of prospective teachers and general students from MU because it was both a prerequisite for admission to the School of Education *and* a course that met a general arts and sciences requirement. It also was sought out initially because of the widespread knowledge belief in the general MU student population that education courses were significantly less rigorous than other courses, even though course number 3013 had an interesting syllabus, demanding readings and an engaging Socratic seminar structure. The unexpected rigor of the class often led a large number of arts and sciences students to drop it without completing. Usually taught by qualified doctoral students and occasionally by faculty members, the course covered a wide range of social issues in education, including, but not limited to, gender, sexuality, culture and ethnicity, class, educational policy issues like school funding, charter schools, school choice and vouchers, basic curriculum theory, ability status, parent and community partnerships, and linguistic diversity. Readings ranged from the theoretical to the practical, and the course provided students with a community practicum as a kind of "lab" experience intended to relate theory to practice. These practica included such experiences as working in an after school program with schoolchildren learning English, a before and after school program for teen mothers at a local high school, or with the local municipal programs for developmentally disabled adults.

The second course, usually taken after formal admission to the School of Education and hopefully in sequence with the former was "Seminar Two." This course was designed to cover the same topic areas as the first, but from the perspective of the teacher, rather than from a societal vantage point. Unlike Seminar One, this course was required to be taught by someone with relevant K–12 teaching experience, and had historically been taught by graduate students who met that criterion. However, beginning with the time of this study, the course was taught exclusively by adjunct or clinical faculty whose specific area of expertise included special education, bilingual education and school and community partnerships. Prior to this, students typically complained that the course repeated things they "already knew" from the first course, regardless of how many times they were told about the revisiting and reinforcing properties of the "spiral curriculum." These complaints led to the redesigning of the course so that it focused exclusively on bilingual and special education, and parent and community partnerships. It often pairs preservice teachers and K–12 students with learning disabilities or limited English proficiency in a "shadowing" practicum.

While the rest of the university was busily overhauling its offerings, the School of Education began doing same. A 2003 evaluation of the introductory seminars revealed that not only are these courses extremely content-heavy and demanding for both instructors and students, they are usually the very first courses in education the undergraduates have, and they require instructors to "guide the exploration of extremely controversial topics with undergraduate students who are just beginning their exploration into becoming teachers, have little experience either with the field of education or with doing challenging, university-level work, and have little experience or desire to explore difficult diversity issues" (MU SOE document). This leaves instructors with a difficult task, to say the least, as students often develop resistance to course material. They often carry this resistance with them to the introductory (and, in this case, often concurrent) methods courses, becoming disgruntled and dissatisfied with their teacher preparation experiences overall.

In the semesters before this study began, the program went through a major overhaul to address the fact that student exit survey responses suggested the need for more coverage of classroom management and differentiation for special education and linguistically diverse students. Possible actions discussed by faculty included increasing field placement hours, emphasizing the practical and explicit applications of methods course material or possibly adding different courses (Faculty discussion handout, 3/20/2002). The last suggestion is especially noteworthy: The students who participated in this study often had the unrealistic expectation that somehow their teacher preparation would provide them with a complete arsenal of skills, so that they would emerge from the program as fully formed teachers with no further learning to do. This may be, as Csikszentmihalyi and Schneider (2000) suggest, a function of adolescent ideas about work and preparation. Young people may expect "one stop shopping" instead of the very beginning of a much richer and more complex professional identity development trajectory characterized by lifelong learning. Klingner (2004) suggests that perhaps a better model for understanding teacher education entails seeing the process as "priming the pump" for later learning in the profession instead of complete and finite "training."

Notwithstanding, the preservice teachers and others surveyed for this overhaul at MU agreed that students' most crucial needs as they entered their first year of teaching were largely technical, ranging from developing and implementing teaching strategies for a variety of learners, to assessment of those students' needs, implementation and understanding of standards, direct instructional strategies for working with students, and scaffolding instruction. Meanwhile, positive comments from administrators in local schools about the preservice teachers coming out of the MU program included praise for students' professional and affective preparation: relating well to parents and students, listening and communicating well with colleagues and others, and being well-versed in educational issues—many of which were factors associated by principals with success in the classroom as first-year teachers. Notwithstanding the preferences of local administrators, preservice teachers answered the exit interview question, "if there was one thing we could do to improve the teacher education program, what would it be?" by requesting a focus on methods and technique rather than professional or affective elements. Of the forty-seven anecdotal statements excerpted in the faculty memo, forty were about decreasing theoretical discussions and increasing "practical" management technique instruction. A selection of representative examples:

1. "Be more practical"
2. "More practice, less theory! Theories don't help!"
3. "Teach classroom management."
4. "Teach classroom management A LOT more."
5. "Add more practical application—classroom management, skills to modify curriculum for special needs, we learned more theory/research than actual methods."
6. "Less theory, more time practicing for *managing!*"
7. "Work on lesson plans, using grade books effectively, not just theory and research."
8. "More emphasis on methods, actual instruction ideas and assessments, with much less talk of theory, philosophy, and ethnically/culturally diversity issues—especially the diversity one. I got it in every Ed. class and have lacked basic instruction needs."
9. "Do more hands-on, practical methodology instead of philosophizing about politics—we're teachers, not lobbyists."

10. "Make the classes more practical in regard to the 'real world' of teaching. I don't think any of us teach in the utopian classrooms that the education courses set you up for!"
11. "Give us more of a feel for the other parts of teaching—paperwork, grade books, planning, and meetings."
12. "Address more practical matters, less theory!"

Meanwhile, seven were related to positive comments (two) or negative comments (five) about faculty and staff. There were no pleas for more or deeper discussion of the theoretical or political. While there is no evidence that students necessarily agreed conceptually with what constitutes the "theoretical" element in their education classes, the dislike of the theoretical and political content is very clear here. It is very tempting to say that these students represent the anti-intellectualization element of the story of teaching as a semiprofession, as argued by Etzioni (1969) five decades ago. While this was not a topic for evaluation and rethinking by the overhaul committee, it was addressed in at least one session, as reflected by faculty email comments. Wrote one faculty member, "It seems to be a really important, albeit old, concern—the theory/practice issues, and the solution is not to just convince students of the importance of theory (as I have tried to do)" (personal email communication, Overhaul Committee, 3/12/2003). These sentiments were echoed—with varying levels of vitriol—in all participant interviews and many observed conversations.

Admissions

Initial admission to the School of Education depended upon a variety of formal measures by which the school attempted to select for persons who will be academically able to complete the program and successfully work as teachers. Informal and affective selection criteria—which are more concerned with selecting for and thus producing individuals who can do the work of teachers—differ somewhat and will be discussed later in this chapter. Lortie's (1975) work claims that it is relatively easy to get into schools of education because formal admission criteria are low, leaving "personality and preference" (p. 40) to be the deciding factors for admission into the cadre of K–12 educators. This claim jibed with the perceptions of the preservice teachers at MU ("admission criteria?" asked one participant in mock-incredulity, "Like, a pulse?"), who were aware of conventional stereotypes of teaching as easy work for those without other choices (Berliner, 2000). However, both these perceptions and Lortie's claims are contradicted by the fact that the undergraduate admissions criteria of the MU School of Education were actually quite demanding. In fact, the average GPA of people admitted during the time of data collection was close to 3.0, and in their majors, School of Education undergraduates had higher GPAs than similar majors in Arts and Sciences.

It is clear that the formal admissions criteria for the MU School of Education were not lower—and are in many cases more rigorous—than other undergraduate professional preparation programs in the preprofessional schools and colleges. Given that, it seems that participants in this study were getting their ideas about the allegedly low admissions criteria for the MU School of Education from popular cultural and personal cache, rather from a more concrete source.

Again, the high grade point averages and test scores for the overwhelming majority of students in the teacher licensure programs refute these assumptions. Yet before celebrating the high standards of the MU School of Education, we can also view "good grades" with some suspicion. As Fried (2000) suggests, good grade point averages may be a sign that individuals are merely good at "playing the game of school." This game, which constitutes figuring out what one must do to "get the grade" and being obedient to those rules, is mutually exclusive with real learning and risk-taking, argues Fried (2000). Similarly, Holland and Eisenhart (1992) found in their study of college women that those more concerned with getting high grades and praise than with "learning from experts" and taking intellectual risks tended to have higher GPAs. This is not to say that good grades are "bad" but rather that there is more to GPAs than high academic performance, especially when good grades are found on a transcript littered with lower level, less challenging courses. For one, people who become teachers are often motivated to do so, at least in part, because they have always been good at school and had positive experiences in the form of good grades and praise from teachers in school (Fried, 2000; Lortie, 1975). For students used to this reinforcement, the grade itself becomes the most attractive objective, with learning falling a distant second (Holland & Eisenhart, 1992).

Even so, there are smart, capable students with good and not-so-good grades in most schools of education. Yet the discourse of the "easy A" remains and must be reconciled with the existence of smart, capable people in schools of education. Law schools, by contrast, do not suffer from such stigma as one expects to find exceptionally smart people there by the dozen. Judge (1982) cautions that beyond individual belief, the low status of schools of education may contribute to this conflict:

> The trouble with [Schools/Colleges of Education] is that they have something to do with teachers . . . and the trouble with teachers is that they are painfully

undervalued—everywhere, perhaps, but especially in the United States. . . . It is precisely here that the contrast with lawyers and law schools becomes most pronounced. Law schools surely derive much of their prestige and success from the importance and prosperity of the lawyer in American life. The social and economic status of the lawyer has advanced in recent decades. Smart people are thus ready to go to law schools, and smarter people to teach in them. (Judge, 1982, p. 29)

So, even if the collective social and cultural expectation that classes in schools of education are easy, full of "easy As" and less intelligent students is by no means supported by the research literature, it persists. In fact, research has suggested that there are other reasons for high student achievement in education classes—that education professors are more effective given their unique pedagogical specialization (Labaree, 2004)—but these do little to combat a monolithic cultural belief system founded on collective devaluing of teachers.

Overview: Preservice Participants at Mountain University

Study participants at Mountain (N = 19) came from the elementary undergraduate and post–BA licensure pools. These groups received the same instructional treatment—they were in classes together, were advised by the same faculty, and identical routes to licensure. All seventeen participants self-identified as white. All preservice participants were between the ages of nineteenth and twenty-four, with an average age of twenty. While the post-BA program typically has students who are not in that age range—and indeed, the students who were on the older end of the age spectrum did come from the post-BA program, during the time frame of this data collection, no older students were observed as part of the cohort. While the post-BA program typically has students who are not in that age range—and indeed, the students who were on the older end of the age spectrum did come from the post-BA program—during the time frame of this data collection, no older students were observed as part of the cohort. The majority of post-BA students at the time of data collection were students who had graduated from MU the previous semester and were continuing on to pursue licensure.

With a few exceptions, participants were similar in many ways to the larger MU population. They tended to be relatively affluent, white protestant Christians with self-described conservative political orientations and a disinclination to identify as or affiliate with feminism. While few voiced divergent perspectives during courses, collected response to political material in methods courses reflects reluctance to engage. For example, in a written response to a reading assignment on teaching about the civil rights movement from *Rethinking Schools*, participants responded in varying ways. Students thoughtfully acknowledged their shock that more people did not know about and understand the civil rights movement, the importance of racism as a reality in US culture and the necessity for teachers to teach about civil rights, however, they were also concerned about teaching the political and framed it as potentially transgressive, even dangerous. A selection of representative statements:

- "Teaching civil rights is a controversial issue; as a teacher I will need to be careful and teach about civil rights in an unbiased way—that it's not right or wrong."
- "How realistic is it [to teach about civil rights] in today's social climate and not lose your job?"
- "It is important for teachers to teach about racism, but it is not always that easy because the issues are very controversial . . . teachers need to address racism from all angles and different aspects to be fair."
- "This is important, but I think elementary kids are too young to learn about it. I'm not sure it is age-appropriate."

In a related classroom discussion about teaching on or about September 11, 2001, participants were concerned: "How do you teach about different things in teaching without being punished?" Another student chimed in, "I heard about a guy—a fifth grade teacher—who showed some footage and got fired." Someone else heard that parents supported this teacher, while another thought they heard that "the parents were behind driving him out." The teacher educator at work in that section skillfully went back to the primary source at hand—in this case a newspaper article—rather than personally disabuse students of these ideas. But the students became quiet after the short flurry of personal horror stories and conversation moved on.

Participants reacted similarly to any political or controversial topic in teaching: that it should be avoided as it represented a threat to their continued employment and their status as "good employees" and "good teachers." When I asked several participants where they got the idea that controversy and criticality would land them in the unemployment line, they said that they knew that there were "lots of teachers out there" and that they were, ultimately, replaceable. This belief was remarkably rigid, even in the face of contradictory evidence—which is very much par for the course with teachers' and young people's beliefs (Csikszentmihalyi & Schneider, 2000; Pajares, 1992). When I suggested that this couldn't be true because it was part of the teachers' work, invariably the participant knew a story of a teacher who

Table 4.1. Female Mountain Participants

Participant ID	Age	MHLE[1]
MUF2S1	19	College degree
MUF2S2	19	College degree
MUF2S3	20	College degree
MUF2S5	24	High School
MUF2S6	20	College degree
MUF2S7	19	Graduate degree
MUF2S8	19	College degree
MUF2S9	20	High School
MUF2S11	21	College degree
MUF2S12	21	College degree
MUF2S13	19	Graduate degree
MUF2S14	21	Graduate degree
MUF2S15	19	GED
MUF2S16	23	College degree
MUF2S17	23	College degree
MUF2S18	19	Graduate degree
MUF2S19	19	Graduate degree

Note: MUFS10 and MUFS4 were both male participants, and as such excluded from this analysis.

had been fired, or a student teacher who never got a job, or whom parents angrily persecuted until she quit. These personal exceptions to every rule became a kind of mythology that was difficult to disprove. I thought of Miss Jean Brodie, or the women of *The Children's Hour*, and the cruel punishments meted out to "good girl" transgressors and wondered if the threat of a failed moral career, too, was part of girl culture as experienced by preservice teachers. Exceptions to this trend were the older students, the two or three at twenty-three or twenty-four years old who had experienced the world of work, however briefly, between undergraduate and teacher preparation. They were cautious, but much less concerned about mythology around disobedience and punishment.

Sample Cases: Kari and Maya

The nineteen female preservice participants at Mountain had remarkably similar demographic backgrounds and self-reported trajectories and stories about becoming teachers, performing gender, and professional attainment. Given their racial, socioeconomic, linguistic, and cultural similarities, as well as their generally uniform high exposure to media culture and resultant frequent references to feminine norms,[2] it is no surprise that girl culture at

Mountain was relatively monolithic. Similarly, faculty and instructor response to that experience was similarly consistent, if weary, and affirmed as
well as quietly challenged both preservice students' penchants for immaturity
and their collective tendency toward political nonengagement and conservatism. There were, however, a few divergent cases from this largely uniform
preservice group; these were mostly among older, post-BA students. To illustrate these trends, the following paragraphs present the in-depth cases of two
exemplary study participants, Kari and Maya. While each are representative
of a majority (Kari) and minority (Maya) of the sample, the chief differences
between them are age and experience. Kari is younger and relies primarily
on a popular cultural and personal experience diet for her reference group,
while Maya is older and has a wider range of personal experiences. Maya's
experiences frame her divergent socioeconomic and political identity and
often run counter to the monolithic face of girl culture as experienced and
embodied by Kari.

Kari

Kari, a twenty-year-old white woman from an affluent, suburban community,
was completing her undergraduate degree in communication and pursuing
her elementary license. She had completed Seminar One and was in the
middle of Seminar Two and Social Studies Methods at the time of data collection. She was a member of a local sorority, to which her mother had also
belonged during her own undergraduate years, and worried a little bit about
life after college, without her friendships and familiar environment. She,
Maya, and the other participants were all enrolled in the same large section
of Social Studies Methods, a seminar that paired planning and teaching
social studies content at the elementary level with multicultural literacy
instruction, and she routinely showed up for the early morning class in her
fluffy shearling boots, white sweat suit with "juicy" printed in large, glittery
letters across the seat of her pants, and dark sunglasses. I would listen for
the jingling of her heavily adorned keychain as she approached my office
for each interview. Smiling, she'd sit down, sometimes with a sigh. "Not a
feminist or anything," Kari characterized the women's liberation as a "bunch
of angry girls who don't like men, who don't want you to do anything traditional. But I'm a girly girl—well, sort of," she continued:

> I was always a tomboy. I mean, my mom couldn't get me into a dress or any-
> thing pink for years. I'd fight her and say I wanted to wear pants! It was a thing
> for my mom because I was the only girl and she really wanted me with all, like,
> bows and dresses. But I wasn't having it. I think I'm like that now. Kind of—

like, I love being a girl, I love getting all dressed up. I don't want to be a man or anything but I'm not, like, made-up to go grocery shopping or anything.

Kari wore a sparkly diamond solitaire on her left hand. I casually asked if she was engaged to be married, ready to offer my congratulations—many of the women in her cadre had become engaged that spring. "Nope," she said, "it's my purity ring—it's like a purity ring—from my Dad. It's kind of part of my church." Like so many young women at MU at that time, Kari explained that she was a member of a large, nondenominational Protestant Christian church in her hometown whose beliefs included the importance of family and the relationship between father and daughter. As part of this belief structure and the rituals of her faith, Kari and her father attended a church-sponsored purity ball during her last year of high school in which she received this ring and promised to continue to live within the values and sexual mores of her church and family. This meant that she promised to be chaste—virginity was implied but never mentioned—until she married. Kari felt that this put her outside of the experience of many of her friends and classmates, who took a much more cavalier attitude toward sexual activity, experimentation, and the opposite sex. But she maintained that this was important in her family, and important for her, and that she sought out friends who were also committed in this way, many of whom were in her school of education classes. That said, she admits she "went a little wild" on the weekends ("but nothing too over the top" she assured me) at parties and with friends, and didn't make it to church most Sunday mornings. Her current interest was in planning a spring break trip to Mexico with sorority friends. She had spent a couple of mornings that week at a local tanning salon in preparation for the much-anticipated beach week and was pleased with the result. "*Girls Gone Wild*, watch out!" she joked.

When I asked her about what she believed about being a teacher, and being a woman, she acknowledged, "Yeah, there are a lot of girls in teaching. All of my teachers were girls. But I'm not becoming a teacher just because I'm a girl. There are many more men in teaching now than before."

My mother was a teacher, for a while, until we came along. Now she substitutes a little bit. That works out awesome for her. And I have an aunt who is a preschool teacher and now that she has kids she runs a daycare out of her house. It's really flexible. And, I know I'm not, like, supposed to say this or anything, but it's not like I plan on working for a career without taking some time, hopefully, to have my own family. And teaching will always be there, I can go and leave, and take care of my own then go back. So it makes sense as a job for me. Not like some other things where you bust your butt and there you are.

I inquired about what kinds of things "bust your butt," and she said that she had friends who were majoring in business, or in the sciences, and while they worked very hard with an array of difficult classes in a demanding schedule, Kari observed that none of them was exactly sure what they would do after college. I asked if she knew any men who were faced with similar problems in those majors. "They don't know. But they aren't worried I don't think. Something will turn up, or they'll just get a job doing something small—I don't think they really think about it."

When I asked about men teaching, Kari was sympathetic. She observed that the one or two male classmates would have a more difficult adjustment than she would. "Teaching, the caring part, comes maybe more naturally to women—men can do it, but it's sort of an uphill climb for them. People assume that they can't or something is wrong with them, so they sometimes just go, 'that's enough' and become principals after a couple of years." When pressed about what might be 'wrong' with them, Kari hemmed and hawed before saying, "You know, people think they're gay, or child molesters or whatever, and that's completely not true, but it's out there and outside people think it even if they don't say anything." When asked about the preponderance of male administrators, and the comparatively stratospheric status and remuneration that those jobs had over classroom teaching, and other feminized spheres of employment, she suggested that while men might have access to higher status and higher pay, they did have to sacrifice the emotional and personal fulfillment that classroom teachers experience. "They make stuff, and money, but do they have the satisfaction? In the end, there's more to it than just the money and prestige. I get to love kids and I'm good at that."

Like many of her classmates, Kari wanted to be a teacher when she was a small girl, and remembered many of her early elementary teachers fondly as loving, caring, and nurturing presences. But upon entering high school and college she became less sold on becoming a teacher. She initially thought about becoming a physical therapist (PT) instead of becoming a teacher, but the flirtation was brief and the practicality of teaching won out in the face of the difficult PT program. She frames this admission in the same way she framed admitting other hidden truths about her decision to teach (for example, that it made sense considering her other aspirations for marriage and motherhood). She said,

> Yeah, I know it's kind of a cop out, but to be honest, the classes were way too hard and I didn't even think I could do it. I just looked at the course cata-logue and it was like, well, too hard. But it's not like it's my second choice or

anything—I want to do it—I'm happy with it. I'm glad I decided to do it . . . and my mom, well, she'd always be like, you'd be such a good teacher. You should think about it. And so I realized that physical therapy wasn't for me and I realized I wasn't going to do it. When I was little I had wanted to be a teacher, and sure it's a sellout but I'm glad I'm back with teaching.

When I asked about what competencies in particular her mother and others referred to when they said she would be a good teacher, Kari affirmed that these were observations made of her with little children. Frequently caring for her younger cousins and siblings as a pre-teen babysitter, her mother commented on how much the smaller children loved her, and how she loved them and understood them. Kari made a distinction between what she did with them and what others did—"I didn't just play with them, and entertain them, I tried to teach them things." However, even with the evidence provided, Kari's mother's endorsement of her daughter's abilities as a teacher were largely intuitive. "She just knew," she said, "she knows me and she just knew I had the gift for it." When pressed for the parameters of her gift—and how she herself knew that she would be a good teacher for young children, Kari said, that she also "just knew,"

> I can just—uh—there's a lot of people out there who have a really hard time connecting with kids and I can connect with them. I can teach them and I can also be their friend and be on the same level with them, so I know how to tell them how to get through this—I like littler kids.

Kari describes herself as "child-like" in many ways, with academic strengths on par with an early elementary curriculum, and says that being "just like a big kid myself" is a tremendous asset in connecting with and understanding children. Like many of the attributes she assigns to good teachers, being child-like is among them; her gifts are innate. Teachers, then, are born, and not made. It is no surprise that while she says she has great respect for her teacher education professors and other mentors, she is dubious about the value of teacher education coursework for making teachers. While she would never admit it, ever-wary of disrespecting others, Kari would probably agree with her program age-mates who see teacher education experiences as buttons to push, hurdles to jump, and largely pro-forma university gatekeeping. She had seen lots of teaching, and knew the basics of how to care for children, but wasn't sure what a lot of the teacher preparation curriculum was about.

I asked what the work of teaching was about. Kari was admittedly a little unsure of what teachers did, exactly, every day. While she was aware of the large amounts of "paperwork" and "planning" as well as "discipline" she couldn't clearly elaborate beyond these general, structural elements. When she was a child, playing teacher, she typically did "paperwork," filled out lesson plans, and disciplined unruly "children" in her imaginary class. "I'm not really sure [what the teacher does]," she says, but, brightening, "While I'm not really doing what I'm going to do yet . . . I feel like how I'm going to feel when I am a teacher, and I like that." When asked how being the teacher feels, Kari smiled, "I'm going to be the teacher everybody loves." The teacher who everyone loves, she says, is typically "young" and "cool" and gentle.

Kari is confident that she can be these things—she has the innate qualities that are necessary for successful teaching—but she wishes that she knew more about how to plan and manage a classroom. In this way, she says, her coursework was a bit lacking. Kari admits that she knows she is basing her entire theory of professional practice and identity on what she remembers from being an elementary student herself ("and it's not like I remember classroom management from way back then!") but she still has concerns about teacher preparation. She talks about it frequently with her classmates.

A lot of times we talk about what we talk about in [teacher education] class and how some of the [teacher educators] . . . present how we're going to be teachers isn't what we see in the [on-site classroom experiences]. I almost feel like it's . . . too idealistic here, what they teach us here. Like, I think it's great, but it isn't what I see. We try and learn, all these great activities, but in the real classroom it's like, "Take out your textbooks and read." I mean, it's great that we have all these high hopes and expectations but it's like we are getting two different stories—the one that's here, and the one that's real. And when it takes me so long to come up with one lesson plan because I am thinking on this higher level that I've been taught I kind of see where the [classroom teachers] are coming from—it's impossible to do that every time. That whole idealistic thing. . . . Our classes [are] a little political but I guess I expect that from this place. . . . It's the ivory tower and all that. Reality is a little bit different. I mean, I really appreciate what they [teacher educators] are doing for us here, but it just isn't going to be practical in the real world. All the theory, it's great if you're going to be a professor, but I'm going to be a teacher of really, really little kids. I'm going to help little kids put their boots on and teach them ABC. The argument is that there [are] politics in everything, that we do politics when we teach, but we really don't. My teachers never did. They just loved us.

But over the course of the semester, political and theoretical issues did crop up. Like many of her classmates, Kari addressed these issues by checking out of classroom discourse. While bubbly and engaging in person, she was often silent, sometimes even with her sunglasses still on her face, in the whole-class portions of her Social Studies Methods course. On more than one occasion the well-loved instructor had to jibe her into removing them, often rolling his eyes in mock desperation and plaintively—but only half humorously—begging the roomful of thirty-some girls (and two males) to stop talking, listen, engage, and stay on task, saying, "I so cannot be the hardass here, folks. Let's get going!" Often in the classroom well in advance of students, he played music, devised interactive, materials-rich activities, and animatedly quoted popular music and culture to this early-morning class in order to wake them up and engage them to think critically. Universally loved and respected by students—and in that regard often held above and apart from the suspect teacher education machine writ large—this instructor was often exhausted at the end of a class with the work required to keep the unruly group focused, present, and working. Whole group discussions faltered. Small group work among students frequently devolved into conversations about last night's television program, gossip about friends and classmates, or hushed discussions of the inadequacies of teacher education courses. Political potency often dissipated in the face of personal experience narratives.

Considering so many were post-BA and could therefore be considered on par with a graduate student population, I observed huge amounts of energy devoted to their engagement in all of the teacher education courses I observed, and the ones I taught. The management-by-entertainment strategy was certainly not universally applied, but faculty were uncomfortable and unsure of what to do with college students who passed notes in class, talked over the instructor, were consistently late or disengaged. This is not to say that the majority of the students were quite this off-task, as most were well-versed in what needed to happen to be considered a good student, but the levels of student nonengagement and immaturity came up over and over again among the faculty and graduate instructors. When I asked about failing students for nonparticipation or noncompliance, the general, but by no means formal, assumption tended to be that very low grades were reserved for academic nonperformance, but the only recourse for immaturity was gentle cajoling and innovative, high energy, or thought provoking instruction. All of the instructors strived to meet students where they were, but more often than not, as one faculty member said, "Sometimes that becomes lowering our expectations or focusing on dispositions, affect. They're good students, great people, but sometimes they just aren't sure what to make of what they need to learn and do to become teachers."

When asked about Kari's own personal and career trajectory, the turning points are many. Important ones include religious confirmation in her church, joining her sorority, meeting her boyfriend, and so on. In the near future she sees future turning points, namely graduating, getting her first teaching job, marrying, and having children. Important people include her parents, siblings, and boyfriend, all of whom heartily endorse her decision to become a teacher, both for her "natural abilities" but also for the flexibility it will afford her. Kari says that she expects to teach until she gets married and has children, and then perhaps to return after her children begin school. She "hopes it doesn't die out," and when I asked what that meant, she elaborated that she was concerned that teachers burn out, and quit, and stop enjoying the work, and that she sees that potential in herself. "It might just be better for me to stay home, a better choice, and I might not want to go back even if I really love it."

Maya

At twenty-three, Maya was among the oldest of the preservice participants in the MU sample, and the only natural sciences major in the group. She also stood apart from her peers in that she attended an undergraduate college other than Mountain, was from out of state, and had had some work experience between completing her undergraduate degree and beginning the post-BA program. She was also politically, socially, and culturally different from her peers. She described herself as a "tree-hugging, liberal hippie from down south," and the daughter of white, working class parents who grew up in a culturally rich but economically poor rural community in a Southern state. She often wore men's clothing and work boots, and with her heavy-lidded eyes, waist-length dark hair and feminist, activist politics, she reminded me of a young Joan Baez. She spoke with a gentle Southern accent, and unlike many of her classmates who lived in the community surrounding the university, she lived about thirty minutes away in a large, racially diverse urban center where, she hoped, she would one day teach the upper elementary grade students of her friends and neighbors.

Maya's childhood and growing up experiences were radically different from her classmates. Her experiences were shaped by her parents' frequent itinerant labor in other parts of the country and longer stints of formal employment in the area surrounding their rural home on a sprawling acreage in the small community where both of her parents were born and grew up. Her parents hunted, fished, and rehabilitated injured wild animals, teaching Maya early on to love and respect nature. "We didn't have money, we didn't have extras, but my parents took care of us—I figure I can live on a teacher's salary no problem!" Maya laughed.

Of her flock of close-knit siblings and cousins, only she would attend college, while the others sought factory or other industrial work. While classmates drew largely on stories of the entertaining qualities of favorite teachers both real and from books and movies, the experiences that Maya shared were deeper and more thoughtful. One day in particular, in small group discussion, a fellow student said that she was confused about what teachers are supposed to do. "Are we [working in teaching] to teach kids, or to love them?" to which Maya replied that teaching and loving can be overlapping tasks. She illustrated her point with a story about losing her family home and possessions in a house fire during third grade. "We didn't have anything. The fire struck when we weren't home and everything was lost—everything. We didn't even have clothes, so people in the community took care of us—they'd leave boxes in the rented place we were staying. My teacher, Mr. Fleet, came to see us at the place we were staying since I had been out of school for a few days." She continued,

> And he said he came to see if there was anything that I didn't have that I needed. And I was like, "Well, I'd just really like to have pictures of my classmates," and so they had the black and white photos that they give out at the school and I came in the next day and the kids had basically taken all those pictures and made me a photo album of all the pictures of the classmates and people had put notes and things especially to me. That was the one thing I wanted, my classmates' pictures. Mr. Fleet organized the whole thing, with the kids, and brought it together and talked to them and everyone treated me right and I never had to say a word. That's love.

And the love was also in their small community, where most of the children from area families stayed in the area despite the decline of the major employers—mines and the railroad—and the loss of economic possibility in the area. Maya even said that she wonders at times whether or not she did the right thing in leaving to take a scholarship at a prestigious small college to the north of her rural community. The college experience was challenging, as she felt unprepared for the stressors of college science courses. "But I always dreamed big," she said. Her parents and friends continually told her how smart and capable she was, her teachers helped create a culture of learning in the school and among the families in the community. "We were always reading, all of us, or listening to music—good music, like the Beatles or Otis Redding. Everyone did it." Although the previous generation didn't typically attend college or finish high school, most of Maya's classmates were encouraged to at least begin classes at a nearby community college after graduation—and a large number of them completed degrees there at the urging of teachers and community members.

Maya completed her undergraduate degree, and then took a job with a consumer advocacy group far from home, "Working with all these Harvard MBA guys who had no conception of reality." After about a year at that job, "Sitting in a desk and twenty pounds heavier and exhausted mentally and feeling really weird and unhappy," Maya gave her notice and went home, where her mother observed her playing with some young cousins.

> My mother said, "Those kids just hang all over you, they love you, you just have a way with kids"—and I do, I have patience with kids and they are fun to me. I always thought I wanted to do something meaningful and change the world, and that made me think, I had never thought of being a teacher before, but, well, if you're a teacher then in a small way you change the world . . . it's in the very small things; showing a kid she can be different by showing how you accept different cultures. I like the idea of being able to go into a classroom and being able to have all these children who, you know, you're giving them skills to get by on, you're giving them tools they need, but you're also giving them a different way to think . . . like the teacher I had who would always have us use paper from the copy room—the other teachers would throw their bad copies in the trash and she would pick them up and hand them out and say, "We'll work on the back"—little things to help people to understand where you are coming from. I got to think about the little things because of the teachers I had and the things they did.

Maya's favorite teachers growing up were the ones that, as she said, changed the world in small ways. Like Miss Lerner, who refused to let any student "off the hook" just because they were poor, or Mr. Fleet, who was thoughtful enough to ask a student what she needed rather than make assumptions about class and need. She defined teachers' work as primarily about presenting children with these "little things"—meaning, alternative ways of thinking about and being in the world that could transform their understanding of the world, and themselves. It was also about caring, and nurturing, and being a loving presence in children's lives.

While Maya did not have specific criticisms of the teacher education program ("It's really fine," she said, "I assume I'm getting solid basics") she did feel some conflict with her classmates, the overwhelming majority of whom were less mature and had less experience in the world outside of college. "Last semester I felt differently," she said. "I was like, 'Oh, I love all these wonderful people [in my classes]! They're so fun! They're so great!' but I don't feel that this semester."

Sometimes—and for the most part I do [generally like them] but sometimes I feel like these women cannot possibly be put in charge of other people's kids. They just are so different from me; I don't understand them, maybe? And while I don't like feeling that way about people, you just get into this mindset that you want school to be such a good experience for every child, that every child enters the classroom and will have a positive experience and then you see people in your classes and you're like, "You're going to be a teacher? Do you have the patience to really think about what you do?" I don't know . . . they're just so different . . . they don't question why, they're just like cows, one following the other along. I mean, please. They want to make the classroom a picture perfect replica of their own "playing teacher" and that's not what it [will be]. There [will be] real, live kids in there and if they don't teach them not to follow, who will, you know?

In a larger discussion mapping her life's important turning points, Maya affirmed that the house fire, going to college and struggling there, taking the consumer protection job (and leaving the consumer protection job), and beginning teacher preparation were all significant turning points in her life because they symbolized her finding herself and learning about who she was. Future important turning points included finishing teacher education and getting a job in her home neighborhood, and possibly looking into summer endeavors, like starting a gardening business. Maya lived with a boyfriend at the time of the interview, but neither he nor his own career or family aspirations surfaced as significant in her trajectory. When asked about the feminization of teaching, or others' focus on its compatibility with family life and motherhood, Maya assured me that, yes, she did consider children and family, but her work was something that was just for her, a pleasure and a vocation independent of other plans. "It's one of the first things I chose for myself," she said, "and that's probably why it fits so well."

Kari and Maya: The Moral Career

An analysis of the stories Kari and Maya, and their peers, told about becoming teachers in teacher education, despite obvious diversions, had several similar signposts along the way. These turning points represent both moments of significance as well as times when the narrator may be demonstrating a point of what Goffman (1959) would call impression management, or realignment with a set of norms that govern social norms and audience cues for what constitutes a "good" performance of the roles of teacher and woman, to name a few. While impression management requires vigilance, the end result is a successful moral career made up of a predictable pattern of connect-the-dots. For participants in this study, table 4.2 reflects the shared and divergent turning points/impression management junctions among participant narratives. Kari and Maya were chosen to be presented as more in-depth vignettes because they easily serve as representative cases of the discernible gender and vocational tropes in the MU data. Shaded areas reflect areas of similarity.

One difference between Kari and Maya's moral career is the diverging endpoint, as well as the points of impression management at which they each explain, confide of reframe specific behaviors. These patterns are illustrated in reference to figure 1.1 from chapter 1.

Kari's moral career begins with childhood aspirations and identification with a teacher, and ends not with teaching, but with teaching as laying the groundwork for marriage and motherhood. In our conversations, she does some careful impression management, beginning with her explanation that teaching remains her first choice as a career despite a brief dalliance with physical therapy, and then with her admission that teaching was about love to manage her contradictory admissions that she really didn't know what teachers' work entailed and that she was suspect of the value of teacher education. Both of these moments of impression management were situated in the enactment of very specific feminine norms, namely that (1) teaching is natural and represents a desirable feminine skill set, and (2) teaching is first about loving, and only secondarily about other concerns. It is possible that the subtext here is that women, with a natural aptitude, are born teachers, rather than products of teacher education. Remembering that a desired outcome of a successful moral career is the enactment and relative ownership of a valued identity, that valued identity, for Kari and those like her, may be an identity tied to gender, but it isn't the teacher identity. It is the identity of wife and mother. Other avenues, such as majors in physical therapy, may be a lot of hard work, and possibly lead to success, but they will not necessarily and clearly lead to *that* particular valued identity, whereas teaching, in the popular culture and media milieu, has been shown to do so. Worse still, there is a possibility that such an alternative avenue could lead to a stigmatized identity, such as academic failure. This becomes gender identity failure for the "good girl" in Holland and Eisenhart's (1992) economy of "As and praise." Similarly, for Kari and others, failure to secure marriage and motherhood, and to be therefore a spinster, also represents an unthinkable stigmatized identity. Teacher meets both needs, and is the primary positive identity that is both practical and available.

Maya's moral career, meanwhile, begins with childhood aspirations that are unfocused, unclear, but generally interested in schooling, nature, and

Table 4.2. Turning Points

Narrative	TP1	TP2	TP3	TP4	TP5	TP6	TP7	Desired future plans
Kari	*Childhood:* Early identification with teacher, teaching	*Beginning college:* Reluctance to become teacher, attempts other options	*Early adulthood milestones:* sorority, boyfriend	*Family Reinforcement:* Parents, others reinforce gendered skills for caring and nurturing	*Aligns self with teaching:* Return to desire to become teacher in face of undesirable other options, but "not a second choice"	*Begins teacher preparation*	*Critical of teacher education*	Marriage, motherhood, possibly leaving teaching
Maya	*Childhood:* Enjoyed school and certain topics (science) but no specific interests	*Beginning college:* Pursues difficult major in the sciences, perseveres	*Early adulthood milestones:* Completing college, finding employment	*Family Reinforcement:* Parents, others reinforce gendered skills of caring and nurturing	*Aligns teaching with self:* Opts to become a teacher after realizing its alignment with her values	*Begins teacher preparation*	*Critical of fellow teacher candidates*	Becoming teacher, exploring interest in science, botany

science. Her journey from that point on is highly erratic, with frequent missteps, learning experiences and renegotiations of self and vocation. In short, she allows herself to fail, and to retrench. The endpoint of her moral career is in the classroom and beyond; she sees the goal as becoming a teacher with divergent outside interests. Like Kari, her sites of impression management are clear: tacit apologies for judging her fellow teacher education candidates, and in some of how she makes meaning from missteps in college and in her first job, where she was clearly miserable. These were mistakes, but in deriving meaning from them rather than internalizing a stigmatized identity, and telling her story as full of thickly agentive turning points, she creates a seamlessly managed narrative and a successful moral career. While I see her commitment to the appearance of niceness, one of Mahalik et al. (2005) identified feminine norms and something deeply embedded in white, middle class girl culture (Greenfield, 2005), her moral career is embedded in a story of becoming a teacher, rather than fulfilling gendered expectation.

Reference Groups and Imagery Frameworks

Kari's reference groups include individuals primarily from her immediate domestic sphere—her mother, family, and friends. Favorite teachers, teachers she knows or thinks about, rarely appear. While she did not make references to popular cultural teachers in the interview series, in observed classroom conversations, she and her friends did reference favorite teachers from the movies and television, mostly as an illustration of classroom management practice. While Kari reflects on how her life has expanded to allow for more friends and experiences, her primarily domestic reference group has remained relatively static in her retelling. Considering that reference groups help us determine who we might be interested in becoming as well as set parameters for what kinds of behaviors and actions are appropriate and inappropriate across different settings and that, as the name suggests, we *refer* to in determining how to act and fundamentally how to begin shaping the moral career, it is no surprise that her moral career is not the story of becoming a teacher but rather of becoming a wife or mother via teaching. The introduction of a new potential reference group, such as in beginning teacher preparation and being exposed to critical political ideologies (such as a closer encounter with feminists and feminism) has doubtlessly had an impact upon Kari's sense of self, but mostly in that she rejected them. Questions remain as to why this new group wasn't at least partially integrated, responsible for ideological questioning or shift. It is possible that the duration of many teacher education programs is insufficient for the necessary depth and breadth of such exposure, though for complex economic and social reasons, creating lengthier programs is often difficult.

Similarly, another way of looking at the figures that populate an individual's narrative about the desired moral career is in analyzing the frameworks of imagery in play. These include culturally and historically specific tropes about professional and gender identities, popular cultural themes and stock teacher images (think about the ubiquitous apple-on-a-chalkboard image). Kari and Maya's imagery frameworks share many similarities as well as important contradictions. For focus, table 4.3 illustrates these tropes as they

Table 4.3. Comparative Imagery Frameworks—Kari and Maya

Norm	Kari	Maya
Niceness in Relationships	The polite girl/good student	*The activist*
	Not a feminist	*The feminist*
	The apolitical	*The politically outspoken*
Involvement with Children	The mother	The cousin/sibling
	The babysitter	The iconoclastic teacher
	The older sibling	The student
	The nurturer	The inspiring teacher
	The "natural" teacher	The nurturer
		The community member
		The transformative teacher
Investment in Appearance	The sorority girl	*The hippie*
	The "girly girl"	*The feminist*
		The activist
Thinness	N/A	N/A
Sexual Fidelity/Chastity/ Morality	The Purity Pledger	N/A
	The churchgoer	
	The wild partygoer	
Modesty	Not a feminist	*The achiever*
	The "natural"	*The activist*
Involvement in Romantic Relationships	The boyfriend	*The person of voluntarily unclear sexuality*
	Teaching as the Marriage-Suitable Profession	
	The heterosexual (assumed)	
Domesticity	Teaching as the Family/ Motherhood-Suitable Profession	The daughter
		The home gardener
	Not a feminist	
	The daughter	
	The future mother or wife	
	The natural nurturer	

jibe with or contradict (in italics) Western feminine norms (Mahalik et al., 2005).

Of the larger group of participants, most imagery frameworks fit in with Kari's column, that is, they were largely jibing with rather than contradicting Western feminine norms as presented here. For Maya, and the handful of participants similar to her, the tropes appearing in their narratives complicated, contradicted, or otherwise did not fit (and therefore appear in italics). Her narrative was simply much less about feminine norms, while Kari's incorporated them centrally.

In terms of thinking about where these imagery frameworks came from, it is possible to construe that individual experience—including the depth and breadth and availability of different reference groups that may or may not contract or reinforce the Western feminine norms implicit in girl culture—is the source. While it was certainly beyond the possibilities of this line of inquiry to definitively connect them with the imagery frameworks in place of particular teacher education contexts, I did collect data on the imagery frameworks at play in Kari and Maya's experiences at Mountain. These include analyses from field notes, observations and artifacts connected with their two methods courses. Table 4.4 illustrates these in reference to the Western feminine norms from Mahalik et al. (2005). Again, italics note points of discordance.

It is important to note that while neither Kari's nor Maya's particular imagery frameworks mirrors faculty or program imagery frameworks, Maya's is certainly more similar. Her conversation about becoming a teacher and her responses in classes were much more aligned with those particular frameworks, and, not surprisingly, her critiques of the program and faculty were few. Kari's meanwhile, like the majority of the sample she represents, differs vastly in terms of political, cultural, and social ideas. Also not surprisingly, her critiques of the program and faculty were extensive. Any programmatic or instructional attempt to encourage Kari to critically reflect on her own schema resulted in the reinforcement of her already rigid belief structure.

Roles and Performances

The individual strives to give an impression that is desirable to themselves and creates the desired effect upon others, the overall pattern of which may be thought of as the shape of the central arrow in figure 1.1 from chapter 1. This arrow, or trajectory, is highly responsive to the reference groups and frameworks of imagery. However, individuals also shape their trajectory based on the roles they choose to "take" or "make." As Goffman (1963)

Table 4.4.

Norm	Program/Course
Niceness in Relationships	The flexible, kind instructor, Meeting students where they are
	The infrequency of failure in education courses
	Political/controversial content
	Teacher as activist/intellectual
	Teaching as political work
Involvement with Children	The child-centered instructor
	The parent
	The transformative teacher
	The critical teacher/anti-racist educator
Investment in Appearance	Emphasis of gender-specific dress code
	Professional dress
	Gender neutral dress
	The activist
	The feminist
Thinness	N/A
Sexual Fidelity/Chastity/Morality	N/A
Modesty	The teacher educator downplaying research
	The activist
Involvement in Romantic Relationships	The heterosexual (assumed)
Domesticity	The parent

writes, "role-taking" (1964) occurs when the individual puts themselves in the role of the teacher, making themselves "fit" into that role as best they can and engaging in occupying that role as it is externally and generally defined. Meanwhile, "role-making" is the process by which the individual makes that perhaps awkward initial fit more comfortable by bringing her own interpretation to the performance. It is easy to say that the last one is more agentive and possibly reflective of a wider range of reference groups and imagery frameworks, while the former represents some restrictions—but in the case of this participant pool, the vast majority of individuals were engaged in role taking, while only a handful were role-*making*.

Looking back at table 4.3, a few important divergences in the two representative samples may be illustrative. For example, Maya's central criticisms of her fellow teacher education students was their "cow-like" acceptance of the status quo, while Kari directed her frustration at figures of authority—and ones that encouraged critical thinking at that. That said, the moral career of the preservice teacher at Mountain seems to diverge in terms of role-making and role-taking. For Kari, becoming a teacher means successfully aligning one's identity with how one perceives the work and role of the teacher (role-taking). For Maya, becoming a teacher involves primarily aligning the work of the teacher with one's identity and value system. So, while teaching becomes an avenue for a valued identity of a particular interpretation of femininity and enactment of feminine norms for Kari, Maya uses teaching to forward her agenda of improving the world through "little things."

Related to both of these are individual interpretations about the nature of teachers' work and programmatic and faculty interpretations (and assumptions) about how individuals become teachers. At Mountain, an interesting wrinkle here was the idea of time. Faculty in both of the methods sections, as well as (implied) in the programmatic literature affirm that becoming a teacher is a process, and that teacher education only begins that process. In other words, preservice teachers do not emerge from their preparation programs as expert teachers, but instead have much learning to do over their professional trajectories. The majority of students, like Kari, assumed that in exchange for tuition dollars they would be transformed, and given the discrete, highly operationalizable skills, to be an expert teacher immediately upon program completion. Her critiques of the faculty were therefore more than just an ideological mismatch but also deep anxiety that as they progressed through the program they were not showing signs of gaining expert knowledge. Hence some of the anxiety about procedural understanding, most of which was based upon their limited (and exclusively structural, procedural interpretation of) understanding of the profession as about the twin tasks of nurturing and management. The basic refusal of faculty and program to frame the work in those terms did not create the conditions for Kari and others to reframe *their* interpretation of teachers' work, but instead to respond to dissonance by clinging more tightly and defensively to their own beliefs. Maya, meanwhile, believed that at least one part of teachers' work was the continuation of what she had already been doing—engaging in the "little things" of iconoclastic, political, and environmental activism—and becoming a teacher, as role-making, was about aligning that profession with this work. Having already had diverse (and divergent) professional and life experiences, she seemed much more comfortable with unclear trajectories and a moral career that involved negotiation, reframing, and a continued and recursive (rather than linear and finite) process of becoming. Finally, Maya's process of becoming a teacher had little to do with gendered identity realization processes or timetables, while it may be said that Kari's was equal parts the story of becoming a teacher and realizing a valued gender identity.

Feminized Profession and Feminized Practices

Both Kari and Maya, and all of their program compatriots, mentioned at least once in interviews that teaching was construed either by them or someone close to them as the work of care. They were all also cognizant of teaching as a "feminized profession" in which men were few and far between. While Maya's mother is the only one in her narrative who seems to hint that teaching comes "naturally" to women, who are biologically more apt for nurturing, the entire constellation of voices in Kari's story echo same, including Kari herself. Maya implies that this is problematic, but does not overtly or critically address it. Kari, meanwhile, addresses her natural gifts directly, and even discusses the obstacles faced by male, and therefore either disadvantaged or suspect, teachers. Similarly, Kari is one of very few participants to even hint at a relationship between biology and power. She affirms that men have avenues to more money, but that affective rewards, many of which are easily attained by women, are more valuable. While acknowledging that "[men] make stuff, and money," in ways disproportionately valued by the culture, Kari still affirms that there are other value systems at work; she asks, "But do they have the satisfaction?" She seems to think not. She also sees, as did many others, the plight of other women attempting to make it in more hegemonic, masculinized professions, and considers herself lucky to have made a much more pragmatic choice, despite popular opinion that it is easy work, and easier still for her because she is female. Is it possible that, in her own way, Kari is retreating to a feminized profession as a means of resistance, as Griffiths (2006) theory of feminized practices might suggest?

In many ways, Kari and others construct teaching as a place where resistant feminized practices are possible. She emphasizes care, understanding, and connection as alternatives to capitalism and the rigid hierarchies implicit in the hegemonic masculinity that defines most other spheres of work. Her resistance, however—if that is indeed what it is—is still not critical. Griffiths affirms that feminized practices may incorporate care and love but that these have less to do with biological aptitude than with creating a space to trouble oppression in the forms of racism, sexism, classism, and homophobia (Connell, 1987; Griffiths, 2006). I wonder how Kari's narrative might change were she to restructure the work of love and care not as biological gifts or imperatives but rather critical choices in resistance to hegemony.

Also, some of her struggle and the dissonance she experiences may have to do with the intersection of care and love (even biologically based aptitudes for caring and loving) and the dominance of patriarchy and hegemonic masculinity in her own life and interpretation of life trajectory and gender identity. While Connell (1987) affirms that there is no such thing as hegemonic femininity, I would argue, as she does, that some forms of femininity are simply more conducive to the dominance of hegemonic masculinity and subsequently less at odds with the practices and products of patriarchy. Kari, admittedly, has very little to lose from living under patriarchy. Even though she emphasizes the importance and power of an alternative framework of capitalist work and reward as care and love, she does so within the established boundaries and gender expectations of patriarchy that one would expect in a university setting. Love, here, can become work, and even transformative work, but it can do so without creating a space for resistance.

Conclusion

Even though extensive longitudinal data was not collected on participants at Mountain, it is interesting to note that while both Kari and Maya (and all but one of their fellow participants) completed their coursework, only Maya became a teacher, and is still an elementary school teacher in a small, southern community at this writing. She is also still an active and highly vocal political and community presence in her small district and community. Whether or not Kari completed her licensure paperwork (many complete coursework but do not finish this step), began teaching and left to pursue other options, or realized her dream of marriage and motherhood, was not possible to determine. Perhaps they both struggled with the idea of care and work, but Kari, being much more wedded to an idea of teaching as nurturing, did not find the realities of the work as palatable as Maya did. As I noted earlier, it is possible to have a successful literal career and a failed moral career, but these findings lead me to consider that the inverse may also be true. Perhaps Kari, and others, have successful moral careers while "failing" at becoming teachers—having determined that work in teaching is not as conducive to their desired identities and trajectory as previously thought. After all, it is possible that for Kari, at least, her story was not about becoming a teacher as much as becoming a wife and mother, and in that sense a successful white, middle class female according to the web of valued identities and roles in her particular sociocultural milieu.

But, as always, the relationship between moral and literal careers is not that simple, and beyond such an analysis are some details about trajectory that must not be overlooked. To borrow some language from Goffman's (1959) dramaturgical turn on data analysis, preservice participants at Mountain University were following relatively rigid and time-tested script for the construction of a valued feminine gender identity. This means that they are making decisions about role-making, role-taking, self, and work that have been demonstrated to be effective by others. Such evidence of its effectiveness in the popular cultural and girl culture reference groups to which they have had access were considered weighty truths and "proof" that the strategies employed would be successful. Like so many, they did what worked. But what about the two or three who represent divergence from that pattern? As Maya would describe it, she was an old hand at being an iconoclast, and perhaps became comfortable with the consequences of diverging from the predictable performance and the proven pathway to valued identity. While those like Kari, ever-ready and always performing, have typically very good grades (albeit often in less challenging undergraduate majors), Maya had fewer poor grades in challenging courses and unchallenging courses alike, had taken time off from school, been directionless, explored other avenues and strayed into the realm of the "nontraditional" student. She came to teaching after trying—and even failing—at a number of other pursuits. "I was never into the whole mainstream thing," Maya would say, "Making myself fit some kind of mold,

> I failed classes; I had careers that didn't work out. I left home and went out on my own and had to go back home after screwing up. I get funny looks because I dress like a dude. I want to go live in a tent in the woods and grow my own food . . . and that makes people [uncomfortable].

Maya and the two other self-described program iconoclasts ("the hippies and lesbians," Maya would joke one day in class) made their own subcultural/countercultural community, as they doubtlessly would in their future work in schools, where, as novice teachers at Valley University (to be discussed in chapter 5), would find, girl culture-cum-hegemonic-femininity can reign supreme.

There are obviously social and historical factors and popular cultural/girl culture influences on what constitutes a valued identity and successful moral career (and the mechanisms by which one might stay "on track" with each). However, the teacher education experience also serves to create opportunities to tell, reinforce and refine these performances and the feminine norms that are implicit in girls' and women's experiences. Teacher educators at Mountain didn't actively participate in the production and reproduction of girl culture through telling and retelling stories, and even pedagogically sought to offer gentle critiques through feminist and other liberatory pedagogies and critical teaching. However, the ways in which preservice teachers were managed and moved through their programs served to reinforce and communicate the Western feminine norms associated with girl culture and the relatively uniform moral career of the preservice teacher at MU. So, one might say that in some small ways, the "hidden curriculum" of teacher education at MU was one of controlling for pacifying and controlling the "fussy" student—silencing the nonstop complaining of the Kari's of the preservice cadre by rewarding relative compliance—even silence—with good will, attention to the primacy of the personal narrative, good grades and, most importantly, little contest to the near-universal notion that the work of the teacher was primarily work to be done by women who were naturally better at providing care and love. However, to give teacher educators some well-deserved credit, as Pajares (1992) and others illustrate, the rigidity of these beliefs and the power of contemporary girl culture are such that taking time from an already jam-packed teacher licensure program to attempt critique could be a fool's errand.

Notes

1. Including tenured and junior faculty, clinical professors, and graduate students.

2. Note that the CFNI did not become available until I had left the MU data collection site, and I was unable to track down participants for more recent administration. It would have been helpful to use that as a measure of adherence here.

~

CHAPTER FIVE

Divining the Hand of Destiny

Valley University

But it just showed me that teaching was a better choice for me. And now
I love it . . . I feel like maybe this is what I am supposed to do, after all.

—Rachel, research participant at Valley University

With an average higher age, more (but not necessarily more diverse) experiences prior to teacher education, and greater overall socioeconomic
diversity, the preservice cohort at Valley University approached the
experience of doing gender and gendered work from a different vantage
point than did MU students. At Valley, gendered skills like nurturing,
connection with children, and so on, were framed as surrendering to destiny, divining "discovered gifts," and newly gendered selves on the road to
finding oneself and allowing these point the way to true [and gendered]
vocation. As will be illustrated in the following sample cases of Adrienne
and Rachel, the intensive teacher preparation at Valley is experienced as
self-discovery and revelation, as Rachel's quote above illustrates, instead of
an affirmation of role-taking, or what an individual "already knows"—or
thinks she knows. Meanwhile, teacher educators at Valley, with their typically more aggressive—but still "developmental"—approach to facilitating
critical reflection and smaller, intensive cohorts also had a different, more
individualized and less uniformly and vocally dissonant experiences with
their preservice students.

Background and Context

Valley University was founded in the early 1860s as part of the original Morrill Land-Grant Act, occupying a picturesque, green campus in a rural New England community with both agricultural and industrial roots. With an energetic research program, Valley has received a Carnegie research rating of "very high," and as of 2007 alone had earned more than $131 million in research awards (University Website, 2008). The Valley University School of Education functioned as an independent department at the University. With its own dean, programs of study and designated faculty, the school has been rated highly by national surveys in higher education as both a "best buy" and, historically, a site for innovative teacher education preparation. During the data collection period, roughly 28 doctorates and over 230 MEds were awarded. Program and course evaluations revealed that students are consistently happy with instruction across the programs, including teacher education.

The TEPP Program

All preservice participants were enrolled in the TEPP program, the primary route to elementary and early childhood licensure at Valley. TEPP was a nine-month, intensive MEd and licensure program in which preservice teachers must complete rigorous coursework while simultaneously completing two internship experiences in local rural, suburban, and urban school districts. The TEPP program had historically been viewed by professionals in the field and aspiring teacher candidates alike as a particularly critical, cutting-edge, and developmentally and social-justice focused program. Small numbers of teacher candidates were typically shepherded through coursework and student teaching internships by a few closely involved faculty, resulting in what one faculty member called a "high touch" program that was difficult to sustain when the program grew larger and began to more closely resemble the batch-processing teacher education units common at many large universities and colleges.

In addition to meeting graduate school admissions requirements, the TEPP program requires applicants to successfully complete a significant number of prerequisite courses and pass the state-mandated teacher licensure examination prior to admission. The majority of TEPP students begin as Valley undergraduates completing the education minor. While there are typically one or two individuals who are not matriculating undergraduates from the education minor (such as graduating seniors from other institutions, or people who are second-career professionals) TEPP's major source of enrollment has been stable for some time, and the time of data collection was no exception.

Unique Economic Variables

Unlike the periods of data collection at either site, the time spent at Valley marked the initial blast of the economic crisis of 2008–present. The impact on the school of education, as in other departments, was significant and appeared so very palpably in my data in the teacher education enrollment figures. Despite historic stability, at the time of this writing, as will be reflected in the concluding chapters and discussion, enrollment in the TEPP program had been dramatically dwindling. For example, during the 2005–2006 academic year, the TEPP program (which at that time did not distinguish between elementary and early childhood tracks) had seventy preservice teachers were enrolled. Many faculty were surprised to find the program attracting (and admitting) such numbers, and discussion about the value of a smaller program began cropping up at faculty meetings. However, the program continued to thrive with sixty-four of that number graduating from the program. In 2006–2007, only fifty-eight students enrolled and completed the program. By 2007–2008, when the program differentiated between elementary and early childhood, separating into two distinct cohorts, the elementary program admitted only twenty-five students. Data for 2008–2009 and 2009–2010 continued to hold at upwards of twenty to thirty admissions, with the prospective 2010–2011 pool being smaller still. While this trend is by no means unique to TEPP and Valley University, it was a significant elephant-in-the-room for many respondents. This represents a further rub considering that the TEPP tuition for 2010–2011 is much higher than the projected average graduate student tuition at Valley, at just over $16,000, not including books, computer software, and data management fees. While this makes sense given overall tuition increases and the fact that TEPP students take more courses and receive more credits than individuals in less intensive programs, the impression of higher tuition still packs an emotional punch for many.

So, the School of Education's loss of state funding resulted in an imperative to find ways to, effectively, do more with less. The actual university-wide figures in lost state revenues was staggering: a $225 million difference between September 2008 and September 2009—compelled $13 million in mid-year cuts during the 2008–2009 academic year, with the university cutting its base budget by close to $14 million over both AY2009–2009 and AY2009–2010. While federal stimulus monies have taken the sting out of some of these drastic reductions, the university chancellor noted in his October 2, 2009, remarks to the campus community, "the absence of stimulus money and the low level of current state support will force us either to conduct ourselves in a different manner or to slash budgets to the point that the campus will no longer resemble the institution we cherish" (University website, 2009).

What that meant in the School of Education was speculated about among faculty and students alike. Faculty worried about the drop in the actual number of admissions, and the TEPP faculty in particular felt torn between the necessity of admitting only those applicants with proven aptitude for graduate study, appropriate dispositions for work with children, and the necessary course and other pre-requisites for admission. However, admitting only those candidates with high marks and completion in those three areas would have left the program without a single functioning cohort. So, as was frequently the case in the past, exceptions were made: individuals without complete applications would be tracked down with repeated phone calls and emails until their materials were submitted properly; individuals without passing scores on certain state teacher tests were admitted conditionally pending passing scores; individuals without the necessary course prerequisites were admitted with the understanding that these course prerequisites would be completed successfully over the intervening summer months, and so on. Many faculty understood that this meant problems down the road—for example, for students conditionally admitted without passing scores on prerequisite state tests would receive waivers to proceed to the first semester of the intensive program without passing those tests (but with the understanding that they would labor long and hard to do so), and those few that still did not pass by December would need to have waivers to continue their attempts during student teaching or risk an incomplete in the program pending their completion. While certainly no applicant without the appropriate background checks, dispositions, or recommendations would be admitted, the gray areas of tests, prerequisites, and other admissions materials matters persisted. While the application process was a labyrinthine endeavor for many program applicants, and frequent missteps due to the rapid pace of change in state requirements were common, the degree to which applications frequently came in incomplete, late, or in disarray was considered by many faculty as a harbinger of difficult times ahead.

While program applicants frequently came from other regional and national undergraduate programs, the majority of students each year were from Valley itself, or neighboring state institutions. Furthermore, many of them came from small, working, and middle class communities and had varying degrees of rigor in their undergraduate and high school preparation. Referred to as "undereducated" rather than unprepared, faculty worked closely to remediate the areas of need for these students, aware that there were often vast differences between the level of professionalism, background knowledge, and cultural capital between some students and others. In the end, faculty efforts were quite successful, with program completer pass rates on state required teacher tests approaching 85 percent for early childhood and 95 percent for elementary candidates during the data collection period.[1]

Graduates from the TEPP program overwhelmingly sought jobs in-state, with very few seeking employment in private or out-of-state schools or school systems. Those who came from in-state institutions, including Valley itself, typically hoped to return to teach in or near their home communities, or in the college town itself.

Teacher Preparation Experiences

Preservice teachers at Valley were organized into cohorts of approximately sixteen to twenty-two individuals depending on the size of overall enrollment that year. After 2007, the early childhood candidates were semi-separated from elementary candidates. In this structure, they took some courses alone, in early childhood–only sections, and some sections integrated with the larger elementary group. Preservice study participants were enrolled in teacher education coursework through the Valley University School of Education for a nine-month intensive period that coincided with demanding field placement internships and student teaching experiences. While required to take introductory coursework in reading methods and general mathematics, the program offered a two-semester structure, as shown in table 5.1. No electives or other free choice options were made available during the program due to tight time constraints. While a few preservice teachers responded that this was not a true graduate program—one said that she felt "infantilized" and "not like other graduate students" who were "able to choose courses and be advised about what they were taking" (student communication, 2008)—the remainder understood the urgency, and the ultimate economic and time payoff, of a short program.

Table 5.1.   Courses Taken by TEPP Students

Fall Semester (Credits)	Spring Semester (Credits)
Human Development (3)	Social Studies Methods (3)
Reading Methods (3)	Science Methods (3)
Math Methods (3)	Special Education Methods (3)
General Methods I (3)	General Methods II (3)
Classroom Internship (5)	Student Teaching Internship (9)

In addition to this demanding, regimented course schedule, the program had also required, in different permutations, a seminar in social justice and a series of Friday morning seminars in everything from education law to critical pedagogy. While both of these supplemental programs ebbed and flowed over the data collection period, the social justice seminar was a difficult point. Students perceived that it was an "add-on" and therefore superfluous (and a frustration given the challenging, critical, and often deeply personal content) whether it was offered as part of the fall semester (as was the case in 2005–2006), the abbreviated winter term (2006–2007), or integrated into social studies methods or other courses (2007–2008). While faculty agreed that the material was important to teacher development, and some students agreed that learning about the ways in which teachers could reflect upon racism, privilege, and oppression to the betterment of their practice as rural, urban, or suburban educators, others felt strongly that it was irrelevant to their needs. While negative student response, typically from the majority of white students, is in line with the bulk of the research literature on teaching social justice and anti-racist content in teacher education (Galman, Pica-Smith, & Rosenberger, 2010), the course ceased to be a standalone offering in the formal study program and at this writing faculty continue to labor to find ways for either its meaningful integration or possibilities for extending the curriculum.

And to all this, faculty were relatively aggressive—meaning, straight-forward—in their expectations for students, even if they knew that many measures (such as offering extensions and waivers to people failing the state tests, had few actual teeth). While certainly approached with kid gloves, to some degree, faculty did attempt to infuse an already overflowing programmatic to-do list with critical content and reflective practice. Many times, this critical emphasis had to do with intentionality on the part of the preservice teachers, to encourage them to move beyond playing with and nurturing children to a level of developmental and curricular planning. As one faculty member said, "Oftentimes, when you go into an [early elementary] classroom, kids are engaged in play-based behaviors, and somebody who interacts positively with him is doing a great job, and that's wonderful, but whether or not that teacher has the ability to think down the line is still up in the air." This often took the form of questioning what it means to move from "loving kids" to teaching them, in gentle and subtle but unmistakable ways. It appeared that some of the preservice students at least began to think about these issues, while some did not. "Not all of them have the big picture," this faculty member continued.

Not surprisingly, the preservice population interpreted this coaxing, and the constant call to reflection ("I have, like eleven reflective journals," said one exasperated student, "I'm reflecting on my reflections!") as a process of individual and career discernment, often having little to do with practice of children (except that one generally loves children, and the practice of teaching about enacting this love). This interpretation, and the incredible pace of the program, may be—in a bizarre turn—responsible for less dissonance among students. They weren't asked to necessarily relinquish their nascent ideas of teaching—that it is about loving and nurturing (and these, as important parts of vocational and gendered identity, were particularly close-held) but rather to build upon it. And that building took on many, if not all successful, forms. An additional critical focus was focusing on teaching practices that are more than just building on one's own apprenticeship of observation. In elementary, and especially early childhood, the fuzziness of memory leads to some very traditional, often outdated, or incomplete ideas about practice. As a faculty member said, "I mean, we don't have memories that are clear from kindergarten, usually, most of us, so you are putting an overlay of what your experiences have been as you're older" and subsequently they become distorted. But the individual doesn't necessarily see the distortion, so what is lost is, again, the intentionality of critical practice instead of oversimplified love and "play."

Overview: Preservice Participants at Valley University

Preservice participants a Valley that are included in this analysis (N = 24) are all white, female English speakers pursuing licensure at the elementary or early childhood level. These are noted in table 5.2, which illustrates the relevant demographics of the participant group writ large.

These participants are demographically distinct from their peers at Mountain, with higher average age of twenty-three, and with somewhat lower overall MHLE's (71 percent at college or above compared to 82 percent for the Mountain group and 25 percent at high school or GED compared with 17 percent same at Mountain). Given the drastically higher rates of tuition, and the longer potential duration of the teacher education sequence at Mountain, it would make sense that a "best buy" school like Valley, and an intensive, relatively cost-effective licensure-plus-MEd program like TEPP would attract more budget-conscious, possibly less affluent students. The data seem to support this trend.

The majority of participants at Valley were also Valley undergraduates, and completed the education minor program as undergraduates prior to

Table 5.2. Preservice Participants at Valley

Participant ID	Age	MHLE
VU1ECE	22	High School
VU2ECE	23	High School
VU3ECE	22	College
VU4ECE	24	College
VU5ECE	24	College
VU6ECE	24	Graduate Degree
VU7ECE	21	College
VU8ELEM	21	College
VU9ELEM	22	High School
VU10ELEM	21	College
VU11ELEM	21	College
VU12ELEM	22	College
VU13ELEM	23	High School
VU14ELEM	28	College
VU16ELEM	27	High School
VU17ELEM	21	College
VU18ELEM	22	College
VU19ELEM	25	College
VU20ELEM	23	College
VU21ELEM	24	GED
VU22ELEM	22	College
VU23ELEM	22	College
VU24ELEM	22	College
VU25ELEM	23	College

applying to admission to the TEPP program. The education minor typically involved an array of social foundations and general methods coursework as well as a low-credit internship in an area school. Students coming from the education minor were typically in good position for admission to TEPP, having been supervised and counseled as to the best way to complete the many prerequisites in a timely manner. However, more and more frequently during the data collection period, very promising education minor students had been applying to, and accepted by, teacher education programs at other colleges and universities, including small local ones. While no data were collected about this loss, faculty did find it a bit troubling, as some very promising students seemed to be consistently siphoned out of the Valley licensure applicant pool in favor of other, possibly more competitive, or more affordable, programs elsewhere. Data were not collected on what their particular motives might have been.

Sample Cases: Adrienne and Rachel

To illustrate general trends in the Valley participant pool, the following paragraphs tell the stories of Adrienne and Rachel. Adrienne is a member of the early childhood licensure cohort, while Rachel is pursuing a license at the elementary level. Their cases are representative of general trends around gender and work in both the early childhood and elementary samples.

Adrienne

Adrienne was a white, female preservice TEPP student pursuing licensure at the early childhood level. She was overjoyed to have recently become engaged to John, her boyfriend from high school, who worked in his family's successful landscape and garden business and whose future was quite promising. I had met John, and he made it clear that was exceptionally proud of Adrienne and her work in school and supported her plans to teach. Her engagement announcement in a local paper mentioned that she was a Valley graduate student in teacher preparation. Adrienne admitted that she had never thought she would stay in the Valley area after completing her undergraduate degree, but that life had taken her down this road and she was delighted that her work could be geographically flexible and allow her to (hopefully) stay in the area.

From a small, supportive family in a middle class suburb not too far from the Valley campus where she lived at home for much of her college career, Adrienne's mother had stayed at home to raise her and her siblings, while their father worked in a staff position at a small semi-urban Catholic college. The twenty-three-year-old Valley graduate was a cheerful and obliging, if not always active, participant in her TEPP classes and a helpful and engaged intern in her field placement. Despite being almost completely silent, and therefore a bit conspicuous, in her small early childhood cohort classes, she did engage thoughtfully when called upon, and steadily and carefully kept up with course assignments and readings. Always a bit sleepy, but carefully made up and trendily dressed, she blended in with the many other young women in the Early Childhood Education cohort and the typical collegiate identity kit. When I complemented her on her matching tote bag and shiny, hot pink flip-flop sandals she thanked me, but then said, quickly and seriously, "Of course, when I am in the classroom I am much more professional in how I dress." There was no denying that Adrienne was absolutely professional. She took her progress in the program very seriously, she said, and her performance mirrored that dedication.

A meticulous student, she had successfully passed all of her state tests for licensure prior to or immediately after admission to the program, and was on track to receive her license the following May. She described herself as a "good student" who had "positive experiences" with most, if not all, of her teachers through the end of elementary school. Secondary schooling was somewhat less enjoyable, as during her first year of high school some routine testing revealed that she "missed out on math and social studies somehow" and "didn't know all the stuff the other kids did." But despite a special focus on remediation in these and other areas, she still enjoyed her friendships, social activities, and other aspects of being a high school student. Still, this experience, and others in college, served to focus Adrienne's desire to teach at the early elementary and preschool levels, "where I feel most confident [with the content]," she added. She was, in fact, quite a diligent, detail-oriented student and not unintelligent—though I could see that she was worried about appearing so to me, and others—but I suspected, and she hinted, at inconsistent, even poor schooling experiences in her past. This was in spite of her near-constant affirmation of love and dedication for her own preschool and early elementary teachers, whom she credits with nurturing her "self-esteem" if not her academics.

I suspected that talking with me made her a little nervous, and asked several times in all settings if she wanted to take a break, or stop talking, to which she cheerfully replied that she was fine. She consistently had difficulty following what I was asking, and answering questions that required some reflection on the relationship between the past and the future. She tried very hard to help me as best she could, checking that I understood her answers multiple times throughout both interviews and signaling the completion of thoughts with phrases like, "That's really all I can say about that," or, "I don't know what else to say here." She seemed to believe that our interviews were something she should have prepared for in advance, but after I corrected this notion she became more comfortable with telling me that she did not know answers to some questions, or could not remember. She described herself more than once as a "people pleaser" and I could see that was true in her eagerness to be of help, and be "correct" with her answers—even to questions where there was obviously no single correct answer. She commented that she showed her professors respect by attending their courses and doing well in them.

The early childhood cohort was nearly always smaller than the elementary cohort (as had been the case historically, though the semi-segregation of that cohort made its small size more noticeable), made up mostly of white, middle class women like Adrienne. Adrienne had been a psychology major at Valley and had spent the year after graduation working as a teacher's assistant in a small day care center. Adrienne opted to leave her assistant position at the day care center and come back to school for the TEPP program because she wanted to move beyond being an assistant, gain a deeper understanding of schools and schooling, and maybe leave the area to work in a different school. Interestingly, at this point it came out that she had participated in the now-defunct undergraduate early childhood program at Valley, which she disliked because of its focus on "rules" that made her uncomfortable.

> Actually, when I first went into the other program, too, in early childhood as an undergrad, I did a couple [internships], and I didn't really like my experiences there. It just—it seemed like there were so many rules and they didn't really—I wasn't allowed to hug the kids. There were so many rules that I couldn't do that I didn't like, and I kind of think I got frustrated with the program. I decided, maybe I'll do something different. Now I'm back. I also haven't had very much experience in schools that have [a curriculum]. But I think most schools don't really look at kids as much as they should.

Despite her misgivings about the early childhood undergraduate program, her primary decision making about coming back to school in TEPP early childhood had to do with reflecting upon both (1) her own apprenticeship of observation and (2) her self-knowledge as an adult. So, (1) her happiest times had been in preschool and kindergarten, though she admittedly could not recall many of the details of those years beyond vague memories of the nurturing teachers she had, and (2) she understood that she disliked politics, competition and upper level academic content above all things—none of which were likely to be present in a preschool or kindergarten classroom—and her desire to teach about social interaction, other people, and social skills.

Like the majority of the Valley elementary and early childhood candidates, Adrienne did not start out wanting to be a teacher. She enrolled as a psychology major because she had wanted to be a child psychologist.

> I don't know, when I was in high school I realized, I don't know why, that I was interested in psychology. I had gotten a few books and was looking through it, trying to figure out what I was gonna major in when I went to college, and I was just reading about psychology and I was real interested in it, and then I knew I wanted to do something with kids, and I just put it together and I was like, "OK, I'll do child psychology." So I pursued that for a little while and thought about it and then I guess I realized that—I don't think I wanted to do it because one, I know you had to go to school for a very long time to actually

get to the point that I wanted to, and I also thought that it would be kind of—I didn't know if I'd be able to take the weight of just going through a bunch of kids that I felt like, you know, you can kind of help. I don't know, I thought it would be too heart-breaking to go through something like that. I thought I would take home a lot of stuff from the kids and who they are and it would be really, really hard to do it.

So, there was a possibility that all the hard work entailed in becoming a child psychologist would not be affectively rewarding in the long run. This seemed like a terrible gamble to Adrienne, who opted to use her psychology degree to become a teacher instead. In retrospect, she says she can see the "writing on the wall" that teaching little children came "naturally" to her and that her ability to connect with young children was not a gift to be squandered. "My parents saw it coming," she said brightly,

> It was just kind of natural for me to do it. And I guess my teachers, most of the people that really know me just think that it's just right for me, that I'd be a great teacher . . . almost everybody has said that I'm gonna be a great little-kid teacher. When I was little they all told me I was a mother type or I'd be a teacher. It just kind of felt like the natural profession for me, I always tried to take care of the little kids on the playground when I was playing when I was little. I would find a little three-year-old and help them down the slide or push them on the swings or something. So I've always been interested in kids since I was a kid myself. I read those books, *The Teenage Babysitters,* and I really wanted to be a babysitter when I was little. When I was twelve I started babysitting. I babysat all through high school, it was the only job I had. I had a lot of babysitting jobs and I just got to know families really well.

After graduation, she had not completed the early childhood undergraduate program, so she could not apply for positions beyond assistant teacher in day care work, but she felt fulfilled nonetheless. "I've been interested in kids my whole life." When pressed about what in particular interested her, Adrienne shrugged. "Well, I guess the social piece. Yeah, the social piece." I assumed that she meant the social environment in classrooms, but Adrienne corrected me—it was her own social development, her social abilities, that she considered her primary skill set and one of her aptitudes for teaching young children.

> I just always really cared about what other people thought and just the respect of other people, respecting their boundaries, respecting their feelings. I think I just thought about that a real lot growing up. I always was really thinking about other people and what they were thinking and how they were feeling, I

guess. It just really—that was just a huge concentration for me in my life and my outlook on life, I think, and I was really in tune with other people . . . that was really important to me and . . . [to] just be around kids. I guess as a teacher, the most important thing to me is teaching them really good social skills and how to respect their boundaries, how to tell other people enough is enough or just really to communicate with others. The whole social aspect is really important to me.

When I asked about what teachers' work in preschool or early elementary classrooms was like, and how it might be the same and different from her experiences in day care, and how she knew, she responded that at first, like many of her peers, she processed what she knew about teachers by "playing teacher" with her friends, and by babysitting for younger children.

I have a little sister who is six years younger, so I help her out a lot, too. I just was—I don't know, actually I used to pretend I was a teacher, now that I think about it. I used to pretend I was a teacher and try to teach my little sister. I'd try to teach her how to read. I just was always trying to teach her different skills—oh, and then I had a cousin who was five years younger than me and I babysat for him a lot, so I started to learn how to take care of him. I just really enjoyed doing that.

She also explained that she was "just an assistant" in her year at the day care center, so that "wasn't really teaching" and didn't inform her understanding of teachers' work. When I asked about her own favorite teachers, she brightened. "I loved my kindergarten teacher, and my first grade teacher," and while her memories were a bit scattered, she remembered having fun, and enjoying the small transgression of a first year teacher:

My first grade teacher was really nice. I don't remember that much about it, but I remember she was a new teacher, and she was very nice. I remember she used to take us out to play kickball when we were supposed to be doing reading. We always had a lot of fun with the things we did. We didn't keep our desks in rows like everybody else thing, she has us in a big circle. We had a Christmas tree in the middle at Christmas. She did a lot of fun things that were different than other teachers. I guess I don't really remember. And I remember she—I don't know what happened, but she only taught there that one year and then she was gone. I remember she wrote us all letters in the summertime, I remember I saved my letter for a long time.

Also like many early childhood candidates and preservice teachers at even the elementary level, she described herself as child-like, and "on a child's level" and that this was also part of her unique aptitude toward being a good children's teacher who could "relate to" and understand children. She went on to describe how, in providing children with feelings of safety and understanding, early childhood teachers are laying the groundwork for future learning from other teachers.

> I feel like if [the children] are very secure and emotionally self-confident in themselves, then they can really focus on their learning better, so they don't have to worry about all the extra stuff, if it's already in place and they know [that they are loved], then they can kind of move past [security issues]. That's my philosophy of what I believe.

So, she constructed the work of the teacher as primarily about loving children, supporting their emotional development, and promoting social skills—and all of these served an educational benefit in the long run.

> So, for example, there's this one little boy in my [internship setting] that if he puts something on the wrong line, he just completely falls apart because he's just worried about something being right, and you see how the little boy is just kind of lost. If somebody's not there to help him . . . to [say] "You made a mistake, it happens," . . . you just get them through that moment. I think it's important for them to know that somebody's there, to have that support in the classroom so they don't feel like they're alone.

Even though she has always "loved kids" and has always felt a unique connection to them, she does find that she is learning more from her TEPP professors and mentor teacher, especially about being mindful of how she talks to and redirects children. She sees the program experience building on her already strong skills in understanding children. "I've always just been really paying attention to that," she says,

> [at the day care center] I saw a lot of different ideas by them of how to direct kids and how to just in the way of seeing them that you might not think that you're already . . . I don't know. I feel like I could put it all together a lot better to explain, but there's a lot just in the way that [my mentors] made me think again, go through my whole thinking of what I do with kids.

Adrienne, and the majority of the other early childhood students, was positive about the TEPP program. While many preservice teachers at the elementary level tend to bristle in the face of dissonance and be quite critical of teacher education programs, curricula, and faculty (Galman, 2009a), this group of early childhood candidates was conspicuously not. Even though

Adrienne couldn't verbally identify the philosophies she felt were underpinning the TEPP program ("We're learning a bunch of different philosophies. It's just still different, I guess. It's just really—I don't know."), or describe which ones she agreed or disagreed with, she did indicate that she was learning from the program. Her one complaint was focused on the differences between how things are done in her internship classroom and how they are framed in the program, and in her own previous experiences. "I think I'm learning a lot [in TEPP]" she affirmed, "But I'm so used to the way we did things at [day care] so it's really directing me in a different way."

> It's harder for me to do just teacher-directed type lesson planning. That's a little challenging for me. I feel like I'm learning a lot. I kind of wish that I— I'm really—I like a lot of my professors who I think are really inspiring, and I like everything that I'm learning from them. It's hard to translate it into the classroom, because I feel like the teachers in my [internship] classroom don't do the kinds of things that we talk about, and so it's really hard to—when you haven't really actually seen something really done, it's hard to try to bring it in and do it, because you're kind of feeling it out, but trying to write a paper about what you did, it's kind of hard. For instance, I mean, just even my last [internship] that I did in kindergarten was just—it was very just teacher [directed]; the teacher talks, the kids listen, she gives them worksheets, they finish it, puts a sticker on the worksheet, and they're done and they move on. There's reading, which is kind of, "Here is the word you're gonna learn this week, try and find it in the book and circle it and underline it." It's not very meaningful, I guess, everything that we're learning about isn't meaningful for the kids. It's just kind of nice to bring some stuff in and say, "OK, I'm gonna try this," but it's hard to do, because you talk about the things in general, or your once-a-week class where you try and go over something and then you try and implement it in the classroom and then you're on to something else the next week, so it's hard to translate it to the classroom. The ones where I had a real demonstration on a class I can do better, just different techniques about shared reading, I have seen, like, in my reading class, it was demonstrated, and I was like, "OK, I'll do that," and I kind of followed almost exactly how [the TEPP professor] did it. That's really hard when you're talking about other stuff, to get it into the classroom when the teacher's doing something that seems like it's completely different.

I suspect that Adrienne rather took for granted the status realities associated with early care and education work—namely, that it was a low-status profession (lower even than elementary teaching) dominated by women and much more associated with child care than formal schooling. However, like several of her peers in the early childhood cohort of TEPP, she took some measure of comfort, even security, in that same low status and the isolated, even cloistered, realm of child care work. She mentioned over and over again in interviews and other observed contexts that she was anxious about competition. It didn't suit her. She disliked classes at college where the dominant mode of discourse was debate, argument, and competition for curved grades, even in what she considered relatively low-stress courses. She felt as if all of the students in a program, or a course, or even a major, were scrambling for the few available resources, be they grades or, eventually, jobs. In the world of early childhood education, she felt confident that there would be no such scrambling and pressure, that "[she] could just relax." Just as she felt moderately confident her TEPP application would be accepted ("Probably more because I went early childhood not elementary, which is harder to get in"), she felt sure of job security in ECE. "Nobody really wants these jobs," she said, "nobody is out there fighting to work in day care or with little kids or whatever." And while one certainly cannot argue with her on that point, her reasons for why these jobs are not aggressively competitive did not directly address gendered work. She, and others, claimed that work in child care is undesirable because of a combination poor cultural priorities and low pay. These attitudes were reminiscent of the elementary level preservice teachers (and, later, practicing teachers) who would accept their low pay and low status knowing that unlike corporate businessmen, bankers, lawyers, and other "money-making" cultural/vocational tropes, theirs was the highly rewarding, potently moral, work of care.

But how did Adrienne and her peers make sense of their status in relation to elementary level teachers? Adrienne was, again, keenly aware of a status and intellectual differential, though reluctant to bring these thoughts to the table. She admitted that she felt she could not have gotten into the elementary TEPP program, and admittedly experienced the level of academic rigor and test performance required of the ECE cohort to be a bit of a rude awakening. Interestingly, she and others noted the presence of even one or two males in the elementary group as significant. "There are some men in the elementary cohort, some men [who are going to be] teachers. But none in our group." Pressed for why that was, she summoned the rather predictable specter of the deviant male in the world of care. "Well, in elementary, some men can teach upper grades," she began, nervously at first,

> But in early, it's all little, little kids, they want to sit on your lap, they have diapers—some of them—and they're just little. It's easier for women. [Me: "why?"] . . . Well, you know, men who teach preschool, or toddler or day care and stuff sometimes end up, people think, you know . . . [Me: "what?"] . . .

well, that they're child molesters or whatever. They're not—but it's kind of like, why would a guy want to do this? And there isn't much teaching—let's face it—it's mostly just playing with them, or loving them, and making their little activities. It's all cute, but most guys aren't into that. They want to teach social studies or math or something and if they like kids, they like the bigger ones that can do more intellectual things. I like the small children, they really love you and you can just enjoy them.

I went on to ask if she thought that women were better early childhood and elementary teachers in general, to which she replied that there were some things men could do better, and some things women could do better ("and that's fine, we don't need to be all same") and maybe in early childhood the work was primarily about nurturing, and things that have "more to do with women." Interestingly, at the day care center where she had worked during her interim year before TEPP, there were two men working with a group of toddlers. These men, Adrienne noted, were great teachers, and greatly beloved by the children. Never in her experience had there been any inadequacies in their ability to love and nurture children, or in their propriety around young children. "They were great guys," she said. When I challenged her previous statement, asking whether or not men might be able to teach in early childhood as well or even better than some women, she indicated that these men were an exception to a general trend and that most likely they would not remain in teaching anyway but would instead go on to administrative positions, or go back to school to train to become upper elementary teachers.

Rachel

"Don't get me wrong," said Rachel, as she sat on the edge of a classroom table in the school of education, balancing to make room for the other members of her methods course small group, "I'm as liberal as the next person, but don't you think homogeneous grouping has some benefits?" Her group members glanced nervously back at the instructor, who obviously wanted the students to critically examine the effects of grouping and other forms of tracking in their small group discussion. Rachel was not afraid to speak out on this, or any other issue, often the lone voice of dissent in large class debates and discussions. At twenty-five, Rachel was among the older preservice teachers in the program, and this sample, at either elementary or early childhood levels. She grew up in an attractive suburb of a major Northeastern urban center, her small family anchored by a stay-at-home mother and an attorney father. Since graduating from Valley three years ago she had worked first as a receptionist at small office and most recently as a counselor at a camp for children with special behavioral and emotional needs. She spent some time volunteering in a fourth grade classroom, lifeguarding, and helping her father at his law office during the spring and summer before enrolling in the TEPP program.

Not surprisingly, and like so many other study participants, while she was delighted to be realizing her goal of becoming a teacher, she hadn't always aspired in that direction. She admitted, with slightly less timidity than some, that teaching was not always her dream. "Sure, I played teacher like all the little girls did—setting up desks with my stuffed animals and dolls, dressing up in my mother's clothes and correcting pretend papers—what we really did was punish our students and pretend that they were talking to their neighbor and not doing their work!" She laughed at her memory of teaching, "of course, we had no idea what we were doing, but it was fun. At one point I even had a chalkboard with real chalk and we'd get covered in the dust. It made my house the place to play!" Despite growing up in the eastern part of the state, she chose Valley over some other smaller schools closer to home because most of her friends from high school were also planning to attend Valley. It was just a few short hours away, but promised to be a new experience and refreshing context for the high-achieving student, who planned to major in business. "I kind of had this businesswoman with the high heels and a suit thing going on, that I was going to finish my undergrad and then go for an MBA, or law school, maybe." But she changed her mind once she looked into the details of the undergraduate business major. "I was a good student in high school, and here at Valley," she said, "so I had the GPA, but I just didn't have, I don't know, the desire to go through it all."

> The courses were, I don't know—they just looked awful. I knew they were important but I couldn't bring myself to make that investment—time, money, hours and hours when I didn't really know about what it was all about. The few people I talked to, they seemed like they didn't really like it either. So I changed my major plan, first to the kind of undeclared general humanities thing and then I got into the honors program [where students could define and make their own majors]. I ended up studying communications with education, and I finished the ed minor. I kind of did the ed. minor thing because I thought it would be good to fall back on, as a back-up plan. My parents, sister, and my boyfriend, and all my friends who know me said I'd be perfect as a teacher—stuff like, I'm so nice, and young and pretty and the kids would love me—I mean, it was a bit much [laughter] but I wanted to do something else for a while [and] maybe work with kids after I settled down, maybe as a counselor or something later on.

After graduating from Valley, she began the job search statewide but was disappointed to find limited opportunities. "Part of it is that I wasn't sure what to do with my major—I did the education thing, that was concrete, but the communications part—I think that I kind of wanted to do business without really doing business, and I thought I could just get an office job that would become business somehow, but I ended up with something not me at all." It was at that point, aware of her misstep, that what she had previously thought of as a back-up plan began to look very attractive. She began with volunteering with an afterschool program, then quit her office job and began working at the day camp and volunteering in classrooms during the regular year. "I had to move back home, it wasn't really a lot of money, but I tried it out and when I knew it was a good thing for me, then applied to TEPP." With her participation in the education minor, she had completed all necessary prerequisites and spent the spring and summer before the program completing her state tests.

Given Rachel's outspoken, often critical perspectives and her strong personality, I expected her to have many critiques of the program, its arduous pace or political bent. However, her experiences in TEPP were largely positive. "I knew what I was in for," she laughed, "this is a fast, short program and I came ready to work." Not surprisingly, she tended to value the most concrete aspects of the program most, such as a classroom management training offered outside of the usual program of study. Among things she did not find valuable was the social justice class, which she felt was "repetitive" because so much of the content had been covered in the education minor. She acknowledged that maybe some students who had not gone to Valley might need it, but she felt that it should have been optional in her case. She also felt like the program should be more restrictive in its admission policies, or else be a bit longer to accommodate those students without basic knowledge about teaching that education minor graduates had. Her impressions of faculty were generally positive, though on more than one occasion, she felt that a few faculty members were "trying to push a kind of political agenda." When I asked what that was, she said that faculty should try to be less "biased" when presenting information. Like Valley students as a whole, Rachel tended to be both less affluent and much less politically conservative than the students at Mountain, but she still was wary of what she called, over and over again, "bias" in how the social foundations of schooling were presented to her and her classmates. "It's not that big a deal," she ended by saying, "just a little something to think about."

Her impressions of classroom life and teachers' work were based more on her own recollections of positive classroom experiences rather than on her internship experiences in TEPP or the education minor:

> I remember my own teachers—how they cared for us, how they really made a difference in our lives by paying attention to us and really giving us their time. I especially remember the ones that made learning fun, like with games. Like my second grade teacher, Mrs. Brown. She would come up with these games where we threw a ball around the room for math facts, and we all got to have lunch in the classroom with her. She really cared, and was really energized, not burned out at all. . . . I know [my teachers] worked hard, but I never saw when they weren't having fun being with us, showing us different things. I know all of this was before . . . [high stakes] testing, so I know that my work isn't going to be as . . . free, loose, like. I remember them, though, and I want to try to incorporate that caring into my classroom.

When I asked Rachel about her impressions of teaching as feminized or gendered work, she said that she knew that gender, and girl culture "subconsciously" contributed to her decision to teach.

> In terms of life, I mean, why women go into [teaching], first of all you see it on TV—all the teachers are women in television, especially in elementary or younger and in the movies, all the good teachers are usually women except in high school where you see, like *Stand and Deliver* or *Dead Poets' Society* or whatever. Then in your own life, that is what you see in your teachers—all women—when you are growing up and I think for me, and for other girls, there is an important connection there. You see someone that made a difference in your life, that cared for you, that looked like you and even though you know on some level you have other choices, that's kind of already in there—programmed—before you even start.

Rachel also said that there was an element of practicality that played into her decision, and that for women, family and marriage impact career concerns in ways that are not the same for men. "And this may sound so antifeminist," she said, quietly, "but I do want to have kids and I do want to be able to stay home with them in the summer and I do want to have their vacations off. That is not the reason why I chose teaching, but it is a great bonus." When I asked where she learned that she would need a career that had this kind of flexibility she said that she had watched her mother, and older friends, struggle with day care, and later aftercare and end up having to choose between working and having children because of the inflexibility of work. This flexibility more than made up for the low status/low pay downsides of teaching, but Rachel was unwilling to interrogate this cover story, telling instead a now-familiar story about teaching as morally superior to financial or status rewards.

> And you know I said to my mom, I could have made a lot of money. I am good at math and I could have been a math major and done really well, but I chose to be an [honors] major and I chose to go into education because I wanted to. I kind of went around a little bit—circuitous—to get there, but I am glad to be here and eager to get into my own classroom. I may not make the big business bucks, and all that, but I am going to make a difference in the lives of children.

I pointed out that at first she didn't want to be a teacher. What had changed? She replied that after a short stint in the for-profit world, she awakened to the importance of teaching. I asked if she had been bored in office work. She laughed, "Well, yes, kind of. But it just showed me that teaching was a better choice for me. And now I love it." But had she fallen back on the "fall-back" plan? Instead of resorting to plan B, Rachel tells her story of choosing teaching as much more thickly agentive, and almost destiny-driven, in retrospect. "I feel like maybe this is what I am supposed to do, after all," she said.

In terms of her awareness of the gendered elements of both teachers' status and work, Rachel had many experiences to share. During the summer before enrolling in the TEPP program, she supplemented her camp earnings by lifeguarding at a public pool alongside a few women and several men.

> Most of my friends, you know, they're women and they know teachers, or are going to be teachers too. But this job was with the general public and so I told the—mostly—guys that I was going back to school to be a teacher, they said it was like a fluff job, that it's not real work, the idea that you go in and you are done at 3:00 in the afternoon.
>
> And it really got under my skin, you know? And then when my friend, who's a guy, when he says that he's a high school teacher I think people are more shocked by a guy being a teacher so maybe they don't react in the same way—maybe they are thrown off by it. They are not expecting a six two and two hundred and eighty pound guy to say he's a teacher. But from me, just this little, like, tiny girl and all, they expect it and immediately downgrade it. Teaching is more of a feminine thing, maybe.

As might be expected generationally (Hall & Rodriguez, 2003), Rachel distanced herself from feminism and feminist politics. "I don't consider myself feminist," she said, "I consider myself an equal, just an equal. You know what I mean? I mean I speak up. I try to represent everyone." I told her I didn't know quite what she meant. Equal to whom? "To everybody," she said, "we're all equal. We're all the same." While I don't think Rachel would have been comfortable telling me that she felt she was equal to men, I believe—based on these interviews as well as my classroom observations—that she, and others, saw feminism as not only pathologized (see the common caricature of the angry, bra-burning, man-hating feminist) but also superfluous now that "we [women] are equal to men," and the assumed apex of our social status development has been thusly reached.

Adrienne and Rachel: The Moral Career

An analysis of the stories Adrienne, Rachel, and their peers told about becoming teachers in teacher education, despite obvious diversions, had several similar signposts along the way, though these were not necessarily in synchronous order. These turning points represent both moments of significance as well as times when the narrator may be demonstrating a point of impression management, or realignment with a set of norms that govern social norms and audience cues for what constitutes a "good" performance of the roles of teacher and woman, to name a few. While impression management requires vigilance, the end result is a successful moral career made up of a predictable pattern of connect-the-dots. For early childhood and elementary participants, table 5.3 reflects the shared and divergent turning points or impression management junctions among participant narratives. While obviously highly individualized, Adrienne and Rachel were chosen to be presented as more in-depth vignettes because they easily serve as representative cases of the discernable gender and vocational tropes in the Valley Early Childhood Education and Elemaentray Education data. Shaded areas reflect areas of synchronicity.

Among many interesting points in Adrienne and Rachel's turning points is the absence of gendered adult milestones as significant in their narratives. When I asked each one of them to comment on the important turning points in their lives, they focused on the professional touchstones reflected in each of their narratives. For example, while each were involved in heterosexual relationships, these did not figure as important in their trajectories; for Adrienne, even her engagement announcement played second fiddle to announcing her status as a graduate student in the school of education. For both of them, the endpoint, however, is the same—and this represents a gendered checkpoint: each wants to become wives and mothers, but not after leaving teaching, or using teaching as a placeholder for those identities. Instead, both hope to be workers, and teaching is a desirable form of work compatible with other gender identity and family goals. Otherwise, their narratives sketch out a familiar and similar tale—teaching as destiny revealed, and all missteps

Table 5.3. Turning Points

Narrative	TP1	TP2	TP3	TP4	TP5	TP6	Desired future plans
Adrienne	*Childhood:* Positive experiences with early elementary and ECE teachers; Negative experiences with high school and some college	*Plan A:* Interest in children, but in child psychology, but reconsiders after weighing reality of work; Dislikes the early childhood undergrad program	*Plan B: Teaching is "Destiny"* Frames as "natural" and the "writing on the wall" of destiny	*Family Reinforcement:* Parents, others reinforce gendered skills for caring and nurturing, retrospective focus on child care as a child	*Initial Employment:* Highly fulfilling assistant work in teaching confirms "destiny"	*Begins teacher preparation*	Balancing work with marriage and motherhood
Rachel	*Childhood:* Positive elementary experiences, memories of playing teacher	*Plan A:* Initially pursues business, then communication with education as "back up" plan in the education minor	*Initial Employment:* Attempts to enact business career trajectory, Realizes poor fit of "Plan A"	*Family Reinforcement:* Parents, others reinforce gendered skills of caring and nurturing	*Plan B: Teaching is "Destiny"* Adjusts trajectory, rediscovers teaching as an attractive option, frames as destiny.	*Begins teacher preparation*	Balancing work with marriage and motherhood

or diversions not mistakes but rather necessary steps toward that revelation. Their patterns of overall impression management are even quite uniform considering their divergent experiences and personalities.

Considered in light of figure 1.1 from chapter 1, the moral career(s) at work are very much the moral careers of "finding the right fit" vocationally speaking, and understanding/realizing one's vocational destiny. In their cases it happens to be teaching, but it could just as easily have been any form of work where they could both "find themselves" and make room for practical concerns, such as marriage and family later on. In this way, both Adrienne and Rachel balance the pragmatics of needing or wanting to work as an economic necessity with the widely held generational expectation that work should be more than a mere "job"—it should also be meaningful and speak to one's particular gifts (Csikszentmihalyi & Schneider, 2000). As per their family and friend reinforcements, and in contradiction with other experiences (all reframed through the backward glance of narrative impression management) both Adrienne and Rachel possess singular, gendered gifts for care and nurturing. Among these are also the expected references to Western feminine norms as operationalized by Mahalik et al. (2005), including but not limited to "involvement with children" and "investment in appearance" (literally, for Rachel, for whom being "young and pretty" is presented as a desirable professional skill). Also interesting is each woman's interpretation of the feminine norm of modesty. While each could conceivably have a wide range of skills, accomplishments and the like to recommend themselves, the sole scores to which call attention are the expressly gendered aptitudes for caring and nurturing and Holland and Eisenhart's (1990) "good girl" attributes, such as good grades. It also goes without saying that each woman constructs her ability to realize teaching is her destiny, not just a "fall back plan" or "plan B" as highly desirable, and each narrative is constructed to highlight points of impression management as thickly agentive turning points, each of which represent a signpost to her awakening.

However, like Kari and Maya at Mountain University, many of these moments of impression management are situated in the enactment of very specific feminine norms, namely that (1) teaching is natural and represents a desirable feminine skill set, and (2) teaching is first about loving, and only secondarily, tangentially, or foundationally, about other concerns. That said, unlike Kari's perspective, which implies that women, with a natural aptitude, are born teachers, rather than products of teacher education, both Adrienne and Rachel emphasize the key learnings to be had in teacher education programs. In other word, "natural" feminine aptitude is only part of the equation. Also of interest are both Adrienne and Rachel's interpretations of what I might call early career missteps—the failure of each Plan A to mesh with personality and each woman's valued identity, either at early inception (Adrienne realizes that becoming a child psychologist may not be appropriate for her) or after a trial period (Rachel sees the business major, and the business world, as a poor fit). Both Valley cases were much more like Maya's at Mountain, whose erratic journey to teaching was unfocused compared with Kari's laser-like precision plan. Also like Maya, Rachel and Adrienne transform missteps into meaningful signposts that are not inconsistent with the desired moral career. Neither accepts nor acknowledges a stigmatized identity (the failed student, the failed worker, the failed independent who must return to live at home) but instead constructs these as necessary episodes in the story of successfully finding themselves. This creates a seamlessly managed narrative and a successful moral career and ultimately the realization of a positive, valued identity.

Reference Groups and Imagery Frameworks

Among participant reference groups, there were also intriguing commonalities: both Rachel and Adrienne seem to divide their immediate reference groups into those who are insiders (meaning, educators or those associated with teaching) and outsiders (meaning those not associated with teaching, or without an understanding of the unique vocational milieu). They also include gender insiders and outsiders—meaning, those who experience gender, and girl culture, as they do (such as friends, other teachers, and family members) and those who do not (feminists, some faculty members). Considering that reference groups help us to determine who we might be interested in becoming as well as set parameters for what kinds of behaviors and actions are appropriate and inappropriate across different settings and that, as the name suggests, we *refer* to in determining how to act and fundamentally how to begin shaping the moral career, it is no surprise that both women's moral careers are about delineating their insider status. This also means highlighting their discovery of their membership in the unique group of people whose destiny it is (and natural aptitude it is) to teach small children. The introduction of a new potential reference group, such as in beginning teacher preparation and being exposed to critical political ideologies (such as a closer encounter with feminists and feminism) serves to further emphasize each woman's active choice to belong to an insider group, and to further demarcate that choice as a means of impression management. Interestingly, unlike at Mountain, the gulf between faculty (who were often quite open and even aggressive with their critical, even political and ideological, beliefs about teaching and schools) and preservice teachers was relatively narrow, leaving both Adrienne and Rachel to assume that predominantly female faculty were therefore insiders to their experience both as teachers/educators and as women engaged in gender performance.

While my initial impression of both Adrienne and Rachel was that they were much less closely aligned with Western feminine norms (Mahalik et al., 2005), I realize that I drew that assumption from the absence of gendered young adult milestones as significant points in each life history narrative. However, an examination of both the available reference groups and the imagery frameworks in play suggest that each participant is actually well-aligned with many of the norms, with only Rachel periodically offering up a conflicting image. For focus, table 5.4 illustrates these tropes as they jibe with or contradict (in italics) Mahalik et al.'s (2005) Western feminine norms.

Just as I did at Mountain, I sought to explore the origins or reinforcements of many of these imagery frameworks by collecting and analyzing data on the imagery frameworks at play among faculty in program materials at the School of Education at Valley. These include analyses from field notes, observations and artifacts connected with their two methods courses. Table 5.5 illustrates these in reference to the western feminine norms from Mahalik et al. (2005). Again, italics note points of discordance.

While there are a few obvious differences among faculty imagery frameworks and Adrienne's or Rachel's, the differences are not terribly stark, nor do they tend to come up except in the most abstract ways in participant narratives. There are certainly more points of discordance among faculty or program imagery and the feminine norms, but there are also many points of agreement, both with these norms and with student narratives. Not surprisingly, neither Adrienne nor Rachel (nor their friends and classmates) had the same kind of vociferous critiques of faculty and program practice as were seen at Mountain.

While the CFNI (Mahalik et al., 2005) was administered to the majority (including Adrienne and Rachel) of preservice teachers in both elementary and early childhood designations at Valley during the data collection period, the measure was anonymous and as a result isolating their individual scores is not possible. However, it is possible to get an idea of overall preservice performance on the measure, as reflected in table 5.6.

These reshuffled and ranked (highest adherence to lowest adherence) indicate that the top two areas of adherence to Western feminine norms for this group are, predictably, "involvement with children" and "niceness in relationships"—both of which were significant for both Adrienne and Rachel. However, while neither indicating an interest in either a thin body

Table 5.4. Comparative Imagery Frameworks—Adrienne and Rachel

Norm	Adrienne	Rachel
Niceness in Relationships	The good student	The outspoken student
	Not a feminist	Not a feminist
	The apolitical	The active participant
	Avoiding confrontation	The good student
	The passive class member	The respectful student/
	The respectful student/teacher	teacher
	The professional	
Involvement with Children	The mother	The student
	The babysitter	The mother
	The older sibling	The nurturer
	The nurturer	The camp volunteer
	The "natural" teacher	
	The idealized teenage babysitter	
	The day care teacher	
Investment in Appearance	The professional	The professional
		Young and pretty
Thinness	N/A	N/A
Sexual Fidelity/Chastity/ Morality	N/A	N/A
Modesty	Not a feminist	Not a feminist
	The "natural"	The "natural"
	The gifted nurturer	The gifted nurturer
	The good student	The hard worker
	The struggling student	The good student
Involvement in Romantic Relationships	The fiancée	The boyfriend
	Teaching as the Marriage-Suitable Profession	Teaching as the Marriage-Suitable Profession
	The heterosexual (assumed)	The heterosexual (assumed)
Domesticity	Teaching as the Family/Motherhood-Suitable Profession	Teaching as the Marriage-Suitable Profession
	The future mother/wife	The daughter
		The businesswoman
		The rejection of business career
		The future mother/wife

ideal or a particular perseveration on sexual fidelity, it is possible that these themes simply didn't come up in the context of the interviews, while they were specifically targeted by the index. Certainly the CFNI paints a portrait of preservice women at Valley as much more aligned with girl culture than the interviews, which were largely about work and gender, could have.

Table 5.5. Imagery Frameworks Observed—Faculty

Norm	Program/Course
Niceness in Relationships	The flexibility of the program, where relationships often trump hard-and-fast deadlines
	Political/controversial content
	Teacher as activist/intellectual
	Teaching as political work
	The teacher as deferent to parents
	The nonpunitive classroom manager
Involvement with Children	The child-centered instructor
	The parent
	The transformative teacher
	The critical teacher/anti-racist educator
	The clinician/practitioner
Investment in Appearance	Emphasis of gender-specific dress code
	Professional dress
	Gender neutral dress
	The activist
	The feminist
Thinness	N/A
Sexual Fidelity/Chastity/Morality	N/A
Modesty	*The activist teacher, activist professor*
	The community leader
Involvement in Romantic Relationships	*The relative irrelevance of sexuality, heterosexuality less commonly assumed among students, faculty*
	The majority married/partnered faculty with families/children
Domesticity	The parent

Table 5.6. Preservice Participant Results from CFNI (Valley) (Ranked)

Feminine Injunction Definition (Mahalik et al., 2005, p. 424)	Preservice Participant Mean Score
Involvement with Children	85%
"taking care of and being with children"	
Niceness in Relationships	82%
"developing friendly and supportive relationships with others"	
Investment in Appearance	71.5%
committing *"resources to maintaining and improving physical appearance"*	
Thinness	64%
"pursuing a thin body ideal"	
Domesticity	64%
desire for or practice of *"maintaining the home"*	
Sexual Fidelity	43%
"keeping sexual intimacy contained within one committed relationship"	
Involvement in Romantic Relationships	41%
"investing self in romantic relationship"	
Modesty	36%
"refraining from calling attention to one's talents or abilities"	

That said, as other research with a similar population has illustrated (Galman, 2006), the areas in which Valley participants had the highest scores may speak to the issue of girl culture, body image, thinness, and power, at least. When Mahalik et al. (2005) were designing and refining the CFNI measure, the "interest in children" subscale, when compared with data from Disorders Index ([EDI]; Garner, 1991), which was used in the design and development of the CFNI, correlates positively with healthier body image and eating behaviors among women. Mahalik et al. suggest that women who are making careers around nurturing and caring for children may experience feelings of "competence and connection" (p. 431) as well as significant social reinforcement (such as offered by Adrienne's and Rachel's families) to such a degree that the pressure to control their bodies and conform to the feminine norms around appearance and thinness is significantly lessened.

Meanwhile, the "niceness in relationships" and "investment in appearance" scores (as well as general tight adherence to feminine norms) may be negatively correlated with an activist or political inclination, according to correlations with Downing and Roush's (1985) five stage model of feminist identity development. This could make sense, as individuals concerned with maintaining "economies of niceness" or systems in which patriarchal patterns of female self-subordination become a currency for social reinforcement and reward (Galman, Pica-Smith, & Rosenberger, 2010) and appearing to be enacting the necessary valued identities for their particular social and gender location, are certainly not going to be the ones rocking the proverbial boat. It has long been suggested that early childhood and elementary contexts actively select for compliance (deMarrais & LeCompte, 1998; Galman, 2006) in these forms, and one way in which this is seen consistently through my sample is the near universal rejection of feminism and feminist politics in specific, and political discourse in general, usually in favor of neutrality or the absence of "bias" (and, implicit in this, conflict). Excepting a handful of individuals like Maya, no participant at either Mountain or Valley wanted to be seen as a "feminist"—something not generationally or otherwise unexpected, given the current trends in contemporary girl culture (Douglas, 2010). These trends in teacher education and the study demographic will be the subject of further discussion in chapter 8.

Roles and Performances

As seen in chapter 4, the difference between "role-making" and "role-taking" had to do with both an individual's interpretation of gender, self, and work and their moral careers. As Goffman (1963) suggests, the process of role-making may involve a wider range of reference groups, and at Mountain, participants like Kari had shallower and fewer reference groups and as a result engaged in more role-taking than role-making. Meanwhile, those with more, like Maya, were more likely to engage in role-making. They made the role of the teacher fit them, rather than the other way around.

In examining the trends among Valley preservice participants, their narratives and trajectories, it is important to remember that both Adrienne and Rachel are enacting not the moral career of the new teacher/preservice teacher/education student as much as the moral career of the young person finding herself and discerning a true vocation. While it is important that this vocation meshes with the valued identity of the gendered worker, the gendered element of nurturance and care in teachers' work is the moral component—it is a way for work to be meaningful, for "discovered," "reawakened," or "realized" self-attributes to be put to work in a way that serves others and of course, a way to showcase pious, moral rectitude in contrast with skewed national priorities and their financial inducements (teaching is important work not dominated by others because of poor social priorities, as Adrienne suggests). In other words, this moral career is about work as a practical necessity, but it is also about goodness. And gendered goodness at that. In that sense, both Adrienne and Rachel are both "role-taking" as well; they are inserting themselves into what is almost a popular cultural folk narrative. In working to become teachers and retrospectively telling a story of self that emphasizes the discovered strengths of caring, nurturing and so on, they are making themselves fit into a specific role as opposed to the other way around. They do not define teaching. It defines them, through retrospective narrative and subsequently impression management.

Similarly, how one interprets self in relation to the role of teacher is impacted by how the role of the teacher is defined, and what individuals believe about how we become teachers. While at Mountain, a rigid moral career and narrow valued identity led to some anxiety around teacher education for Kari, while more flexibility and centeredness in role-making gave Maya a different experience. While Valley participants echoed Kari's concerns at one point that in exchange for tuition dollars they would be transformed into relatively expert teachers immediately upon program completion, this belief died quietly with continued exposure to the teacher education context. Instead, the majority of participants at both elementary and early childhood levels seemed to have found some comfort, some feeling of completion, in the knowledge that they had, in fact, chosen their vocation correctly. They expressed relief that they enjoyed the children at their internship sites. They worried less about what exactly the course content was and whether or not it agreed with the way they remembered teaching because the primary work of self-discovery and vocational realization was done. Some small conflicts arose here and there—over clarity of assignments, particular placements, and so on, but these were relatively minor. After the narrative of self-discovery was constructed, the rest, it may be said, was all downhill.

Conclusion

Interestingly, while both Rachel and Adrienne understood that to be a teacher is to accept not only a smaller paycheck but also lower, even semi-professional status, they both affirmed that there were both pragmatic as well as moral reasons for accepting what they both ultimately saw as a trade-off. Teaching, they affirmed, is an inherently moral task and is a vocation rather than a mere "job." On one hand, in examining the way participants thought about, maintained and gradually built a narrative that showcased the desired valued identity, it is no surprise that they had to cast their aspirations, or last-ditch choices, in this light. They effectively create an alternative value scale, one that emphasizes caring, nurturing, and devotion to children (who may be considered, if Tolstoy was to be believed, the lowest status citizens of all and the most voiceless) over money, power, status, and competition. Furthermore, teaching makes sense if you reject the bad social priorities and the skewed domestic ideologies they represent—one need only make that leap, and tolerate the ignorance of those who cannot.

While I did ask why it seemed like more women were able to make that leap, none of the Valley sample seemed ready to attribute unique value—beyond biological aptitude for nurturing—to women, or subaltern men, or anyone who does not seem to benefit or buy into the structures of hegemonic masculinity. Instead, both Adrienne and Rachel—and nearly everyone else—distanced themselves from feminist-ideological praise of women, or even recognition of the revolutionary potential of feminized practices (Griffiths, 2006) as resistance to these "bad priorities" out there. Instead, their moral system hinges on a patriarchal interpretation of performance and work. I felt like Rachel, especially, was on the cusp of beginning to connect patriarchy—rather than arbitrary and blameless priorities—with teaching as low status, gendered work. But I didn't push it. Neither did many of the faculty, who despite their very critical approach to practice and individual reflection on practice, were wary to disrupt these fledgling narratives and the work of impression management inherent in creating a valued identity out of a potentially stigmatized one.

However, before I give emergence and pragmatics their complete due, I must affirm that I see these women as making some questionable null choices. Let me explain: many Valley (and elsewhere) preservice teachers see that their interests as relatively compatible with patriarchy, and, in a pragmatic move of accepting this compatibility, they opt to choose a less difficult path and stay on, as chapter 1 suggests, "the windy side of care." But there must be some kind of guilt, some backpedaling ("it's not like it was a second choice—I always knew I would teach," they said over and over again about other aspirations abandoned to this path). To wit: in framing their choices in the discourse of "destiny," the culpability, both personal and external, for such nonchoices is squarely out of their hands. Like Williams (2005) said of one trend in contemporary girl culture, "a passenger—which is the most a princess can hope to be—is never in charge. It's a hard lesson for women to learn, and it's one that men knew all along" (p. 188). Destiny, even vocation, can make passengers of us all, and "postfeminist" (Douglas, 2010) girl culture finds ever new and insidious ways to make the passenger seat seem ever more desirable. Not the least of which is the framing of teaching as a critical, transformative, and even revolutionary task. But to do this, one must not be terribly invested in either "niceness" or "interest in appearance" or teaching, as it turns out —and as we shall see at Prairie College, in chapter 6, where the Mountain and Valley patterns of work, gender, and identity are turned on their head.

Note

1. This was until passing the state requirements became attached to program completion, and those who did not pass the state tests were no longer considered program "completers"—at this point, pass rates for completers were at 100 percent.

CHAPTER SIX

~

Planning for Temporary
Experience and Other Horizons

Prairie College

I think everybody at Prairie is going for the same goal, to make a positive impact on the world, and people go about it in different ways depending on what their major is. And you get people who want to be diplomats or environmental scientists and when you say, anything, a doctor or a teacher, they can see the positive social effect you might have with that. I don't know. It's about service. At other places it's about competition, it's about money, and status. I think teaching is important, but there's no getting away that it's a low status profession.

—Interview with Samantha, Prairie College participant

While both Valley and Mountain Universities were large, public research institutions with independent schools of education and relatively profitable teacher education programs, Prairie College was a very different setting. A small, private, politically liberal religious college with an explicit social justice ideology, Prairie College enrolled students who typically self-selected to attend the college and opted to study education learned, and embraced, what was referred to as the "Prairie Story of Teaching." This "story" presented teaching as more than a mere job; instead, it was framed as profoundly agentive, transformative activism aimed at creating a more just world through relationships with students and a critical vocational identity. This is evidenced in the above quote from my interview with Samantha, a student in education at Prairie, whose story is told in this chapter. While Prairie participants— only 50 percent of the total original corpus of data were female—framed elementary teaching in this way rather than as the gendered work of care, very few (if, realistically, any) of them would ultimately pursue classroom teaching as a long-term career goal, and most embarked on primary level teaching knowing that it would be a temporary experience on the road to other work and other selves.

Background and Context

Prairie College is a small liberal arts college affiliated with the Quaker faith, located in the American Midwest. As I indicated in chapter 3, I was fortunate enough to be able to spend an extended period of time at Prairie as a visiting faculty member teaching a course in educational foundations while conducting my research. Being a community member in this way afforded me the opportunity to become familiar with the Prairie student and faculty culture and the school itself, as I lived on campus among faculty and students alike. At the time of data collection, the college did not have a formal school of education, and instead prepared prospective teachers by offering an interdisciplinary undergraduate minor in education that offered curricula focused primarily on foundations of education. Similarly, the college did not grant a teaching credential. Instead students took a variety of seminars, most of which did not necessarily include a classroom internship, though some students did engage in a semi-structured field placement experience prior to completing the minor. Students moved through the minor course of study at their own, often idiosyncratic, pace, and with a range of completers and non-completers at various stages in their progress, it was difficult to determine who among them would do what.

Established in the mid-1800s to provide "a guarded religious education for the children of Friends,"[1] at the time of its inception, Quakers still separated themselves from the world in a number of ways: by their manner of dress (simple clothing), the way they talked ("plain language"[2]), and by the extraordinarily strict code of morals and behaviors under which they lived. Today, a significant number of children from liberal Quaker families receive their education at Prairie, and the college tries to incorporate their concerns around peace and justice work and socially liberal values into a significant part of the curriculum. These liberal Quaker parents are happy to see that the dominant spirituality on campus is aligned with their liberal interpretation of Quakerism (one that sees worship proceeding from a basis of silence and that is open and welcoming to all kinds of people and their traditions). Yet, while not all Quakers nationwide are liberal Quakers of the sort that are represented at Prairie College, even Quakers from the other side of the ideological fence would agree that virtually all Quakers will unite the basic tenets of their belief system, which include a commitment to education, and a high value assigned to the work of teaching.

In contemporary times, and during the time of data collection, Prairie College was primarily an undergraduate liberal arts college community consisting of 96 full-time faculty and 1,170 students (56 percent female, 44 percent male), 7 percent of who were international students. The college was nearly twice as ethnically diverse as Mountain University with 22 percent of student so identifying. While statistics are not available on socioeconomic diversity at Prairie College, it was my observation that aggressive strides had been made on the part of recruitment, admissions, scholarships, and budgeting personnel to find ways to attract economic diversity to the campus. Adjusting for time and inflation, Prairie tuition at the time of data collection was significantly higher than either Mountain or Valley Universities' rates at $31,782 including room and board.

Prairie College adhered to Quaker philosophies, including an explicit social justice agenda which was integrated into all teaching, administrative, and social aspects of college life. All meetings—from weekly faculty meetings to departmental meetings to hiring and admissions department meetings—followed Quaker practice, as "silent meetings." This meant that the meetings did not have a rigid agenda, but rather began in silence, inviting those who would speak to do so of their own accord while everyone else listened until moved to speak on the themes of the day. Another Quaker structure in wide use was the idea of "consensus"—meaning, there was no place for "decision by vote" at Prairie College—rather, everyone must come to consensus instead of simply accepting what some called the tyranny of the majority. This often takes a very long time, but is an accepted Quaker practice. As Quakers do not make oaths, there are no oaths of allegiance, or honor code statements. Nor is anonymous critique allowed: even faculty evaluations at the end of each academic semester require a signature from the student.

The education department at Prairie College had gone through many incarnations before assuming the form at work during the period of data collection. While at one time the college had both elementary and secondary licensure programs, eventually this dwindled to only a secondary program, which would be discontinued in 1994 and replaced with the education minor. Students who completed the minor (or any other Prairie student interested in exploring teaching) were encouraged to pursue a master's degree at another institution after their undergraduate degree at Prairie was completed. This was called "four-plus-one"—four years at Prairie and one year somewhere else. At the time of data collection, a new, intensive and very small in-house Master's in Teaching program had been newly instituted to provide the "plus-one" at Prairie. This small program and its handful of enrollees were not part of the Prairie sample included in these analyses, as MAT students were at the secondary level and were largely older, second-career individuals.[3]

While grade point averages, written statements, test scores, and letters of recommendation are all part of admission to the Mountain and Valley Universities' schools of education, what I call "ideological matching" and self reflection seemed to be the most significant part of the selection process for admission to the undergraduate education minor at Prairie. The primary admissions assessment was made based upon a conversation with the chair of the education program. This was accompanied by letters of support from faculty and an informal assessment of college grades, though these are of less importance. The chair at the time of data collection added,

> By the nature of the application process, we ask an awful lot about their ideas about teaching, and about children. They read about the nature of our program, we ask them to read Parker Palmer's *The Courage to Teach* in advance—when you read books like that, if they don't appeal to you as books that are helping you to shape your identity as a teacher, then it's pretty clear that you're not designed to be in this program. So, it's heavily self-selection and then constant reinforcement that this is one of the most wonderful things that you can possibly do with your life.

This self-selection based on ideological matching at first seems as though it would limit enrollment; however, the majority of students similarly self-select to come to Prairie as undergraduates in the first place because they are attracted to an opportunity to learn in an environment very much aligned with Palmer's philosophy and the Quaker ideology. The reinforcement the faculty describe happens through course readings and the conversations about teaching that take place at Prairie. These conversations and experiences are all in accordance with what many faculty associated with the education minor call the "Prairie Story of Teaching,"

> When you're reading Palmer, *The Courage to Teach*, you're talking about teaching as an identity. There's nothing in there about teaching as a role—it's through and through identity, as is [Robert] Fried. We reinforce that teaching is who you are, not about the methods. And, when students ask about methods, we say, "it ain't about methods, it's about you!" That's very difficult for them to understand, but they come around and understand that it's not really

about method or technique but rather about who you are, your relationship to your teaching. The Prairie College story about teaching clearly expands beyond the classroom and includes spending lots of time with students—even here at the college—and thinking about students when you aren't normally thinking about them. Faculty members walk over to the dorms to ask students why they aren't applying for Fulbrights. I once was giving the final examination for the educational foundations class and a student didn't show up, so I got my coat, got into my car and drove over to his apartment, walked in and woke him up so he could take the exam. He mentioned that story in another class years later as an example of what caring teaching looks like, and how teachers in K–12 education should relate to their students.

This story is reflected in the courses, discussions, and the general milieu of the institution. In the materials advertising the education minor, teaching at Prairie is characterized in terms of Quaker principles, among them, "awakening the teacher within," respect for persons, integrity, simplicity, consensus governance, equality, peace, and justice (Prairie College Education program Website, 4/2002). The offices and website alike are festooned with a quote from a member of the English faculty:

It is worth acknowledging, in all humility, that though there are many great, beautiful, noble callings for human beings—ministry, healing, protecting the powerless through law, making art, music and literature, the most wonderful things that human beings are privileged to do—none of them is more valuable to the human race, to the future of the planet, or to our own souls, than the work of teaching. (Prairie College Education program website, 4/2002)

Furthermore, the "Prairie Story of Teaching" is not restricted to applications solely in the preservice teacher preparation arena. The Prairie College mission statement—irrespective of the teaching program in particular—includes a reference to the "process of awakening the teacher within . . . shaped by the distinctive perspectives of the Religious Society of Friends [the Quakers], the openness to new truth and the willingness to search" and the conceptual framework of the education minor reflects this. Reflection and identity-development are also central, with multiple quotes from Fried (2001) and Palmer (1998) throughout the document, focusing on "outstanding teachers' recognition of excellent teaching coming from their "identity" and "integrity,"

and that good teachers understand their "calling" to be teachers and discover the "life-giving ways of relating to the forces" or identity that "converge within each and every person" . . . "good teaching comes from good people" and the task of education is to address the "living core of our lives." This task is especially important to teachers, Palmer asserts, because "we can speak to the teacher within our students only when we are on speaking terms with the teacher within ourselves." No teaching will ever really succeed unless "it connects with . . . students' inward teachers." (Prairie College Education Program Conceptual Framework, 2002)

The education program emphasizes "the teacher as an informed reader of educational texts, well able to probe assumptions and values, to evaluate them, to understand what it is to be in a position of leadership . . . with respect for the consciences of others and lack of coercion . . . in the Quaker spirit of servant-leadership and consensus building" (Prairie College Education Program Conceptual Framework, 2002).

The structure of the education minor included taking a variety of education courses—none of which were encumbered by the byzantine requirements and enormous coverage pressure included in obtaining a license, state teacher education standards, worry about completer rates on state teacher exams, and the like. What resulted was a great deal of freedom, very little of the dissonance between theory and practice and a focus on individual discernment. To reiterate, the students who self-select to attend Prairie and to minor in education do so on an ideological basis. They are already a "good fit" with the "Prairie Story of Teaching" before they begin coursework and critical discussion. Course offerings in education are heavily elective and vary tremendously from semester to semester. Titles like "Moral Education," "Experiential Outdoor Education," "Education and Imagination," "Educational Foundations," "Theory and Practice," and "Human Development" dot the course catalogue and are cross-listed in a variety of majors. However, the formal minor program is actually a very small way in which Prairie College produces teachers. Much of the message about teaching is modeled by professors. One faculty member illuminated:

> They [emphasize] how teaching is important, that teachers are passionate about what they do and that there is such a thing as excellent teaching, that excellent teachers lead lives of passion and commitment and excitement where they get to know students really well. Our students see that in all of their courses—be it in biology or physics or English, and they think, "you know what? That looks pretty good to me. I would like to do that, too." So when I think of Prairie producing teachers, my first thought is not—maybe it should be, but it's really not just the education program. My first thought is that it is the whole ethos [of the college].

It should be noted that my data suggest that while Prairie is very good, in fact, at producing teachers, what it is ultimately producing are probably more professors in higher education than elementary or primary teachers. It follows as well that there were almost as many men in the education minor group as women—something unheard of at larger public university settings like Mountain or Valley. While many—mostly the women—would continue on to teach elementary or secondary school, the majority of even these would leave after one or two years to enroll in graduate schools. Many of these would become teachers at the college level, as had been modeled by their engaged, committed, and highly talented faculty. Without the formality and paperwork of a licensure track, individuals with an interest in education and schooling, but not necessarily in becoming teachers, could participate in a low-commitment way through the education minor. Nonetheless, it is still true that many more females voiced an interest in elementary level teaching, and many more went on to actually teach, according to my follow-up data. However, the ways in which Prairie college education minor women interpreted and interfaced with girl culture and gendered work were still radically different from the majority of Mountain and Valley participants. This has to do, primarily, with self-selection to Prairie, and its campus culture.

Student Culture and Economic Concerns

The college as a whole is guided by Quaker practices in teaching which focus on a semi-Socratic process of "awakening the teacher within" and on drawing out the knowledge students already have in a kind of quasi-constructivist-meets-spiritualist approach. Faculty embrace these tenets to varying degrees, but most of the related faculty who work with education minors are active Quakers, hailing from Prairie College themselves or another similar Quaker institution. Most of the students at Prairie embrace Quakerism or, if not formally the religion, then the Quaker values of peace and social justice. Similarly, most also embrace the highly egalitarian Quaker position on gender equality. However, not all students embraced Quaker tenets of faith, justice and, ostensibly, liberal Western gender equality and feminist politics. This showed itself primarily in an increasing political and social conservatism from a growing and increasingly vocal minority of Prairie students. Students and faculty alike were taken aback by what they saw as exemplars of a trend toward conservative, often hostile, dissent among students around issues like the Iraq War, which broke out during the data collection period, as well as a rejection of pacifist politics. The seeming gap between the historically ideologically matched Prairie student and this new, conservative student was referred to by the faculty as representative of a "bimodal distribution."

The "bimodal distribution" was political and social to be sure, but faculty also used this term to describe the disparity in attitude, maturity, and academic preparedness among students. While "typical" Prairie students tended to be more socially liberal, academically proficient and certainly more likely to be Quakers themselves, this smaller emerging group, despite being intellectually able and promising, were usually undereducated and underprepared for demanding college curricula. They struggled with material more than adequately prepared students found unchallenging. Teaching to groups like these was difficult, and a source of discontent for faculty members. These students also tended to reject critical political content, but not in the context of intellectual debate, but rather in "checking out" of class participation, becoming withdrawn and silent. While this pattern could have easily been mistaken for poor academic performance, it was materially different in my experience and others'.

As seen at other campuses experiencing what could be called the conservative student renaissance of the early 2000s, self-identified "conservative" Prairie students would tentatively discuss how they felt silenced in classroom debate and how they disliked the campus, their professors, and fellow students. None of these students were represented in the education minor sample at Prairie, not surprisingly, as the culture of aspiring to teach seemed to be associated with positive identification with faculty and ideological matching with Quaker tenets.

Economic Factors

Even though the data collection period at Prairie was well before the economic crisis of 2008, Prairie was experiencing financial hardships that had bearing on admissions and subsequently student culture. Many faculty members told me that because of financial and other difficulties Prairie accepted the majority of its applicants, and that a commitment to first-generation students, particularly those from the small town in which the college was situated, resulted in their admission in large numbers. The public schools in the area had significant challenges, with a near 60 percent dropout rate and a staggering near 40 percent teen pregnancy rate. Students coming from these schools and this environment, as well as from similar settings in both rural and urban settings could hardly have the kind of college preparation and privilege possessed by fellow students from Chicago's affluent lakeshore areas. However, Prairie made extraordinary efforts to support and encourage its students from all backgrounds by providing academic assistance, financial aid and grants, and additional training and mentoring for professors.

But the feeling remained. "The school has changed significantly in the last three years," said one senior I spoke to in passing, "it's becoming a more conservative place." Different people I talked to attributed the reasons behind this change to different causes. Declining admissions standards was a common suggestion: Prairie lost a tremendous amount of money in the economic decline following the terrorist attacks on September 11, 2001, and combined with the past few years of slightly dwindling enrollment and high tuition, had to begin admitting more and more of its applicant pool. Faculty and students alike suggested that admission was now as high as 80 percent; however, in an inspection of the Final Report of the Strategic Planning Committee (2002–2003), I found the following:

> Our most significant and distinctive strengths have to do with clarity of mission and vitality of program and community life. Our most important weaknesses and challenges, on the other hand, take financial form. We struggle to find the resources we need to sustain the distinctive educational experiences we offer. Compensation of faculty and staff has fallen below the levels of peer institutions. Program budgets are cramped; faculty and staff feel too busy[4]; some buildings look shabby. These financial challenges derive from persisting weakness in enrollment. We do not intend to have a large enrollment, but we struggle even to reach our target enrollment of 1200 students. The shortfall of 100 fewer students means [approximately] $1,500,000 less for the operating budget. Our strategic plan begins with an argument that the college should continue to use 1200 students as its planning basis. To lower our enrollment would be to weaken the college's foundation for quality, this is crucial, so we are placing it first. With enrollment as our most important strategic problem, in the last three years we have increased the size of our applicant pool . . . our yield on admission has been at about 30 percent (the percentage of students we admit who actually enroll) but we have to admit more than 80 percent of those who apply in order to have [the bare minimum] of matriculants, even though admitting such a high percentage of students risks admitting students who are not prepared to thrive at Prairie. And even admitting 80 percent of the applicants leaves us with too small a class. (Prairie College Strategic Plan, 2002)

The reality of the actual acceptance rate at the time of this study was unclear, but the near-universal perception of faculty and students alike was that this was part of the problem of the "bimodal distribution." Many students transferred to other schools (attrition being another theme in the Final Report) and some faculty also decided to leave Prairie. The headline of the Friday, April 24 *Prairie College Sentinel* was, "Numerous faculty members choose to leave Prairie." (2003)

Overview: Study Participants at Prairie

Study participants (N = 9) were all undergraduates enrolled in the education minor program, and constituted a minority within the twenty-five to twenty-eight students estimated to be enrolled or taking courses in education minor at the time of data collection. Of these, I collected data on a total of twenty-one students, and the nine participants included here are parsed from a larger body of participant data which also included two women of color and ten males.[5] While the presence of so many men in a teacher education pool is unusual, our collective astonishment must be mediated somewhat: (1) this was not a licensure program, and as such it did not distinguish in any formal way between elementary and secondary (where there are typically larger numbers of male candidates); (2) participants identified strongly with the mostly male, all professorial faculty rather than with early memories of elementary or even secondary teachers; and (3) based on some longitudinal data, the overwhelming majority of these men did not, in fact, go on to become teachers, most opting for graduate school programs in other areas. Of the nine females included in this analysis, meanwhile, only one indicated a possible interest in secondary education, and she ultimately decided on elementary level preparation before later abandoning her aspiration to teach altogether upon admission to a PhD program in the humanities.

The general faculty perception of why students enroll in the education minor is expressed in emotional terms (it is, said one faculty member, "Passion to help young people—passion from the heart"), intellectual terms ("They were excited about the readings for the course, real intellectual excitement"), and in the language and implied ideologies of the "Prairie Story of Teaching." Says one faculty member, students would "sit and talk to me about their future careers in teaching and what they wanted to do for children, their goals academically and pedagogically . . . they are [going to be] Prairie-like teachers out there in the world, according to the Prairie philosophy." All study participants identified themselves with the traditional type of Prairie student rather than those represented in the "other side" of the bimodal distribution. They had an excellent, usually elite, high school education, and matched well with dominant campus ideologies.

These participants are demographically distinct from their peers at Mountain and Valley. The average participant age was considerably lower at nineteen and with much higher Mother's Highest Level of Education (100 percent at college or above, with the majority at the graduate or professional level, compared with 71 percent at Valley and 82 percent for the Mountain group). In keeping with their egalitarian economic justice ideology, Prairie offered many students generous financial aid packages to offset the costs of tuition, so the high cost of tuition cannot be said to select for more affluent students and against working class and poor students. Furthermore, given the students' accounts of how their highly educated but socially conscious

Table 6.1. Female Prairie Participants

Participant ID	Race	Age	MHLE
PS1	W	19	Graduate Degree
PS5	W	19	Some College
PS8	W	20	Graduate Degree
PS9	W	19	Graduate Degree
PS10	W	21	Graduate Degree
PS12	W	21	Graduate Degree
PS13	W	20	Graduate Degree
PS14	W	19	Graduate Degree
PS20	W	18	College Degree

Quaker parents were not always engaged in high income brackets—for example, one participants' parents, both physicians, worked in rural medicine services and as a result she received a need-based financial aid—it is possible that MHLE could be misleading when it comes to an assessment of actual financial status. It remains an adequate, however, if not very good, indicator of cultural capital.

Sample Case: Samantha

To illustrate general trends in the Prairie participant pool, the following paragraphs tell Samantha's story. While Prairie students' experiences in life were quite widely varied, their interpretations of those experiences, and their attitudes around teaching, gender, work, and identity were quite uniform, and are reflected in this vignette.

Samantha wore a brightly patched green corduroy dress, long underwear, and Doc Martens work boots in the cold Midwestern winter weather on the quiet weekend morning she came to talk with me. Her face was free of makeup, and her blond hair hung down to her waist. "I'm off to the library after this," she said, plopping her heavy book bag onto the floor. Midsemester exams were approaching and I assumed, given the size of that book bag, that her stay at the library would be a long one. A nineteen-year-old Spanish major and education minor, Samantha grew up in a middle class college-town suburb of a large urban center in the Midwest with her graduate degree-educated mother, immigrant European father, and university professor stepfather. Her father had only a high school education and returned to Europe shortly after the divorce to continue in his family's agricultural business. "I think he finally got a GED, but he doesn't like to talk about it much," she noted. "Higher education, college, isn't part of his world, or necessarily valued." As an older sister of several younger siblings, she said, laughing, that

"I'm the only girl, and the oldest, and I think that explains a lot—I think you can't help but be the responsible one in the family if you're the oldest." In her assumed role as responsible eldest sibling she identified strongly with her teachers, excelled in school, winning a partial scholarship to attend Prairie.

Samantha's earliest memories about schools and teaching were her grandmother's stories about being taught by the nuns in her parochial school. She said that these stories illustrated the difference between babysitting, or care work, and teaching. "The nuns were supposed to be teaching her—but all they did was give her a book and then sit back down at the desk, watching her and the other kids but not engaging with them in any way,"

> Teaching is supposed to be about knowing more or having more or difference experiences from someone and using that to help them learn. There was none of that. My grandmother didn't get to finish high school, but she worked really hard to make sure that my mother did well—and that her teachers didn't just babysit her but actually taught her something.

Samantha was very bright, obviously serious about her academics and while not a Quaker, deeply invested in the Prairie ideology of vocation as social justice. In pursuing the education minor and contemplating becoming an elementary teacher, she was hoping to contribute to the lives of children in need toward a more just society. "I'm very political," she said, "and part of that is knowing that I have to do something with my life that makes change." She reflected on her own life as a trail of turning points leading to her current position of aspiring teacher. One important turning point in Samantha's life was her parents' divorce, which also constituted one of her earliest childhood memories. After her father left the family, a move to a new and more affluent neighborhood creating class and racial awareness, later framed by her experiences in critical coursework at Prairie.

> I remember we moved in with my aunt and that was like, that was kind of weird because everyone else had a dad and we moved from like a townhouse, and like people lived upstairs from us and the neighborhood was much more part of our lives and then we moved to the new house and it was much more upper class and apart from all the people. I know it sounds weird to say this but there was no diversity on my block. Like, my school, I had so many kids of color in my kindergarten class and then we moved and the people there were upper middle class and all white and everyone had a mom and a dad and everyone had more means than we did and I remembered that this was kind of weird in school because everyone else got what they wanted like right away from their parents. And I felt entitled, all of a sudden, to whatever I wanted

from mine. But she couldn't do that. She couldn't provide that for me so that was different from us.

Samantha says that she knew at that point that she was different, and as a result bonded with her grade school teachers who, knowing her situation "looked out for me." Samantha firmly believes that this early trust and identification with her grade school teachers created an environment which, combined with her role at home, made her into a high-achieving student.

The sudden absence of her father, compounded by the presence of several small siblings, created a new, and not entirely welcome, role as second mother. Unlike many other study participants who relished their roles as surrogate mothers, caregivers and babysitters to their younger siblings, Samantha found the experience somewhat difficult.

> My mom was a single mom, I was like, six, and she needed a lot of help around the house—I wasn't the most helpful but it was still this feeling that it wasn't the "five of us" but instead it was she and I helping the little boys.
>
> I always felt like I had to watch them or give them advice or something or if they were being bad I had to, like, "that's not okay" or whatever. I don't know. And they would say, "You think you're mom but you're not" like they still say stuff like that to me, "You just wish you were mom." Like, what? What's that supposed to mean? [laughter] I don't know. But my mom got married again when I was nine and then when I was eleven, my very youngest brother was born. And so, um, he was kind of like, a child of mine too because there is such a significant age gap there. Sometimes I did feel like he was my child.

Subsequently, these experiences created a different outlook from that of many friends: "[Friends] say, 'well, you know, when I have kids . . .' and I'm like, it's kind of like I already have them." While her college experience was rich and valuable, Samantha often regretted that she was not at home to teach her youngest sibling. She phrased it this way over and over again—rather than care or nurture, her interest was to teach him. Paramount among the necessary teaching was to share with him her perspective on the emerging Iraq war. "I feel like I'm in a position where if I did want to teach him about how I think that the war is wrong, I could, I could talk to him about that and I feel like the earlier people are exposed to other ideas the better."

Meanwhile, school and her relationships with her teachers became increasingly important, and being a good student became an important part of her developing identity.

I knew the teachers looked out for me because I would always, like I would always go help a teacher with something inside—like, our art teacher would let us help her clean out the closet and keep beads if we found [them]. That was her way of being nice. And my second grade teacher, Mrs. Gerhard, was my favorite teacher in elementary school. Because she was German American like me, we had something in common, and she used that as a bridge to talk to me more than other people. I always got my reading done faster than other people and she would give me something extra to do. At one point she had me helping this Polish boy who had just moved here from Poland and had a hard time reading. She would have me help him; that way she found something for me to do so I felt useful. I used to get all the work done that way.

Samantha saw a clear connection between her wanting to help and please her elementary school teachers and being a second mother to her siblings at home. However, she does not see the underlying personality trends as necessarily benign.

My teachers could tell that I was mature—I was born older. Not that I want to brag, but it's true. I've just had more to think about things, and had more on my mind, had to be worrying about everyone else, all the time. It's hard to get out of that pattern if you're used to it. Maybe that's why I think about being a teacher—I just pay a lot of attention to other people.

These relationships with teachers directly informed her vision of wanting to become a teacher herself, and her experiences at Prairie made that vision more critical. She reflects on "playing teacher" as a young girl, saying that it was highly unrealistic and more related to her psychology as a child and popular culture at the time than any enjoyable replica of future vocation.

I would be the teacher and my friends would be the students and I would make them sit in rows and I would discipline them. It was more like doing what I said and then it turned out to be not so fun and they wouldn't want to play that game. But, um, when I was little we saw teaching as making people sit in rows telling them what to do—the idea came from TV or something—probably—because my teachers in the classroom were all really nice. In addition to television, we had a need to be in control and it's not the kind of thing you get when you're little, so in playing teacher I was like "I want people to be paying attention to me" how do I keep them paying attention? "Be quiet! Don't do that!" You know. That was one of the first things you go to, just being bossy or whatever so that you can get them to do what you want them to do.

Unlike so many of the other program participants, Samantha's family was not wholly supportive of her decision to pursue a college education. She saw this as a cultural phenomenon, rather than a value judgment, and took it in stride, even turning a critical eye toward higher education practices in the United States.

> The way I hear their stories it makes sense that [my father] didn't continue his education, whereas where I am from everyone goes to college and you don't ask questions. It's assumed: four year college. And it's like if you're taking a year off you're going to die. "But it puts you behind in the whole rat race!" people scream. For [people my father grew up with], they see that and they think that people too often go to college when they don't need to, and they spend all this money and then they aren't happy—and I think that's true. I think there are a lot of people in my neighborhood who went to college realize that this isn't what they really wanted to be doing but they were just fulfilling their parents' dreams. Because that's what you do. So I think that's what my father's people are against when they're against higher education—they're against people just finally going without needing to or really thinking about it. Not even wanting to but doing it because it's a rite of passage. And spending a lot of money in the meantime.

When she told her father and brothers that she planned on attending college, they urged her to think critically about the job she saw herself obtaining after degree completion. "What job do you want to get for yourself that you need a college education? Huh? Tell me that!" they asked.

> [My father] actually got really agitated about it. Then I was like, "I want to be a teacher . . . " and my dad was like, immediately, "Oh, okay. No, you're right. That's a respectable job. That's good." And my father respects it because he sees it as a useful job, that there will always be a need for teachers, and job openings for teachers, given that education is compulsory in the US. And that's totally different than the way it is here. Instead of seeing it as all the Prairie students do here, like "you can change the world!" like through, you know, "You can change the life of a child, you can *make* it equal." Like I can personally address the inequalities in the system. Both ways of thinking make sense.

Samantha's mother saw a teaching career much more along the Prairie ideological lines, that interest in children and improving their lives was the primary and best motivation for a career in the classroom. Samantha acknowledged that this was much more in line with her thinking, and part of her motivation to complete the education minor and become a teacher.

A lot of people's problems as adults come from things that happened when they were young, which is why I want to teach elementary school. You can help that child before patterns are set, before violence takes over their lives. If you can teach a child to read before they get frustrated with school and get to a breaking point I think you can change so much. In our society too—I think that so many of our problems could be helped if we worked with our children and took care of our children more.

Her decision to teach was further solidified by an intern experience at a local elementary school during her senior year in high school. A fluent Spanish speaker, she worked one on one with monolingual Spanish speaking elementary school students to provide conceptual help in mathematics. Interestingly, her other experiences with children prior to this—babysitting, and so forth—which were primarily about care giving rather than teaching—were not especially enticing. "Helping the kids my senior year was kind of the moment when I decided to be a teacher," she said,

> because before I thought, "oh, gosh, I wouldn't have patience for little kids," I used to work with little kids at church, so I'd help out and there would be so many of them and they would be running around and they were different ages and you just couldn't control them and [exasperated sound] they would give me a headache every morning. So I used to think, "Oh, gosh, I *can't* deal with kids." They're cute but just too much. A lot of those kids all together running around and the littler ones are all over each other, and you, and they can't find anything to do and you're like, "Please, please . . ." So of course I didn't think I had the patience for children. But then, when I worked with these kids senior year that was the point when I realized that it wasn't that hard a stretch for me if you're teaching them instead of running around after them.

Samantha's experiences at Prairie further fueled her understanding of and desire to teach children of color, especially Spanish speakers. She took a class in Chicano literature that opened up a greater understanding of racism, white privilege, and schooling. Her education minor courses emphasized creating a classroom that was welcoming to all students but avoided essentialism or forcing students to speak for all members of a given community. Many of her ideas are from reading memoirs.

> We are reading [books] about ways in which kids didn't feel comfortable—like *When I was Puerto Rican* by Esmerelda Santiago is one. And we already read the sequel to this book, *Almost a Woman*, she was talking about her educational experiences, not all of which were good. So a lot of books we've been reading

in my classes, a lot of them describe those same situations where the teachers were the bad guys and I'm not going to do that—hope not.

Her experience at Prairie has been as positive, and her relationships as strong, as those in elementary school.

> I love my teachers here, too . . . I have a relationship with my teachers here, we have small classes, and in high school I was still looking for that kind of relationship like I had in elementary school with my teachers because everyone was always knowing their teachers, and being friends, like they'd look out for me. It was nurturing. It was family. They all knew me. I liked them. I felt like they cared about me. And at my high school we had 4,000 people. It was huge. And it was more difficult for me because the whole first year I was lost in the crowd and I wasn't anyone special. And I think that's important in teaching. That's why I chose Prairie because the classroom setting was smaller and teachers would care.

While teaching is not typically constructed as the gendered work of care at Prairie, reactions outside of campus culture varied. Samantha reflected that when she told people that she wanted to be a university professor, everyone responded very positively, describing how an intellectual life would be difficult at first, but suit her well in the end. But when she told people outside of her family and circle of college friends that she would also like to teach elementary school, they typically responded with statements about how caring she was, and how "cute" that would be. Meanwhile, within campus culture, most friends said that in teaching she would be able to "make a difference" while in the classroom—but seemed to hint that her stay there would be a temporary one. She noted,

> At Prairie, people here are like, that's great. We need good teachers. I think everybody at Prairie is going for the same goal, to make a positive impact on the world, and people go about it in different ways depending on what their major is. And you get people who want to be diplomats or environmental scientists and when you say, anything, a doctor or a teacher, they can see the positive social effect you might have with that. I don't know. It's about service. At other places it's about competition, it's about money, and status. I think teaching is important, but there's no getting away that it's a low status profession.

When I asked where this idea might come from, or how it might be communicated in the culture, Samantha was clear that her ideas were probably different from most people's because she had strong relationships with teachers, and that her belief system and the Prairie story of teaching emphasized teaching as a higher form of service.

> But most people [outside of those circles] think it is just easy—they get those ideas from media culture that has no idea what teachers really do. The media portrays the role of the teacher unrealistically on [television] shows because teachers are never teaching, just relating with students, and other teachers. In clip art, for a teacher, it's usually with a hat and funny glasses pointing at a chalkboard where it's got numbers or something up there and it's always someone in front of a group of people. Or someone doing most of the talking or, like, *Welcome Back Kotter* or *Saved by the Bell* where the teachers are mostly doing counseling and always doing it at high school level and it's supposed to be dramatic, interesting—nobody thinks teaching little kids to read is interesting. They think it's babysitting.

Samantha also started volunteering recently as an adult ESL tutor. In developing her own identity as a teacher, Samantha says that the hardest part to learning is to "worry less about myself and more about the student—last year I was worried more about what I look like and how I'm doing than what the students are doing." Samantha says she knows that teaching would not be the end of her vocational road. "I might really like doing that for some time," she said, "but I can see myself, after a few years of teaching, becoming a linguistics professor, or teaching teachers. I have lots of interests that could build off of classroom experience."

Samantha: The Moral Career

While all of the Prairie participants had widely varying personal experiences—some grew up in racially homogeneous suburban environments similar to Valley or Mountain participants, while others like Samantha had an entirely different life experiences, habitus, and cultural cache—the fact that they all self-selected to attend an ideologically specific college like Prairie may have been unifying. This unification, much of which may have had to do with cultural and class capital, could be one reason why the stories Samantha and other women at Prairie told about becoming teachers, and their valued identities and moral careers, were so very similar. The typical turning points demarcate increasing ideological and professional discernment—they move from relative uncertainty about teaching (childhood play, early identification with teachers) to increased clarity (adolescent and adult experiences), criticality (learning to reflect and critique at Prairie), ideological matching and eventual plans for teaching, and most importantly, the moral career of the professor/attorney/doctor whose teaching experiences enrich that future occupation. As Samantha said, she knows she will teach, and that in this way she will contribute to a more just world, and that those rich experiences will inform her future career. In other words, like the Mountain participants for whom teaching was a means toward enacting the moral career of the wife and mother, teaching is also a means to an end for Prairie students—toward socially conscious, ideologically matched, higher status work as professors, doctors, lawyers, and similar. Through this carefully managed moral career, they have found a way to affirm the social and moral value of teaching at the elementary level without necessarily creating long-term valued identities as teachers at that level, with the subsequent social and economic status issues. Instead, they will become teachers (and professionals) like their parents and Prairie faculty, and use teaching as a moral springboard to remain consistent with the Prairie ideology.

In this regard, impression management is key. It is important that the work of early and elementary teachers not be disparaged, nor the social and economic status issues inherent in becoming a teacher appear to compete with the moral importance of teaching work. Effectively, by carefully maintaining a vision of becoming teachers—and leaving the profession—as morally and ideologically consistent—Samantha and others have their proverbial cake and eat it too. The end result is a successful moral career and valued identity both at Prairie and outside of Prairie.

It is especially interesting that the mechanism by which participants might ford the gap between graduating from Prairie and becoming a classroom teacher was not a subject of concern. I suspect that enrollment and completion of plus-one program somewhere else (or obtaining an emergency license in a high-need district, or teaching at a private Quaker school) is assumed. Given the status of teaching and the wide availability of teaching jobs at the time of data collection, it was certainly not unrealistic for the bright, capable Prairie graduate to assume it would be relatively easy to get work as a teacher. Regardless, much more thought was typically given to how a period in the classroom would be massaged and integrated into a meaningful experience in the following professional degree program and subsequent employment as, in Samantha's case, a professor.

Like the participants at Valley, there were few, if any gendered milestones present in Prairie narratives. When I asked about important turning points, these were almost all exclusively ideological—very focused on emerging meaningfulness and discernment. Considered in the terms of figure 1.1 in chapter 1, the typical Prairie participant's moral career could very much bet

Table 6.2. Turning Points

Narrative	TP1	TP2	TP3	TP4	TP5	TP6	Desired future plans
Samantha	*Childhood* Positive experiences with early elementary teachers, cognizance of class, racial/ethnic differences	*Adolescent, other experiences with children, schooling* Begins early career discernment, identification, etc.	*Begins education at Prairie* Develops both teaching and non-teaching interests	*Prairie Story of Teaching* Reinforcement Identifies strongly with Prairie ideology	*Ideological negotiation:* Encountering other popular cultural ideologies, defines own position	*Elementary Classroom teaching* Short duration, temporary	*Post-Teaching* Obtain professional degree and pursuant higher status employment building on themes of teaching experience

the moral career of the socially just professional, with time as a classroom teacher serving to shore up those commitments.

As for the very limited references to either contemporary girl culture or Western feminine norms as operationalized by Mahalik et al. (2005), including but not limited to the Valley participant's top scoring "involvement with children" and "investment in appearance" they go virtually unregarded, except in brief reference to others' beliefs. For example, some of Samantha's acquaintances—notably outsiders to Prairie—associated teaching with caring and nurturing. But this was very brief. In fact, one process of discernment that was very important to Samantha was learning about the differences between "babysitting" and teaching, with a great preference for the latter (whereas many other participants at other sites drew parallels between the two). Also conspicuously absent was the belief that teaching was in any way a natural or biological skill set, or that it was about the work of love and care. For Samantha, it was absolutely about affirming a child's self-worth and self-esteem, but to listen to her talk about that work and those tasks, she sounded much more like the Prairie faculty and their work as teachers. Considering that most of the faculty in the education minor were male, in departments outside of a formal school of education, and that their teaching work at the college was not scripted as feminized any more than any other academic department, it is not surprising that Samantha and others—who identified their teaching so strongly with their professors' university teaching—would not see that work as feminized either.

Imagery Frameworks and Reference Groups

There was little to no gap between the imagery frameworks prevalent in faculty discourse and official Prairie materials and artifacts, and the narratives of individual students. However, interestingly, the areas where the most plentiful imagery appeared were in the top two CFNI subscales of "niceness in relationships" and "interest in children." While there were also several examples of discordance there, even discordance, especially in the act of speaking-back-to, are significant. Of all of the three participant groups, those at Prairie were least closely aligned with Mahalik et al.'s (2005) Western feminine norms, as illustrated in table 6.3. However, this is not surprising given the ways in which Prairie's theological and social bent self-selected for similarly minded students, and how the ideological match selected for in the education minor further solidified that coherence, also in table 6.3. Italics, again, indicate discordance.

Table 6.3. Comparative Imagery Frameworks—Samantha and Prairie Faculty

Norm	Samantha	Faculty/Prairie
Niceness in Relationships	The good student The teachers' helper Attentive to other people *The vocal outsider* *The political activist* *The feminist*	*Political activism* *Civil disobedience* *Pacifist politics* *Social Justice* Highly personalized instruction Strong relationships between teachers and students Quaker respect for others
Involvement with Children	The responsible older sister Children, and teaching as "cute" The caregiver Relationship-based The teacher/tutor *The professor/teacher of adults* The teacher vs. babysitter Teacher media caricature The teacher who "looks out for" children who need help The political teacher	Caring teaching independent of gender/nurture Personal and individual Teaching as a calling Relationship-based Teaching as "within" *The professor/teacher of adults*
Investment in Appearance	*Comfort with "being different"*	N/A
Thinness	N/A	N/A
Sexual Fidelity/Chastity/ Morality	N/A	N/A
Modesty	"Doesn't want to brag"	N/A
Involvement in Romantic Relationships	N/A	N/A
Domesticity	The responsible older sister *The reluctant surrogate mother/helper post-divorce*	N/A

Even though it was not possible to get formal CFNI data for participants at all three data collection sites, reviewing both the CFNI scores at Valley, and analyses of narratives and other data at Mountain and Prairie, the sub-scales, "involvement with children" and "niceness in relationships"—both of which have revealed themselves to be prominent with other groups of preservice teachers (Galman, 2006)—are among the most plentiful themes, both concordant and discordant. Many of the other subscale norms simply did not come up in the data (though there may be more to this than meets the eye, as was discussed in chapter 5).

However, the discordant imagery is of interest when it comes to the connections between the "niceness in relationships" subscale and its negative correlation with activist or political activities (Downing & Roush, 1985), which is perplexing in the Prairie context. Both Samantha's own and the institutional/faculty/program narratives affirm the peaceful, but undeniably political, sociocultural norms of participating in Prairie culture. While the Quakers, and even non-Quaker participants like Samantha, were all very nice people, they did not necessarily privilege "niceness in relationships"— meaning, retreating from conflict or discomfort—over a social, political, and activist agenda. With its rich history of pacifist politics, as a refuge for conscientious objectors, and at the forefront of social justice work, Prairie was a place where political engagement—and the framing of teaching as such—was paramount. The impact of this ideological climate, and the self-selection among students who would attend Prairie and the education minor (remembering that the "bimodal distribution" was not a demographic factor here), also served as a filter for feminine norms and girl culture as known in popular media and girls and women's experiences.

Unlike both Mountain and Valley, Prairie was not a feminized environment, even in the education minor milieu, where females only very slightly outnumbered males. As such, what we might call girl culture at Prairie was experienced a bit differently. One significant difference was that Quaker, and therefore Prairie, ideology around gender, equality and feminism was explicitly addressed at both the spiritual and campus policy level. The Quaker Testimony of Equality affirms the equal status and value of women and men in religious and secular life, and aggressively champions women's rights. Indeed, Quakers and Quaker social and religious institutions have been at the forefront of the feminist movement throughout the twentieth and twenty-first centuries. So, it is no surprise that feminism is not a bad word among Prairie participants, and my question about feminist political identification was consistently met with, "Of course I am! How could I not be?" When I told Samantha, and others, that I asked that question because they did not mention feminist politics specifically in their narratives, and that because most other young, white, female preservice elementary teachers would not thusly identify, they were shocked. As Clare, another Prairie student, interested in preschool teaching, would tell me, "I don't see how any woman, or man really, can look at how far [we've] come as women and a society and not give some credit to feminism, to women having more rights and legal protection." I wonder if this erudite response could be chalked up to Clare's background as a history major, or Samantha's—or any participant's—privilege of exposure to a top quality liberal arts education. But there was a predilection for political involvement that showed signs of reflection, and action. As least two participants were developing a gender or women's studies focus in their undergraduate program. Two more volunteered as tutors at a women's center near campus.

Conspicuously missing from participant narratives at Prairie was elsewhere near-universal moral career endpoint (and often a great deal of perseveration) and valued identity of the ideal wife and mother. While wanting to marry or partner and have children and a family is by no means mutually exclusive with feminist politics or professional attainment—indeed, as Greenfield (2005) writes, it can be a site for action of the most profound kind—it is intriguing that the "moral career of the future wife and mother" dominated the majority of study participant narratives at both of the larger sites, without appearing at Prairie. Furthermore, at Valley and Mountain, marriage and motherhood were not equated with action, and seen not only as goals to be enacted but as reasons for choosing teaching—and for leaving (or, as I suspect, being quietly and passively drummed out of) other professional aspirations. It is possible that because, at Prairie, for reasons related to ideological self-selection, MHLE, and cultural capital, and egalitarian and reflective teaching practices at the college in general, young women were not drummed out of other professional avenues in the same quick way as was seen time and time again at Valley and Mountain. At both of these larger program sites, participants told about how they had initially planned to pursue careers (and some, even, tentatively pursued) in areas other than teaching—as physical therapists, psychologists, physicians, and businesswomen. All of these initial pursuits were notably *not* among the feminized professions, and all were abandoned due to "boredom" or that they "looked too hard" or that the young women, in one's words, expected to "work their butts off" and still not achieve success in that field and subsequently be "left with nothing." This is not to say that teaching, as a career that is flexible and compatible with marriage and motherhood, is in any way semiprofessional or subordinated to the more masculinized, high-remuneration professions abandoned by participants. However, it is notable that only after "choosing" to abandon plan A in favor of teaching, that participants began to champion the pragmatics of teaching as a route to more historically female domestic involvement and domestic ideologies, and subsequent framing of teaching as the gendered work of care.

I do want to affirm that how the majority of participants are retrenching and re-authoring their professional lives are ultimately agentive and pragmatic. I do not want to suggest that they are surrendering, or retreating, or giving up dreams. Rather, I suspect, and will explore at greater length in chapter 8, that they are perceptive veterans of life under patriarchy—they see the writing on the wall, understand the dominance of hegemonic masculinity in the workplace, and make other choices to stay on the windy side of care.

Conclusion

However, this question remains: why do all of these young women become so easily discouraged, bored, or alienated in the fields of their original plan A? Are they panicked about missing out on motherhood and family? Do they see participation outside of the known and feminized as quixotic and dangerous to the identity and moral career? It may be a point for future study to illuminate these women's experiences with plan A and how their alienation, boredom, and checking out began. We know, for example, that while more women start out pursuing degrees and careers in the science, technology, mathematics, and engineering fields, more men complete in those areas. The instructors of those classes and faculty in those programs are certainly not standing at the front of the classrooms, or advising centers, exhorting all females to give up and leave, but the pattern remains, and is all the more insidious for its spectral, silent qualities. Valley and Mountain participants interpreted their choices to turn to teaching, and the supportive (and typically also feminized) schools of education and faculty as part of value systems that recognize the moral and vocational importance of working with children even if the larger system of social status and financial remuneration does not. This often manifests itself in the language of "fit"—and while the converse, the language of alienation, does not explicitly enter the picture, it is certainly part of their early experience.

Women at Prairie similarly affirm a moral commitment to the work of social justice; they maintain an ideological moral career which may or may not include classroom teaching. Theirs is not the moral career of marriage and motherhood (and compulsory heterosexuality), though many certainly hope, as many men do, to have the blessings of family life along the way. To revisit Williams (2005), Prairie women seem to be less passenger-like; destiny and biology simply do not figure into their stories. Instead, they each talk about discernment, preference, and their own sense of vocational clarity. This is Quaker discourse, to be sure, but somewhere along the line these women began to separate biology and vocation in ways the others did not.

This also had to do with participants' available reference groups and experiences. Despite varied life experiences the Prairie participants were all of similar age, had similar positive experiences with learning (if not with schooling), and had similar MHLE's with typically professional parents. Even with different pre-collegiate late adolescent experiences, the women's reference groups were as similar as their turning points and narratives. The strongest reference group, and those to which they had begun the most fervent anticipatory socialization, was undoubtedly their own collegiate faculty. This reference group was even more frequently mentioned in terms of both projected teaching identity and long-term moral career than the K–5 teachers of their own early identification and subsequent apprenticeships of observation. Considering that all three participant groups had equal apprenticeships of observation and therefore almost equal access to elementary teachers as reference groups, the degree to which they actively constituted an object for imagined selfhood varied: Valley and Mountain participants identified strongly with their own elementary and early childhood teachers, while Prairie participants did imagine themselves as enacting the relationship-building, individualized, and political/activist teaching lives of Prairie faculty.

Given the professoriate-as-reference group, it is less surprising that the Prairie participants, like Samantha, were engaging in what Goffman (1964) calls "role-taking" rather than "role-making." I was surprised by this, given my immediate assumption that given the "Prairie Story of Teaching," and student self-selection for agency would create the conditions necessary for widely varied role-making of all kinds. Again, the difference between "role-making" and "role-taking" has to do with both an individual's interpretation of gender, self, and work and the nature of the desired moral career. As Goffman (1963) suggests, the process of role-making may involve a wider range of reference groups, so there are, effectively, more choices on the "menu" for how to perform the role of teacher. For Prairie participants, they modeled so consistently and intently on the Prairie faculty as the primary reference group for becoming teachers that the field, effectively, narrows. They are no longer role-making—making teaching fit them and their predilections and crafting the moral career accordingly. Instead, they are role-taking, literally taking up the performance of the teacher role by striving to become like the Prairie faculty that they so (and rightly so) admired and esteemed. Gender roles, and gendered interpretations of work, have nothing to do with it. Nor does imagining the work of the teacher—Samantha was concerned that it might be a "stretch" for her to work with very small children, until she realized that teaching was different from babysitting or care giving, and teaching looked much more like what her professors did. A reassuring thought given the unspoken subtext here: with a spectacular education and brilliant future prospects, why would Samantha, or anyone like her, want to enter into the harem-like isolation, uncertainty, de-professionalized, and deskilled poverty of NCLB-era classroom teaching? I suspect that, even for the dedicated, the call to teach is much more palatable if it is a temporary learning experience on the road to better things. Similarly, it is possible that the kind of critical, transformative and powerful work Samantha and other Prairie education minor students hoped to do in classrooms is becoming difficult, if not impossible, given the contemporary face of schools and schooling. This reality may drive some to exercise their passion for teaching in the comparable, but less constrained, world of higher education.

What remains, however, is a troubling thought I introduce only with hesitation and difficulty: without the disenfranchisement, boredom, insecurity, or alienation that drove Kari, Adrienne, and Rachel (and to some extent, Maya as well) from their initial areas of interest, who would fill the halls of the education schools? It seems that even the inducement of the ideologically powerful and profoundly professionalizing "Prairie Story of Teaching" is not enough to convince Samantha and others like her to become teachers in deed as well as thought. It is worth observing that Samantha seems to be less affected by the tenets of girl culture and dominant Western feminine norms, and in that respect, without the lure of the "natural," perhaps she is simply a bad candidate for public school elementary-level teaching? Is it possible that in the NCLB era, teaching has been deskilled to such an extent that the nature of elementary teachers' work has become the province of those who "can't do" or, more aptly, those who believe they can or should not? Does elementary and early childhood teaching, then, rely at least to some degree on toxic girl culture, and, if so, tacitly approve of (and possibly even reinforce) its influence on young women's experiences and interpretations of gender, identity, and work?

Notes

1. Adherents to the Quaker faith call themselves members of the Society of Friends, or simply "Friends." This information was provided by the Prairie College Quaker historian during a series of interviews in January 2003.

2. Friends at this point in history used the pronouns "thee, thy, thou, and thine" instead of "you" as a measure of democracy and equality. As several hundred years ago class distinctions made via pronoun: "you" was reserved for people in superior classes to the speaker, and "thee" for those inferior. The Quakers refused such distinctions (Interview, Prairie College Quaker Historian, 1/2003).

3. Because this analysis is focused on the experiences of the noted demographic in teaching (young, white, middle class females) this group has been excluded from analysis.

4. Indeed, halfway through my semester there, we were all asked to take a Busy-Ness survey, meant to assess how busy we all were. However, nearly everyone was too busy to take it.

5. As in the case at Valley University, while the experiences of the two women of color and the men are valuable, informative, and rich, this analysis is focusing specifically on the experiences of young white women in preservice teacher education and has been limited to reflect those population parameters.

~

PART III

NEW STORIES OF LOVE AND TRANSGRESSION

~

CHAPTER SEVEN

For Goodness Sake,
Consider What You Do

Teacher Educators and Preparation for Literal and Moral Careers

For goodness sake, consider what you do,
How you may hurt yourself—ay, utterly

—*Henry VIII*, Act III, Scene I

While teacher educators were only tangential informants at each of the data collection sites, their perceptions of preservice programs and students were valuable in developing a more nuanced understanding of the experiences of preservice participants as a whole, and about the complex and contradictory relationships between teacher education faculty (who are also overwhelmingly female, white, middle class and have typically been PK–5 teachers themselves) and preservice teachers (who are embarking on entering the profession their mentors have left). These teacher educators' experiences represent both intentional and unintended critique of the image of the iconic teacher and assumptions about women and work. This is observed and interpreted from the vantage point of valued feminine identity, and the Western feminine norms (Mahalik et al., 2005) performed by preservice participants as discussed in chapters 1 through 6.

It is important to think about teacher educators as walking a very fine line in the midst of the phenomena I have described. To illustrate, consider the quote, above, taken from Shakespeare's play, *Henry VIII*. In it, Cardinal Wolsley reminds the soon-to-be removed Queen Katherine to be thoughtful of her actions—to think beyond her immediate reaction and consider instead the nature of the audience. He begs her to consider the intentional, and the unintended consequence. He then continues, warning, that in her world of contradiction, natural responses may be the most treacherous. So also teacher educators must practice constant vigilance amidst contradictory impulses: Teacher educators, myself included, paradoxically also colluded (however unwillingly) with preservice participants' visions of valued feminine and vocational identity, often actively reinforcing iconic imagery and the moral career of the "schoolmistress" in particular. These two patterns may seem contradictory, but accepting contradiction is an integral part of beginning to understand the complexity of contemporary primary-level teaching as feminized work. This chapter presents data related to the white, female teacher educators[1] who worked with the young women at each study site. Discussion begins with Valley and Mountain contexts, which featured similar trends. Analysis of the Prairie context, which is markedly different, follows.

Teacher Educators: Background

As Sandra Acker wrote in 1995, "The research literature of teacher education is remarkably silent on topic of teacher educators themselves" (p. 141). Fifteen years later, the landscape is much the same. Demographically, as outlined in chapter 2, the existing literature suggests that most primary level teacher educators are white, middle class females, and of these, those who do the brunt of the labor-intensive work of teacher licensure are untenured (e.g., pretenure, adjunct, and clinical) (Cole, 1999; deMarrais & LeCompte, 1998; Fuller, 1992; Grant & Gillette, 1987; Suarez-Orozco, 2000; Vare, 1996).

Cole (1999) found that untenured teacher educators found themselves often hamstrung between a variety of masters, hearkening back to Judge's (1982) critique of graduate schools of education, where academic and professional identity teeters between questions of scholarly legitimacy, sweeping externally imposed mandates and ultimately the question of where their work should be located and for whom they should be working. As one of Cole's participants observed,

> Pre-service teachers come in with a very clear sense of what teaching is, and if we give them what they expect and what they think they need, they will value that but we will be perpetuating the status quo. If we try to shift [our orientation] and teach to transform rather than transmit, then that is not what they are seeing in schools, so the [teacher education] program appears irrelevant. . . . We have to work in both [schools and universities] at the same time. (p. 292)

Cole also found that pretenure teacher educators struggled with the pressures of the tenure system and the blind alley of understanding institutional norms and politics. At least two of the teacher educators involved in this study, facing similar difficulties with the above, decided to leave academia in the months that followed data collection. They simply couldn't make the contradictory demands of teacher education, a balanced home life, and the academic tenure system work. One voiced her frustration that she was "supposed to be an expert" in teacher preparation in her given area, but it seemed to her that "every day [communication from the licensure office] had some new thing that needed to be done, and it's not up for debate." She observed that the overall conditions of dissent had a gendered element, even in a heavily feminized arena such as primary teacher education:

> It's just "do it"—you know? I've studied this for a long time . . . and I feel like if I had tenure I'd feel better saying that these demands are not at all what the research says about good teacher development. I know some of the [male faculty] do things other than licensure work, and [those that do] find ways to kind of . . . noncompliance . . . with something they don't believe is right. And nobody really goes chasing them down about it. Some people [in administration and licensure] even come in and give me a hard time in front of my students . . . and the way they talk to my students about licensure sounds punitive [and] undoes what I am trying to teach them.

This participant and others mentioned on multiple occasions that they left (or contemplated leaving) university life because they felt "alienated." This sounded a lot like the preservice participants who chose teaching after bad experiences in other pursuits in college. Interestingly, while the faculty members did not claim to be "bored" as many preservice study participants said they were when talking about their respective vocational plan As, this may be only a difference in semantics; what they are both talking about is fundamentally burnout (LeCompte & Dworkin, 1991). Like Kari, who would have gone into another line of work were it not for the alienating nature of her coursework experience, pretenure teacher educators may decide to say, as one of Cole's participants said, "To hell with it" (p. 293). Such are the fundamental feelings of meaninglessness and frustration associated with burnout. "I just want to do my work," said one Mountain teacher educator, "but instead it's an expectation that I'm going to take care of everybody, fill out their forms, chase them around [for assignments] when some [students] should probably just fail the class [etc.] and if they do it shouldn't be my fault!"

The gendered element of the expectation of care (and ultimate responsibility) was apparent to many of the female teacher educators who contributed to the study, and while many found it symptomatic of sexism as found in feminized professions, others saw the expectation of care as one of the principal hallmarks and strengths of any school of education. All teacher educators suggested that both the expectation and the work of care were emotionally, intellectually, and physically exhausting.

When I asked if there were other professional arenas where they could use the additional energies, many said that they would probably devote additional time to scholarship, some for the purpose of disseminating what they know and have learned about teacher education, others to shore up their employability and to give themselves more professional leverage. At least one indicated that mobility depended upon a durable publication record, something that she and others deemed impossible given the wide expectations of teacher licensure work. More than one Mountain and Valley participant offered critiques of the tenure system itself, saying that it didn't fit in the feminized sphere of primary teacher education. She felt like the caring, high-availability, personalized care of one-on-one preservice preparation was "more than hand-holding . . . it [was] the right way to do things . . . [and] if that means I don't get reappointed, that's fine [because] I'm doing [teacher education] the right way." When I observed that the moral high road may not lead to tenure, she quickly said that "tenure isn't everything." I wondered if she was really so devoted she would cut off her nose to spite her face, and jeopardize the literal career in favor of the moral one.

Patterns in Higher Education

It is not surprising that in higher education in general there are higher levels of pretenure attrition among female tenure-line faculty, and significantly higher numbers of clinical and adjunct females compared with tenured and tenured-system males, across most departments and at most universities, both historically and currently (Hirakata & Daniluk, 2009; Jackson & O'Callaghan, 2009; O'Callaghan, 2009; Spanbauer, 2009). Schools of education, meanwhile, are feminized environments in that there may be more women working in the school to begin with, but even here, women make up huge numbers of nontenured positions related to licensure, supervision, and program work, while a smaller, minority population of tenured and tenure-line males occupy the majority of positions of relative privilege and status uninvolved in licensure, but focused instead on research (Glazer-Raymo, 2001; Liston, 1995). Nonetheless, schools of education garner praise for their numerous female employees, as observed in a recent report from Harvard University where the school of education was held up as a model of success and foil of the troubled, male-dominated business school. The *Harvard Crimson* reported that,

> with women making up only 29 percent of its junior faculty, the Business School faces one of the largest gender imbalances at Harvard's graduate schools, according to the 2009 annual report issued by the Office of the Senior Vice Provost for Faculty Development and Diversity. At the other end of the spectrum, almost 60 percent of junior faculty at the Harvard Graduate School of Education are women. (Merrigan & White, 2010, p. 6)

It was intriguing for me to observe this trend at all three sites involved in this study: there were simply more females involved in elementary teacher education at the pretenure, clinical, and adjunct levels, with many more males among the tenured professoriate, and nearly all of them working in areas outside of elementary teacher education (or if working in teacher preparation, doing so as "service" to the teacher education program, with their primary affiliation located in a typically higher status—meaning, less feminized, with more males and more abstract affiliation with children and teachers—administrative, measurement, or other research area). The large numbers of women in elementary and early childhood teacher preparation makes some contextual sense given the feminized history of the profession (e.g., those who taught PK–5 are typically those that comprise the teacher education faculty in that area) but the presence of a large, arguably exploited underclass of pre- and untenured, female, primary teacher preparation faculty may reflect more than just historical patterns.

And these realities do not escape the notice of the preservice teachers in the programs at both Mountain and Valley. Like the elementary teacher who implements all the testing and disciplinary policies districts and buildings can dish out for no other reason than that she was told to do it (and she has been selected for her adherence to the Western feminine norm of obedience) and has been similarly led to believe that as a worker she is easily replaceable and should, subsequently, be grateful for her very job, primary teacher education faculty may be more and more often being selected through a similar sieve. During and following the 2008 economic crisis, schools of education began hiring more clinical and adjunct faculty to teach in teacher licensure than ever before. Research suggests that this may be indicative of not only dire economic realities but also low institutional commitment to teacher education (Boyd et al., 2008). It goes without saying that women have been and continue to be overrepresented in the elementary and early childhood areas, but as postrecessional economic and prioritization forces demand the hiring of fewer tenured faculty, more pretenure and mostly adjunct and clinical faculty, the fundamental ability of teacher educators to engage critically with the demands of coverage and licensure may decrease. This is not to suggest that PK–5 teachers, pretenure, and clinical, and adjunct faculty are unquestioning, acritical, or sheeplike, but rather that they are terribly, terribly vulnerable. In the words of one of Cole's (1995) participants, the women in teacher education who make up the cadre of temporary or contract positions subject to frequent renewal or the threat of termination "are treated like dirt and have no say in anything" (p. 286). While these are strong words not intended to reference beyond the context of that particular study, the feeling of increasing powerlessness and intensification was palpable among respondents from both Valley and Mountain. However, at these sites there was significantly more sympathy for administrators, many of whom were perceived by faculty as having found themselves in an impossible position brought on by either economic (Valley) and political/licensure pressures (Mountain and Valley).

Power, Compliance, and Transgression at Valley and Mountain

It is against this political and economic backdrop that teacher educators at Valley and Mountain did the work of teaching young women how to negotiate primary level teaching as a low-status, feminized profession. This was both an overt and hidden curriculum taught in the margins, and by narratives and degrees. One narrative that came up time and time again in teacher educators' stories at both of these institutions was about negotiating the differences and similarities between teacher educators and their preservice students; it was made problematic because, in reality, there was not much space, at all, between the two, save time. For the teacher educators, who left teaching for a variety of reasons (at both sites mostly related to wanting more or different intellectual challenges, autonomy, status, salary, and power to affect positive change for the profession, and even the dumb luck of opportunity) it is about telling the story of leaving the classroom to those whom they have a vested interest in leading *into* that very place.

Second, contesting the common popular cultural and occupational folk narrative of the teacher as taken-for-granted and devalued female worker had special resonance when preservice teachers saw that the faculty with whom they work in schools of education may have been having a similar experience. When teacher educators had to implement program requirements that were obviously contradictory to their own teaching stance and interpretation of teachers' work, preservice teachers invariably saw the limits of teacher education faculty authority and connected this to the nature of teacher education as feminized work. As several preservice teachers at Valley and Mountain remarked, they didn't understand how their professors could talk about teaching as social justice, about high quality assessment, about student-centered instruction and, in the words of one Valley student, "drop everything to drill us for the [state licensure examination] when that has nothing to do with what we're learning, or what they think is important to teach us, and they don't say anything about it but it's kind of obvious." Another added, with a half-smile, "They're really not in charge." Still others bought into the idea that schools of education were inherently lower quality; they thought that because professors had little control over licensure requirements, that they were somehow lower quality academics, or "not really professors" as one said, because they "have no say" over the nature of their work.

For preservice participants, these observations made a strong argument for the practicality of compliance as a coping and survival strategy. If power and autonomy, even with the PhD and a faculty position, are still unattainable, then the perceived sacrifices (and identity risk) of leaving the relative safety of the classroom and the teacher and mother moral career are just not worth it. So, finding alternative economies of interaction—such as exchanging financial remuneration for children's love, and the driver's seat for the security of being a perpetual girl culture passenger—becomes even more palatable. This effectively reinforces the moral career of the teacher as iconic "schoolmistress," for whom appearances are paramount, and "exit strategies" hinge on skill sets outside of those valued by a competitive, hegemonically masculine workplace. More than once in this study and in casual interactions with colleagues I have heard teacher educators opine to return to the classroom, where life was easier, struggles (and choices) fewer, and work more defined and perhaps even less political and alienating.[2]

But even in the midst of this structural collusion on the part of teacher educators there is also space for transgression from the obedient, insecure iconic teacher as both "schoolmarms" and "seductresses," who disobey the most fundamental laws of girl culture to exploit the "third spaces" (Anzaldua, 1987) in schools of education and teacher preparation.

The Teacher Educator, Iconic Schoolmistress, and Transgressive Schoolmarm/Seductress

To review, white, middle class, female preservice teachers exhibit many of the same behaviors Holland and Eisenhart (1992) saw in their white, female college student participants: a marked need to please, to conform, and to be seen as "good girls" to the exclusion of conflict, critique, or political stances and activities (Galman, 2006). In keeping with contemporary girl culture, and its emphasis on appearances, they hope to be schoolmistresses: young, feminine, attractive, heterosexuals whose primary motivation to be a teacher is being loved in return by children and laying the groundwork for marriage and motherhood. She also appears to be politically conservative, and distances herself from feminist discourses (Hall & Rodriguez, 2003). She believes that teachers are born, not made and that women, as "natural" caregivers, make better teachers of children than men most of the time. For them, the central qualification for elementary teaching is to know how to love, and political or critical work is unimportant (and even at cross-purposes) compared the work of care; therefore teacher education coursework is a necessary hurdle, a ticket to punch at worst, and a journey of individual discovery and the honing of the valued identity of schoolmistress, rather than essential skill building, though that certainly is a bonus provided, it is concrete and focused on management. One can imagine that the iconic schoolmistress would have a high score on Mahalik et al.'s (2005) CFNI. Powerlessness, or rather the appearance of it, is a virtue.

The schoolmarm and seductress, meanwhile, represent transgression from the above in the form of power. The schoolmarm, a spinster, focused on herself and her work rather than on marriage and motherhood, would rather be heard than seen, and has little vested interest in appearances of beauty, or even of heterosexuality, and offers obedience to no one. Her presence throws many Western feminine norms into question, and she has abandoned the valued feminine identity in favor of the freedoms (and power) associated with transgression. The seductress, meanwhile, is equally powerful in transgression. To revisit the chapter 2 discussion of Farber's (1969) assessment of legendary fictional seductress, Miss Jean Brodie,

> A Svengali of the boarding-school, Miss Brodie is a strange mixture of idealistic aesthete and fascist, sexual libertarian and fierce authoritarian. . . . Though Miss Brodie is a monster, she is appealing too, for her desires are only more extreme forms of desires we all have. She refuses marriage because she will not accept a subservient role in her society; she insists on creating a meaningful life that is hers alone. Her dedication to teaching is ultimately selfish—she wants dominion, power to control other destinies, the satisfaction of molding human lives in her own image. (p. 63)

These are, quite clearly, *not* "good girls." But even though popular girl culture teaches that young women should avoid these stigmatized feminine identities at all costs, there is a lot of power located there—and while it is risky power, it is recognizable in the narratives of girl culture, mostly as a cautionary tale (but the kind of tale from which one cannot easily look away). And this kind of power, the power that puts self first and appearance last, was frequently observed in teacher education contexts at Valley and Mountain. While not always positively received by preservice teachers (who obviously had a vested interest in the primacy of the schoolmistress as desirable trope), I believe that "misbehaving" teacher educators planted important seeds of transgression.

Even though preservice teachers knew, and voiced, that their professors of teacher education were, in the words of one young woman, patently "not in charge" in schools of education, transgression and its lessons were visible in other ways. The following sections illustrate two composite instances of teacher educator transgression at Valley and Mountain[3] in the form of stories about their own lives, leaving teaching, and work and life in the academy.

The Schoolmarm: "Being a Bitch Already"

It was during those five to ten minutes before class that Anna, a preservice elementary teacher placed in a nearby third grade classroom, walked into the university seminar room, sighed loudly, and plopped down in her desk. "It's official," she said, loudly, "I am really, uh, really having issues with my cooperating teacher." Some of the other students laughed, already familiar with Anna's problem. "She's just *so* not the teacher I want to be. Not ever. I'm trying really hard, but it's so, she's just [pause] such a bitch sometimes!" Anna looked at Dr. Sarah F____, the junior faculty member teaching that evening's methods class. She sucked in a little bit of air, "I'm sorry for the language, Dr. F____, I mean, but there's not another word I can use at this point." She shook her long black ponytail forward in mock despair and put her face in her hands. Sarah turned from the blackboard, where she had been laboring to set up an ancient overhead projector. "What's going on?"

Another student, Simone, laughed, "It's really true. Anna's teacher isn't so nice."

"She's just, she's so, so, *mean* to everyone," Anna continued.

Sarah sat down. "What do you mean?"

"It's like she doesn't even care what you think about her—she is so, so blunt. You know, like, she just puts it all out there, with kids, with parents, with me. She doesn't care who she upsets. Like, I come in with a coffee and she's like, 'You're late, but I see you had time for Dunkin Donuts,' and I'm not even late but I feel bad and did she really need to say that?"

Sarah listened, then asked, "But is she a good teacher?"

"I don't know—the kids really love her."

"But is she a good teacher? That's not always the same thing."

"Yeah, yeah she is."

"Even though she's not so nice?"

"Yeah but, like today I was supposed to have this big lesson plan done to teach and we ran out of time and I worked really hard on it and she wouldn't let me teach it and was like, 'Well, that's the way it is sometimes. We're on a schedule' or whatever. I worked so hard! She actually told me to 'suck it up'!"

Sarah folded her hands in front of her face. "But that is the way it is sometimes, right?"

"But did she have to put it that way?"

"No," Sarah said ("I was thinking about my teaching evaluations sinking lower and lower at this point," she said to me later), "but what can you learn from this?"

Anna half-laughed, exasperated, "How to be a big bitch, basically!" The other students, now gathered around the exchange, laughed uneasily and looked at Sarah.

Sarah laughed, too. "Sure! Sometimes you've just got to be a big bitch already. Nobody says you have to be nice all the time and if you are nice all the time you're probably not doing your job." She looked around at the young women, most of whom had stopped laughing. "There's a difference between mean and assertive, guys." Anna didn't seem to know if Sarah was joking or not. "I'm being serious here," she continued, "you can be nice all day long and everyone might love you but that's not your job, is it? You guys don't always like me, right?" At this point the conversation ended as the rest of the class filed in and the instructional period began. In a short conversation later on, Sarah wished she had time to really talk about niceness with her all-female class. "What it does to them, this always being nice stuff. It's the same niceness that keeps them from asking for a raise . . . from breaking up with the bad boyfriend."

The Seductress: Putting Self First

The question had come up twice before. "If this is all so great and we're, like, changing the world and all that," asked one student, "why did you leave teaching?" The break had just started, and while some students ventured out into the hallway to make calls on their cell phones, a few stayed behind.

Dr. Catherine H_____, an elementary teacher educator and an untenured, junior faculty member, swallowed hard. She later admitted to me that she was never sure how to answer this question—after all, she knew that on some level she was both trying to "sell" careers in teaching, encourage program completion, honor her students' idealized visions of self-as-teacher, and at the same time challenge them—she sighed, "People who say it's a lot have no idea." At first, she later reflected, she tried to answer by saying that she never left teaching, but just changed what kind of teaching she did. That didn't work out as students obviously didn't buy it. They knew the differences between teaching at the university and teaching in a classroom, and it wasn't an apples-to-apples kind of comparison. So one day in class, when this rather forward student asked why, she told them. "I left," she said, "because I got tired of being told what to do, and I wanted more." The students were uncomfortable with the answer, and became quiet, waiting for more. Catherine explained that while she loved teaching, and loved the children, the conditions of working in districts and institutions were not a good fit for her. "I'm actually not sure how to tell you about this," she admitted, "but even though I was good at it, I didn't like it." She scanned the room. "Am I making any of you uncomfortable?" A few students looked at the floor. One peeked in from the hallway to listen.

The young woman who asked the question in the first place said, "Well, I mean, it makes us wonder about what we're getting into!" This was punctuated with a nervous laugh. Other questions followed in staccato:

"Don't you miss the kids?"

"Summers off?"

"Did you worry about getting another job?"

"What about all that work to get there and going *back* to school . . ."

Another observed, "not everyone is smart enough to become a professor."

"So you did your time in the trenches and then got the hell out of there," said the first student, again, intending to sting.

And another, "What do you mean by 'more'?"

Catherine responded, "I needed something for myself. I'd watch the kids go off at the end of the [school year] and do other things and I suddenly realized that being happy for [their] success wasn't enough for me. I needed to do other things."

The student who asked the question slowly mumbled, "Beyond summer? I mean, I always thought I'd do my thing in the summer, be with my kids, all that stuff."

Catherine nodded. "Yes, beyond summer." Catherine reflected later on that the preservice teachers, her colleagues, and her research really did give her such joy, she didn't miss the little children at all. When I asked later if she would admit that, she said she wasn't sure that "it would serve a point." She already felt nervous enough teaching teachers when she wasn't a master teacher herself, with only a few years in the actual classroom, "in the trenches," as the student had put it.

Teaching to Transgress

Part of these small transgressions—and they represent just a handful of exchanges, notably in the margins of official program time (break times, before class, and so on—never part of the official curriculum)—is that they emphasize the humanity and fallibility of the teacher educator. So much of classroom time is devoted to an already overstuffed curriculum, but it is also devoted to programmatic unity and the cover stories that these entail. Delving beneath the cover stories, to learn what many teacher educators really think—even if this contradicts the best interests of programmatic coherence and a united front—is rare because these stories may deviate sharply from the "stock story" of identity told over and over again. They are risky, because they do not fit in the carefully managed moral career of, in this case, the teacher educator.

As the author/narrator of our own stories, we engage in creating autobiography when telling our stories. Bruner (1991) describes the autobiographical process as one of building an *idea* of self that is itself the work of crafting a desirable identity. He writes that "a narrator, in the here and now, takes upon himself or herself the task of describing the progress of a protagonist in the there and then . . . he must by convention bring that protagonist from the past into the present in such a way that the protagonist and the narrator eventually fuse and become one person" (p. 5). Something must happen that brings about that unification, and according to Bruner, autobiographers and even casual tellers of the story of self utilize familiar literary techniques and devices to do so.

Bruner believes that autobiography is an outgrowth of fiction, not the other way around (1993, p. 30). He continues, "Autobiography is not only about the past, but is busily about the present as well" (1991, p. 7). One illustration of this aspect of story is in Clandinin and Connelly's (1996) work with teachers' stories. In this study, they found that different stories were present in the "landscapes" of teacher professional knowledge, and that individuals told different stories about themselves and their knowledge with different purposes (and different role performances) in mind. While the theoretical works, methods text and policy around teaching methods constituted a "sacred story" (Connelly & Clandinin, 1996, p. 24) (which is to say, a story that is not openly contested) of teaching, the day-to-day reality of the classrooms in which teachers actually practiced constituted a "secret story" of what "really happens" which is shared with other teachers in secret settings and third spaces. Lastly, the stories told by those same teachers who move out of the safety of the classroom into a larger community. In these stories, which Connelly and Clandinin call "cover stories," the teachers "portray themselves as experts, certain characters whose teacher stories fit within the acceptable range of the story of school being lived in the school" (p. 25). Deviation from the cover story—both by teacher educators who "out" themselves as schoolmarms, seductresses and the like—and preservice teachers who admit teaching was really plan B—are significant transgressions that are often relegated to unofficial spaces. These stories make deviation from the schoolmistress trope possible, and may destabilize the dominance of the "good girl" as desirable worker.

Some Thoughts on the Unique Case of Prairie College

When it comes to preparing teachers, institutional context matters (Goodlad, 1990). In these data, Prairie represented a unique case among the three sites for a variety of reasons, namely that as the only small liberal arts institution represented, faculty and students' experiences were radically different than their peers' at the two larger institutions. The stories of gendered tropes, of faculty frustration, of transgression and care, simply didn't show up in the Prairie College sample. The way in which students were prepared for literal careers was very similar to the way in which they were prepared for moral careers—thoughtfully, planfully, beautifully—but without the pressures of licensure, accreditation, and coverage, and the status issues associated with graduate schools of education (Judge, 1982). At Prairie, the mostly male, tenured, professoriate working in teacher preparation as service was of a completely different ilk than the overwhelmingly untenured, female, education school faculty working in most teacher education programs. The Prairie faculty's commitment to the social ideology of their institution, and their genuine belief in the potential power of the Prairie student as a teacher, was what fueled their voluntary and entrepreneurial participation in that education minor program. Becoming a teacher at Prairie simply wasn't constructed as the same gendered endeavor because the kind of teaching to which even the education minor students aspired was not the semiprofessional, feminized universe of primary level teaching; instead, those who wanted to teach wanted to do so at the university level, typically as tenured professors at small liberal arts colleges where they could enact the "Prairie Story of Teaching" in a venue similar to their primary and collegiate anticipatory socialization among social justice-oriented professional parents and later, liberal arts professors.

Tenure-line college and university teaching in the disciplines (as opposed to interdisciplinary, state-run fields like education) is far from feminized, as defined by Etzioni (1969): it is not considered, culturally or otherwise, to be semiprofessional. It is not numerically dominated by females (if anything, the reverse is true). It does not have low levels of autonomy and high levels of bureaucracy. Similarly, for students, the "Story of Teaching" that dominated Prairie left a great deal of room for interpretation, ideological self-selection limited the participant pool and the realities of becoming teachers were so remote from the discernment process—which focused not necessarily on the moral career of the teacher, but rather on teaching as a temporary stopover en route to other vocational destinations and identities. Prairie faculty had not always been teachers themselves, and for those that had, the experience of teaching paved the way to the experience of becoming an elite liberal arts professor, and the question of why they left teaching was not frequently discussed, possibly because it was simply not a topic for debate. Many participants accepted the rationality of leaving teaching "after a few years" to pursue bigger and better things, so the question of why their faculty mentors had done so was moot. Similarly, while the occasional male primary level teacher educator garnered greater interest at Mountain and Valley (questions abounded about his experiences as a teacher, especially around negotiating suspicions of sexual deviance, but speculation about why he chose to become a teacher in the first place was shallow—he did it, they assumed, to become an administrator or professor later on, unlike female faculty who became teachers because they loved children and only stumbled into the professoriate) the abundance of male faculty at Prairie did not. They simply weren't a rarity because they were elite liberal arts professors first and teacher educators secondarily, and this first category was not (and is not) feminized.

To say that the aspiring primary level teacher at Prairie was not gendered may be a stretch, but considering that the faculty involved in teacher preparation were predominantly male, the program made up of equal numbers of male of female students and the work of the teacher about critical, intellectual social justice and relationship rather than care and love, this may be a relevant argument. To add to this, the female participants did not, themselves, particularly buy into the Western feminine norms underpinning contemporary, generational girl culture but instead tended to identify strongly with male tenure line faculty—and these not necessarily in education. This could be a function of their strong side-bets (Dworkin, 1987), as they were not alienated, "bored," or otherwise drummed out of the arenas of their original aspirations but instead added a minor in education to existing plans. They simply had more choices, different and more varied reference groups and imagery frameworks, and they ultimately enacted different moral careers than their age-mates at Valley and Mountain, for whom the valued identity, and vocation, were so profoundly gendered and linked to girl culture instead of Quaker culture.

Learning Gendered Work: Self-Sacrifice, Dollars and Cents

As Weber & Mitchell (1995) suggested, we do not know much about teacher educators themselves, but data suggest that many of them are teacher educators because of their strong moral commitment to the work despite lower salaries, lower status, and so on. Like so many preservice study participants, they often talk about the moral weight of vocation to counter examination or action around mobility and remuneration—and more than once preservice teachers involved in the Mountain and Valley samples mentioned how their teacher educators' language around the meaning of care made those intrinsic rewards more socially valuable than any extrinsic reward. While some participants agreed wholeheartedly with this assessment and incorporated these patterns into their own narrative of role-taking, others sensed the taboo nature of contradictory speech. As reflected in the sample cases from Mountain and Valley, so many said, "I don't know if I should say this," inviting me into the spaces behind the cover story of wanting to be teachers not for the moral weight of the work but rather for the more mundane and worldly realities of summers off, flexible schedules, and reasonably stable employment. I began to wonder, how are teacher educators—so critical in other regards—actually reinforcing Western feminine norms, and many aspects of Greenfield's (2005) "toxic" girl culture, in their insistence upon the moral rectitude of being poorly paid in exchange for working toward making a difference. It is an economy of self-sacrifice. I am reminded of a doctoral student of mine who wanted to take an unpaid, and clearly exploitative, internship. She asserted to me over and over again about what "great experience" it would be. I told her that under no circumstances does she work for free; graduate credits or other, more direct financial remuneration, is a must. Most men don't work for free. Many women, meanwhile, feel like they should be so thankful for the possibility of even the scantiest employment that they should accept lower or nonexistent wages. This is even more pronounced in the feminized professions, where meaning is conflated with remuneration as an economy of necessity for the preservation of valued identity.

Many of my colleagues in teacher education, also white, middle class women, would probably be uncomfortable with my unrelenting focus on dollars and cents. To be honest, I am a little uncomfortable writing about it. I am, after all, as well-socialized a white, middle class "good girl" as anyone. However, money is, to some degree in a capitalist system, power. Nice girls aren't supposed to talk about money, to demand money, to pursue money. They are supposed to bow out of the power race in pursuit of higher meaning, love, care, and pure vocation. So, the language that preserves the valued identity in the face of being shortchanged and sacrificed on the altar of meaning is that of moral rectitude, and social justice itself. We simply take it for granted that "good works" must be done by those who can afford to get by with less (or are worth less). "When I tell people I'm going to be a teacher," one Valley participant said, "They say, 'Ohhhh, that's so great,' with this look like I'm becoming a nun or something."

A recent article in the *New York Times* reported 2010 Pew Research Center findings that a surprising number of people in the United States and other industrialized, Western contexts believe that "despite affirmations that the sexes should be treated equally . . . men should get preference when it comes to good jobs" (Shannon, 2010). Admittedly, this view is even more common outside of Western contexts, but it should not be totally unexpected in the United States. As Etzioni claimed in the late 1960s, the historically feminized professions, like teaching and nursing, remain semiprofessional mostly because of their association with women, and women's low level of social status and subsequent lessened need for financial support and exclusion from the power structure. As men received preferential treatment in every other area of work, including preparation for higher earning professions, women opted for the valued identity found in the vocational-value discourse of the feminized professions. If you aren't allowed or are discouraged from playing and winning at the status and money game, an alternative economy of love, care, justice, and meaning is both a very attractive and quite pragmatic option. This isn't to say one cannot do good works, be invested in social justice practice, love and care and make a living wage, or that one must abandon the former to pursue the latter, more hegemonically masculinized financial value system. However, it is of key importance that teacher educators refrain from dichotomizing. "The message we get," said one Valley participant, "is that we chose to make no money in exchange for feeling good about making the world a better place . . . and we're encouraged to see anything else [including leaving teaching] as a sell-out . . . like the only way to be good is to work for nothing in the inner city somewhere."

Conclusion: What Do You Make at the End of the Day?

In one observed methods course, the instructor began that day's class by telling a story about a businessman and a teacher. I had just received something similar in a forwarded email, and it went something like this:

> A first grade teacher and a businessman were in an elevator. They began to talk about what each did for a living. The businessman told the teacher how he had an MBA from Harvard, owned his own business and in fact was on his way up to his penthouse office suite in that very building. "What do you make?" asked the businessman, curious about what kind of salary an elementary school teacher could earn these days. "I make dreams come true," answered the teacher, to which the businessman chuckled, "but can you live on it?" The teacher stood tall, "I make children smile," she said, "all you make at the end of the day is money."

The students in that class smiled and felt inspired by the story. A few wrote it down and said they would share it with their cooperating teachers. It was an inspiring story, rooted firmly in American popular culture and its celebration of the scrappy moral underdog standing strong in the face of a smug, fat-cat businessman. It was a wonderful departure from the usual mythology of the teachers who teach because they "can't do" or similar. But it's no coincidence that in no iteration of this story was the businessman a businesswoman, or the teacher a man. That, and the moral of this and so many other teaching stories, still sends a powerful message about teachers' work.

Teacher education, like the elementary school building and culture itself, is profoundly invested in the status quo and works to discourage transgression and encourage obedience, even if they do not necessarily "consider what they do" in deliberate, malicious ways. One of the ways in which this is communicated is through the pastoral control modes of vocational meaning, gendered filial piety, and accountability. The very language of accountability is problematic because it is difficult to contest. While preservice teachers (and scholars in education) have grappled with defining the true nature of teachers' work, teacher educators' work is similarly fuzzy around the edges. Neither a professional weeding-out system, nor at a pace that encourages careful discernment, teacher education has, and continues to have, a wider and wider "subjective warrant" in the contemporary economic and social climate (Lortie, 1972, p. 38), meaning—"wanting to teach becomes justification for doing so," especially when the warrants of other professions may be increasingly stringent and therefore lose applicants through self and institutional discouragement (p. 39). However, this places an undue burden on teacher education programs, and even more on the teacher educators who are charged with making teachers out of whomever appears at their door, regardless of their understanding of doing, or being, the teacher. Without the programmatic "teeth" of a more stringent warrant, teacher educators (already among the lowest status stakeholders in the academy) are further hobbled. Responsible for preservice teachers' performance on an expanding array of exit examinations, accountability measures, and similar but unable to exert more than minimal control over who enters the profession, they are left to operate via inefficient systems of pastoral control.

As Meiners (2002) found, one of many problems with the way certain gendered vocational roles—such as the incarnate "Lady Bountiful"—comes into play in teacher education is that her influence is at the fore of a racist, heterosexist, classist endeavor to regulate which bodies make acceptable teachers and which do not. So, teacher education programs do not select for potential students with an academic or other formalized pre-enrollment sieve, but rather an affective process encouraging self-selection through a series of bureaucratic and programmatic ordeals, the process of regulation operates by cooptation and manipulation rather than by brute force (Schutz, 2004) because, fundamentally, brute force is both unattractive and unreasonable—and simply not an option. When there are no "sticks" one is left to reinvent and cleverly use an array of carrots. In exhorting preservice teachers to think carefully about the vocation they have chosen, a carrot can also make a very convincing stick.

All three sites experienced struggles of varying degrees of severity during the time of data collection. Mountain University was in the midst of a curricular overhaul aimed at strengthening and improving their programs, Valley was in the throes of the recession and its terrible toll on state universities, and Prairie faced its own economic woes associated with admissions numbers. All three were forced to compromise in one way or another: Mountain University, which relied upon its lucrative, successful, and high enrollment teacher education programs was left trying to find ways to address student concerns about rigor and content despite the fact that many faculty felt the student critiques were less than valid, and, in the words of one graduate instructor, "Basically asking us to jump—and we ask, 'How high?'" Valley, meanwhile, faced dwindling enrollment and the rapidly changing face of the teaching profession from a "teacher shortage" to a "teacher glut" economy and looked for ways to be proactive while also acknowledging somewhat lowered admission standards to keep the programs afloat. At the time of this writing, Valley faculty were also grappling with adopting a controversial teacher accountability and testing measure which was embraced as a possible strategy for advanced competitiveness (and economic survival) by administration but horrified the faculty. Prairie also faced a similar admissions crisis on a larger, college-wide scale.

The issues of teacher accountability and the model of "continuous improvement" suggests that teacher education institutions and accreditation boards recommend increased scrutiny, testing, and measuring of accountability for teachers without observing or addressing the domestic ideologies that are antecedent to who becomes a primary-level teacher in our culture. The fact that the overwhelming majority of Valley and Mountain participants chose teaching after abandoning alternative moral careers is something that cannot be overlooked. Similarly, that the majority of preservice teachers reject feminist politics and activist, intellectual interpretations of teachers' work, and are themselves overwhelmingly white, middle class females who will teach children of color (Zumwalt & Craig, 2005) should warrant some concern. How is it that teacher educators, and teacher education institutions, actively cater to individuals who "awaken" to teaching as a gendered destiny after having been alienated elsewhere? Are they critical and reflective of this point, or could this become a quiet recruiting tool in the desperate post-recessional economy? Similarly, do schools of education (and the K–20 endeavor writ large) have something to gain in terms of accountability and control from contemporary post-feminist fantasy?

Notes

1. While there were a small number of male (< 3) and an even smaller number of teacher educators of color at the study sites, I'm restricting my commentary and analysis to the data from the overwhelming number of white, female teacher educators (> 15) at all sites. The exceptional case would be Prairie College, where the majority of teacher education faculty were white males.

2. At one point during my doctoral program, I began to perceive some of the alienation and burnout among faculty and friends in teacher education, their powerlessness, the discourse of insecurity and scarcity, and I actually applied to go back to teaching fifth grade at the elementary school I had left when I went back to graduate school. I remember weighing, in my head, the differences between the low-autonomy reality of the classroom teacher at the dawn of the standardization (and soon to be NCLB) era, and the scary stories and experiences of my friends in higher education. In the end I decided to stick it out and finish the degree, but I had to give away all

of my file boxes of lesson plans and elementary teaching materials that very day—otherwise I knew that I would return to the classroom out of fear of what was to come as a teacher educator.

3. I do not identify at which university these occurred, lest those individuals be identified.

∼

CHAPTER EIGHT

Sweet Are the Uses of Adversity

Wise Fools, Radical Love, and Resistance

Sweet are the uses of adversity,
Which, like the toad, ugly and venomous,
Wears yet a precious jewel in his head;
And this our life, exempt from public haunt,
Finds tongues in trees, books in the running brooks,
Sermons in stones, and good in every thing.

—*As You Like It*, Act II, Scene I

During July 2010, Michelle Rhee, chancellor of the Washington, D.C., public schools summarily fired over two hundred "underperforming" teachers. Her reason for dismissing these teachers was that they were not producing student gains according to a newly implemented growth-model accountability measure called "IMPACT."[1] As American Federation of Teachers president Randi Weingarten wrote in response,

> Chancellor Michelle Rhee's signature education philosophy appears to be that you can hire and fire your way to better schools. Rhee fired more than 75 teachers last year under her old evaluation system. Last November, she used a budget crisis as an excuse to dismiss another 266. Today, the initial implementation of the new IMPACT system already has resulted in terminations of more than 200 teachers. Questions have been raised not only about the validity of IMPACT, but about the chancellor's penchant for firing teachers rather than providing supports to develop their skills. (Abramson, 2010)

In other words, it's a lot of very sudden "stick" (and a merit pay "carrot," discussed next) possibly better suited for the Skinner Box than the nuances of teaching children. The media, well-accustomed to the narrative of the teacher-as-scapegoat and the normalization of largely punitive policies enforced from outside the profession, referred to the masses of the fired (and the nearly three hundred fired the previous year, as well as the nearly eight hundred other D.C. teachers labeled "minimally effective" and under surveillance for the next year) as "lousy teachers" who are "given the boot" (*Wall Street Journal*, July 27, 2010), and "bad teachers" schools were forced to keep under "progressive" employment procedures (*Newsweek*, January 26, 2010). In Rhee's own controversial words, she justifies the fall 2009 mass firings, saying, "I got rid of teachers who had hit children, who had had sex with children, who had missed seventy-eight days of school. Why wouldn't we take those things into consideration?"[2] (*Newsweek*, January 26, 2010).

It's difficult to contest such discourse—the "bad" teachers, the "lousy teachers" who are truant, allegedly abusive, and even "had sex with" children do not encourage sympathy—it effectively paints would-be defenders into a rhetorical corner. Rhee's words also echo stock popular cultural imagery of the bad teacher as failed, deviant female: the seductress, an abusive, burned-out schoolmarm, ineffective, unintelligent, and dangerous. Wall Street denizens, largely responsible for the recent economic collapse, have been described in kinder terms. It is no surprise the innocuous, apolitical, obedient schoolmistress remains an attractive trope to parents and media, and a safe harbor for teachers anticipating hasty termination, and a ruined moral career, should they "fail" at being a teacher and get caught up in a moral panic.

It has also been widely speculated that Rhee's move also helped the beleaguered D.C. public schools close a budget gap, even after accounting for the cost of merit pay rewards. Similar money-saving schemes have been attempted in some districts via questioning the rules around teacher seniority. To wit: a variety of arguments are made to justify how older and more experienced, higher-earning teachers could be laid off or compelled to retire and replaced with less experienced and less expensive ones (Abramson, 2010; NCTQ, 2010; *Washington Post*, March 27, 2008). That older teachers ("schoolmarms") are demographically and politically distinct from subsequent generations (of "schoolmistresses") is clear, with more progressive politics, confidence, and experience and less inclination to put up with deprofessionalizing and deskilling "reforms" (Dworkin, 1987; Galman, 2006). That the new teacher hires, mostly young, white women, are more closely aligned with both Western feminine norms and contemporary neoconservative politics, and as NCLB veterans themselves more likely to acquiesce than resist, is certainly a distinct possibility (Galman, 2006). That the popular cultural (and girl culture) narrative depicts the "schoolmarm" in the same way it does most older women—disposable, dead-wood-to-be-cleared-away, and so forth—cannot be a discounted factor in the contemporary narrative contesting seniority as a variable in personnel decisions (Greer, 1993).[3]

Meanwhile, teachers who do show measurable student growth get to both keep their jobs and may receive a merit pay increase based on student gains. It goes without saying that the ends may justify a variety of means and that competition will be fierce to teach in those classrooms and schools where children are most likely to achieve academically.[4] As districts in Florida considered a similar merit pay scheme, a teacher wrote a letter to the editor in the *Palm Beach Post*:

> If this is what my pay scale is based upon, then please give me all advanced students whose parents are well-educated and pushing their children toward college. Please do not give me any ESE students or non-English-speaking students. Just give me the cream of the crop. Then I can guarantee that my students will set the standard for their classmates and my pay will be at the top of the scale. No one will be happy, but who cares? I will be able to pay my mortgage and put food on my table. And I will have been legislated out of a noble profession that I once loved. (*Palm Beach Post*, March 17, 2010)

The letter writer received more than one aggressive, personal attack in the rebuttal comments that followed the printing, many of them using the language of the failed feminine moral career (accusing the writer of not "caring" enough, not being "capable" of care, of not "loving" her job and the students adequately, and so forth). It goes without saying that teachers need to make more money, but offering a performance bonus that comes at the other end of at-will firings is hardly professionalizing.

But in the midst of this gloom and doom, as Shakespeare so deftly put it, even the most formidable adversity may yet serve a positive purpose. The problems of primary level teaching and teacher preparation as "women's work" or "feminized professions" subject to all the above ills are not intractable. Indeed, I suggest that like Shakespeare's toad, there is also a precious jewel to be found in the midst of ugly experience and equally venomous girl culture. Instead of the rush to masculinize, measure, and mete out punishments via discourses of accountability or "merit," I suggest that redefining twenty-first-century primary teaching as gendered work means identifying and valuing feminized practices

(Griffiths, 2006) that may have emerged or be actively emerging as a form of resistance to hegemony, including the neoliberal discourses of merit pay, teacher-proofing and the other machinery of a racist, classist, and sexist state. They may be operating as a quiet, even tacit, response to hegemony in the margins of increasingly regimented, deskilled work spaces.

Feminized Practices as Resistance

To review, feminized practices, as defined by Griffiths (2006), are independent of the feminized professions but they may develop in the enclaves of female numerical dominance (even in spite of, or possibly because of, the male-dominated leadership structures of the feminized professions). Writes Griffiths, "The feminization of teaching, insofar as it exists, is to be welcomed because it provides a space for resisting hegemonic masculinity" (p. 387). As discussed in chapter 1, feminized practices, per se, within feminized professions, can be defined as "any practice . . . seen as fluid, leaky and viscous [with] different practices seep[ing] out into each other as a result of the embodiment of their individual members" (p. 387). Whereas hegemonic masculinity emphasizes individualism and competition within a rigid hierarchy, feminized practices represent an alternative: fluid practices which "leak into each other," and which have "permeable" boundaries, in which seemingly contradictory approaches can be simultaneously equally effective, and in which the individual, child-centered approach emphasizes many ways to reach the same goal (p. 396). Similarly, responsiveness, or "viscosity" means that practices are slow to evolve, not reactionary, and they respond "to internal and external changes" in a way that makes these practices not only more flexible and nonhierarchical but also more receptive to change and diversity in such a way that it attempts to meet the needs of and be inclusive of many, excluding none, and incorporating the divergent practices of many. This serves to create communities of practice in classrooms and schools instead of competitive, hierarchical systems.

If we think about accountability, both in teacher education contexts and, especially, in the primary schools (in the form of merit pay, high stakes testing, NCLB, IMPACT, and other measures) as the face of amelioration by masculinization, making the schools look more and more like the hegemonically masculine ideal, then feminized practices are especially well-suited as a form of resistance to (and subversion of) these. The following discussion seeks to frame what feminized practices look like at the Mountain, Valley, and Prairie sites, and how subversion is fostered, even in the midst of adversity and collusion with Western feminine norms, girl culture, and similar.

Feminized Practices at Mountain and Valley

Viewed through the lens of feminized practices, Mountain University and Valley University can be seen as places where fluidity, leakiness, and viscosity were being actively eliminated through the pursuit of rigor, standardization, and control. While these trends toward what can be called "masculinization" are probably common university-wide, schools of education can maintain (even inadvertently) spaces for resistance in which feminized practices are maintained. As described in chapter 7, these spaces may be located in the seemingly inefficient practices of the schools regarding admission, evaluation, and matriculation. These include the wide subjective warrant and widely divergent and individualized admissions policies in place in both institutions, the seemingly arbitrary sense of student evaluation and the process toward graduation, all of which cast "problems" at each site when in fact they represent arenas of more fluidity and flexibility than any other area of life at the education schools. While faculty and administration alike complain that these three practices are "messy" and in need of alignment/accreditation/standardization/heightened control (mostly in the form of more regimented and rigid completion/graduation requirements attached to state tests and removed from teacher educators' hands), these are actually sites for greater individualized, inclusive, responsive practices. They only appear messy from the vantage point of Tayloristic institutional control and streamlining.

Individual practices are somewhat different. Some of the preservice teachers appeared to be engaging in feminized practices, but upon closer inspection were also at the forefront of hegemonic masculine norms. Kari, whose "role-taking" experience was representative of the overwhelming majority of the preservice primary level teachers at Mountain, was deeply invested in alternative economies of love and care, rejecting other reward systems, her interpretation of love as feminized practice was not critical. Indeed, as noted in chapter 4, she was comfortable with patriarchy and may have even seen that she benefited from it. Her interpretation of love and care was biologically based and reflected a one-dimensional, rigid interpretation of the feminine and of the teacher. Indeed, like many of her classmates, her beliefs about teacher education were rooted in efficiency and practicality: teacher education, for them, was about imparting discrete skills rather than theoretical principles, in a timely fashion rather than one that is individualized or terribly time consuming. Employability and linearity, rather than the evolution of self, or vocational discernment, seem to weigh most strongly in such a priority system.

Resistance, it seemed, was framed most clearly as resistance to the teacher education program's intent to challenge preservice teachers' beliefs, rather than even tacit resistance to hegemonic masculinity. Teaching was about learning a set of formalized skills and conforming to those monolithic skills and the similarly inflexible image of the teacher. As for those few students like Maya, for whom "role-making" was the task at hand, the process of becoming a teacher more closely resembled Griffiths's ideas of viscosity, fluidity and leakiness; for Maya, becoming was a circular, recursive process, and the teacher identity was itself fluid and malleable, made to fit the contours of her own critical consciousness and vocational objectives. For Maya, the work of the teacher was an avenue of resistance to normalizing cultural pressures and creating more choices—not less—both for herself and for her future students. That said, Western feminine norms are themselves, like any normalizing system, rigid and exclusive rather than flexible, evolving, and inclusive. They encourage role-taking rather than the more viscous role-making process. That Maya was possibly less aligned with these norms seems fitting as well.

The overall trends for preservice students at Mountain and Valley were similar. While role-taking dominated the ethos of professional identity and role development for Mountain students, the preservice teachers at Valley were focused much more on individual vocational discernment, and self discovery. In this individualized respect, their process of becoming teachers sounds much more like role-making—except insofar as the selves they are "discovering" are remarkably uniform and have to do with discovering their biological aptitude for care. A little bit like Columbus "discovering" the New World, Adrienne and Rachel's respective Hispaniolas were hardly new territories, but rather reincarnations of stock postfeminist rhetoric. Like their age-mates at Mountain, they created alternative (but not necessarily critical) economies of work as remunerated by biologically based, gendered care and love. These may represent the beginnings of feminized practices, or they may represent the absorption of patriarchal ideology about biology, work, and worth.

The faculty at Mountain and Valley found themselves in similar straits— they were in the midst of working to increase the rigor and standardization of the primary teacher education program at their schools of education, but had not necessarily bought into all that this entailed. That very act of balancing different selves, objectives, and systems requires individuals to become comfortable with multiple contradictions and slow-moving systemic change. Being mostly untenured, lower status members of the academy required to answer to the state for teacher licensure, they may feel compelled to comply with mandates and reforms with which they do not agree, as well as to find ways (through scholarship, through third-space conversations with students such as described in chapter 7) to resist the march of hegemony. By hanging on to some degree of control in the admissions, matriculation, and evaluation processes, where fluidity, viscosity, and leakiness are the guiding principles of practice, such resistance may be maintained. While this may be frustrating for administration, and for the Karis of the student body, it is nonetheless a site for promising practice—both in terms of offering alternatives to role-taking, encouraging productive dissonance, and preserving space for growth and change amidst increased pastoral, and disciplinary, controls. This includes nudging students and pushing their boundaries as well, despite the bulging demands of course coverage and the possibly unwarranted weight of teaching evaluations that judge "niceness" before instructional quality (Galman, 2006). Call it subversive, radical love or grassroots resistance—it was omnipresent and maintaining its momentum in the slow, leaky, and viscous way that only feminized practices can.

Feminized Practices at Prairie

Yet again, Prairie represents a unique and divergent case. While Griffiths (2006) affirms that feminized practices do not need to be enacted in a predominantly female environment, like the elementary classroom or other feminized professions, one must give the devil his due and point out that teacher education at Prairie was no more feminized that your average elite liberal arts college. However, that said, the absence of formalized, rigid licensure requirements and the pressure to standardize may have created a space for more feminized-type practices to thrive. It is also possible that the Prairie College ideology may be less inherently judgmental of "messy" processes or "inefficiency" and more tolerant of individualism than other institutions may be.

In welcoming divergent experience, individualized trajectories and encouraging alternative trajectories, it is possible that the Prairie ideology and progressive Quaker ideologies may themselves actively encourage feminized practices. Samantha's narrative certainly suggests that her progress toward both personal and vocational discernment is themselves fluid, leaky, and viscous. She is comfortable with a nonlinear progress through life, with an evolving sense of self, with multiple—even conflicting—aspirations. The very faculty with whom she works at Prairie embody contradiction and responsiveness; they encourage others to become primary level teachers, while they are not primary level teachers (and some never have been), openly admitting that one need not "sign on" to a particular vocation for longer than one is called to do it, if at all. Quite literally, it is possible that it is the "thought that counts" at Prairie, and that pressure aside, individuals may grow in alternative practices that resist hegemonic thinking and being in the world.

This is by no means a suggestion that we collectively abandon teacher licensure in favor of a more individualized; "viscous, leaky, and fluid" feminized approach to learning to teach. However, I would suggest that the contemporary strategy of radically tightening control of teachers (e.g., mass firings, more stringent requirements, more surveillance, and less autonomy or security) and actively discouraging collectivism and professionalism (merit pay, high-stakes testing) could bear some morally imaginative scrutiny. Similarly, teacher educators should be wary of importing such tight controls into their own domain under the guise of "accountability" and its familiars.

Feminized Practices and Girl Culture

Feminized practices can be found among preservice teachers and faculty in the nonfeminized environment of Prairie College, but not in the heavily feminized environments of the Mountain and Valley schools of education. The stepped-up intensification of hegemonically masculine practices associated with standardization, licensure, control, and the like certainly could have an effect, as this was the case at both of the latter, and conspicuously absent from Prairie. However, it is also possible that collective adherence to contemporary girl culture, and by extension, Western feminine norms, can negatively impact how feminized practices are valued and interpreted as this kind of girl culture is at its heart may represent a kind of hegemonic femininity.[5] Adherence to girl culture and the associated feminine norms may, in part, impact ideological preservice self-selection to specific teacher education programs and to the profession in general.

I acknowledge that popular girl culture in the US context is diverse, rich, and by no means wholly oppressive. That said, current trends, as Brumberg writes (2002), nonetheless reflect a trend toward controlling bodies and aspiration: "American popular culture is especially dangerous for girls . . . everywhere," she notes, "we see girls and women looking in mirrors, nervously checking who they are" noting that for all our impression management, we are not a terribly reflective or self-aware society (pp. 88–89). Instead, we collectively encourage girls and women to focus on, as Mahalik et al. (2005) defines as one of the quintessential Western feminine norms, a nearly obsessive interest in "appearances"—of niceness, of love, of idealized self.[6]

For many preservice teachers, though not all, becoming teachers is part of envisioning this externally focused female perfection, which is to say, *being* the young, pretty schoolmistress, Meiners's modern "Lady Bountiful" (2002) instead of *doing* the work of instruction, though this certainly may change over time. The beginning preservice teachers with whom I work assert that good primary level teachers are "pretty" and "young" and love their students, nurturing their nascent identities and self-esteem. They hear the language of loving children, of vocation, of highly flexible work compatible with childrearing and gender norms echoed in teacher education program materials. When it becomes clear that the work of the teacher is less about looking and acting the part of the social mother (Cortina & San Roman, 2005), but rather critical, even political work that resists many of the most pervasive tenets of this face of girl culture as we know it, many preservice teachers become disenchanted with teacher education, possibly because it demands constant reflection, and also because the work of critically examining oneself and one's identity is difficult and unfamiliar territory for the NCLB-era high school graduate (Galman, 2006). Teacher educators themselves act simultaneously in resistance to and collusion with this aspect of girl culture, and I count myself among the guilty in this regard. Too often I see our overburdened, accountability-drowned programs perseverating on female-specific dress codes and behavioral compliance policies, while we sideline important conversations about what it means to politicize the work of care and problematize students' interpretations of "loving children" as self-centered aesthetics rather than real critical care (Valenzuela, 1999). We also often fail to critique our own driving needs (because we are also statistically mostly white, middle class women) to be liked, to be "good girls" in the Holland and Eisenhart (1992) sense, and to valorize other pervasive Western feminine norms, often to the detriment and silencing of other women, especially women of color.

In a recent *New York Times* article, Peggy Orenstein quoted Deborah Tolman's work on girls and sexuality; "By the time they are teenagers," she said, "the girls I talk to respond to questions about how their bodies feel—questions about sexuality or desire—by talking about how their bodies look. They will say something like, 'I felt like I looked good.' Looking good is *not* a feeling" (June 7, 2010, MM11). So also, vocationally speaking, enjoying doing the work is very different than enjoying performing gendered tropes that are associated with gendered identity. Putting the appearances before feeling and doing has created the devastating synesthesia that is the hallmark of mainstream girl culture, fueling "postfeminist," neoliberal rhetoric, among other disturbing contemporary discourses (Douglas, 2010).

I would like to think that in actively, overtly valuing feminized practices we might find an inoculation against the troubling intersection of girl culture and teaching as a feminized profession. It seems that in failing to frame teaching as the work of biologically based care and love, as well as its wholesale rejection of this contemporary face of toxic girl culture, Prairie College has created an environment where feminized practices might flourish in more than just the margins. It could be said that Prairie College, and possibly the progressive religious ideologies that drive it as an institution, have created an alternative to this kind of girl culture and its gendered connection with teaching.

Playing the Wise Fool:
Practical Recommendations for Teacher Educators

This chapter began by sketching out "the uses of adversity"—in other words, the difficult professional context in which contemporary preservice and inservice teachers and teacher educators find themselves and the possible positive products of such experience. Remembering the Wise and Foolish Virgins from the first chapters of this book, who differ in their focus on adherence to feminine norms, moral careers and impression management strategies, in the following paragraphs I will suggest that teacher educators might resist reifying either "wiseness" or "foolishness" by embracing contradiction. A simplistic read depicts the "Wise Virgins"–like Kari, Adrienne, Rachel, and others—as setting out explicitly to do the work of love, expertly performing a culturally valued feminine gender identity and planning to reap the rewards associated therewith, and the "foolish virgins"—like Maya, Samantha, and others—as being unafraid of missteps and less invested in the gendered work of love than in critical and transformative classroom politics. But their stories and experiences illustrate how the tropes of "wise" and "foolish" are too narrow and too simplistic to totally represent the experiences of gendered work in preservice preparation. In short, as participants in popular and, even tangentially, vocational and girl cultures, all the participants were both wise and foolish, and teacher educators should both be aware of this hybridity as well as work to trouble contemporary girl culture and its insistence on one-dimensional reference groups for girls and women.

Creating teacher education, and the teaching profession, as a bastion for feminized practices and resistance to hegemony might also go a long way toward transforming the work of love into an alternative girl culture built on radical—meaning critical—love. To do so ultimately turns the

Wise/Foolish dichotomy on its head, creating what I like to call the "Wise Fool," who, like the Falstaffian "holy fool" is "shamming vices and enacting parodies [with the] inner intent of [sisterly] self-humiliation and [motherly] truth-telling" (Battenhouse, 1975, p. 32). In thus attempting to radically reconstruct (rather than dismantle in the manner of a straw man) wiseness and foolishness, the Wise Fool and her radical practices recontextualize teacher education as an experience in subversion; queering schools and disrupting contemporary discourses on gender and work. So, to revisit early chapters and Griffiths's (2006) theory of feminized practices, it may be that feminization of the teaching profession is not a problem—but rather a solution to the very real problem of hegemonic masculinity in teacher education and schools alike (Connell, 1995)—and that feminized practices, when separated from the ever-prepared objecthood of girls in contemporary girl culture, can be a form of resistance enacted, wisely, knowingly, but with the freedom of the fool.

Adversity creates the Wise Fool, and through her a model of imperfection for children and others. Playing the "Wise Fool" means becoming comfortable with contradiction in both how we work and what kinds of femininities and masculinities we inhabit. This includes the contradictions inherent in doing the gendered work teaching and teacher preparation in the feminized professions, as well as the contradiction of doing our work with care and love, but not in such a way that care and love become an end unto themselves, and a biological imperative. We cannot all teach in small, private religious institutions where alternatives to contemporary girl culture are built-in, and licensure pressures are optional. We probably wouldn't want to, as creating a significantly more diverse cadre of new teachers for the next twenty years depends on high quality teacher education happening across a wide array of private and public colleges, universities, community colleges, and alternative licensure programs. But in managing the hand we've been dealt—standardization, regulation, and an increasingly young, white female preservice pool—need not be incongruous with progress.

Practical action suggestions for teacher educators as Wise Fools trouble girl culture–driven moral careers and support transgressive trajectories, identities and practices mean valuing the practices that may seem arbitrary, poorly aligned or even "messy" in their own departments and across the profession. The Wise Fool talks openly about teaching as a historically feminized profession and labors to make it more—not less—feminized in its practices by valuing leakiness and embracing viscosity as defined by Griffiths (2006). It may seem incongruous with the era of efficiency and standardization, and an example of uncomfortable disobedience for precarious, junior teacher educators, but I suggest that wise foolishness is the key to loosening the vise grip of control and the primacy of obedience in the world of gendered work.

Valuing Leakiness

We can frame feminized practices as leaky, meaning that they have fluid, shifting boundaries and may incorporate a variety of seemingly contradictory, individual, and even idiosyncratic approaches to reach the same goal. I suggest that to emphasize "leakiness" in the gendered terrain of teacher education programs and practices, we might begin by (1) creating breakable rules and (2) emphasizing the unmeasurable.

Make Breakable Rules, Then Break Them

We must become comfortable with creating program policies that are more user-friendly—meaning, allowing for more interpretation and manipulation on the part of the teacher educator who works in the program they govern. Fundamentally, these policies, or "rules" must be "leaky" enough to allow for interpretation, and rule-breaking if necessary. While teacher educators and administrators often worried that their ultimately very flexible policies lacked "teeth" and sought ways to "enforce the rules" (faculty interview), what is most valuable about the policies and practices at most sites was just this flexibility and the ethic of care (Noddings, 1984) it implies. For example, the teacher educators at Mountain and Valley mostly practiced the principle of leakiness in the common practices of breaking the hard-and-fast licensure "rules" to accommodate promising students who may not have otherwise completed or been admissible into programs, but who showed every other indication of being able to meet program performance criteria through alternative means. Making breakable rules doesn't mean not having standards, but it does mean relinquishing some degree of control, taking some risks, and emphasizing that one size—or one hierarchy—does not fit all.

Additionally, creating a culture where rules and policies exist to serve those who use them, versus requiring individuals to retool themselves into the model provided by rule schemas, might bring open contestation of the Western feminine norm of obedience. Teacher educators and preservice teachers alike are in some ways—both at the University and primary school levels—are selected and reinforced for obedience and conformity, and program and tenure or promotion policies provide further emphasis.

Emphasize the Unmeasurable

As some of my colleagues in elementary teaching used to say at the beginning of high-stakes testing and NCLB era, "what isn't measured, doesn't count." But rather than trying to measure more things, re-emphasizing the importance of, and allocating space to, the unmeasurable is essential. Placing an emphasis on those things that cannot be readily entered into an accountability engine does not mean throwing up one's hands and abandoning the central usefulness of data collection for program improvement altogether. What it does is begin to place more equal emphasis on both the measurable (rubrics, assignments, adherence to standards, etc.) and the unmeasurable (vocational discernment, identity development, perceptions of the work of love and care) and by doing so creating, promoting, and encouraging a discourse that supports the latter.

One of the reasons the discourse of love and care (both as gendered, biological aptitude in the world of gendered work and as critical, transformative practice) remains a covert, hidden story is because what it means to do contemporary "women's work" is not part of the official discourses of most schools of education. The defensive rhetoric is there to be sure: emphasis on the nobility of the profession, faculty and students alike rally around the morality of doing socially just work in a largely morally bankrupt, money-driven culture, and so on. But the conversation about why all the classrooms are full of young, white women, or what it means to do gendered work, and what our collective moral careers might really be about—there is no space (or, often, language) for this kind of talk. We know that a major contributor toward the reproduction of unexamined, even incorrect preservice teacher belief systems is silence (Galman, Pica-Smith, & Rosenberger, 2010). Students and others might dismiss the unmeasurable as "fluff" or "theory" and unnecessary for professional development, but *it's what doesn't get talked about that doesn't count.*

Another central issue with measurement is that a clear and operationalized idea of what teacher competence necessary looks like in the preservice context is difficult to make universally measurable. A "good novice teacher" might be one who has certain dispositions, or who can write a lesson plan and deliver it according to what counts as competence, but student growth over time is difficult to measure in the preservice period. So, the things that get measured are often polluted: because everyone seems to get the highest rating on their lesson plan, the ultimate measure of who gets to be the "good teacher" has much more to do with other things, including effect, gender performance, and compliance.

If love is to be radical, and real, and not just something women "do" naturally that dictates teaching careers—we must talk about it as an official discourse. The same goes for the largely marginalized moral career of the preservice mothers-to-be, the elephant-in-the-room of semiprofessional "women's work," and the spectral absence people of color from teaching and teacher education.

Embracing Viscosity

Efficiency and responsiveness, while not mutually exclusive, are not always compatible either. Embracing "viscosity" means valuing practices are slow to evolve, and resisting the efficiency-driven need to react quickly and automatically according to uniform policy. A slow, radically individualized response is certainly less efficient, and profoundly at odds with the dominant hierarchical business model. However, adopting more flexible and non-hierarchical practices could create spaces for resistance to hegemony, and ultimately create school and workplace cultures that are more favorable to change and welcoming of diversity. "Viscous" practice, with its seemingly chaotic, molasses-like pace, can incorporate the needs and practices of many as it goes, rather than simply enforcing the rule of majority or the prescribed path of the "norm." Two steps toward creating more "viscous" teacher preparation contexts include (1) radically individualizing program practices, and (2) adopting a policy of intentional inefficiency.

Radical Individualization

I have a wonderful colleague who refers to her work in teacher education as "high touch"—meaning, that she works to have a personal relationship with each and every student. While the language I use is that of radical individuation, rooted in feminist (and feminized!) practices, both approaches acknowledge the indisputable truth that in work with human beings, batch processing just doesn't work. While it may be unreasonable to suggest that each individual preservice teacher be required to design and independently structured, unique path to licensure, a radically individualized approach would emphasize a more individualized path to becoming a teacher that is independent of the lockstep routine of university courses followed by field experiences and licensure. Instead, as suggested by the Coalition for Essential Schools and others, some preservice teachers may benefit from alternative models more tightly tied to apprenticeship-style, field-based learning in classrooms featuring individual learning experiences based on mentor relationships with other new teachers. Still others may benefit from a more theoretical, even abstract, foundation in university courses prior to fieldwork such as offered at Prairie College. Others may wish to include a variety of interdisciplinary coursework. The issue at hand is that sameness in a program is ultimately unnecessary. The primary rationale for prescribed progress is rooted in Taylorism, and continues out of adherence to history as well as to control variables and avoid personal and bureaucratic hassle ("We have to make it the same—otherwise the [students] compare notes and think that one group is having it easier than the other and they start screaming that it's unfair" said one teacher educator). Uniformity eventually boils down to a lowest common denominator, which is ultimately unfair to everyone.

Of course, as I have illustrated in previous chapters, teacher educators are already physically, intellectually, and emotionally overworked, as one frustrated Mountain graduate instructor said, "babysitting" preservice teachers who "simply don't seem to understand that they are in graduate school." Her instinct, and the natural reaction of so many, is to create more rigor: in admissions criteria, in program assessments and benchmarks, and to create bigger, more formidable programmatic "sticks" with which to club the incompetent or inefficient. That said, true viscosity—and the circuitous, highly inefficient but highly effective "high touch" approach of radical individuation—demands the highly unintuitive step of doing the inverse. As is the emphasis at Prairie College, doing the time-consuming work of building licensure programs on relationships rather than benchmarks is essential. So also is the appropriate tenure and promotion valuation of this approach, both in terms of the expectations and specific contours of what constitutes teaching load and scholarship output for teacher education faculty.

Adopting a Policy of Deliberate, Intentional "Inefficiency"

This recommendation is intentionally framed as polemic. Of course we want our teacher education programs to be efficient—if efficiency means that they use resources maximally and well to produce highly competent teachers. However, the contemporary use of the discourse of efficiency is increasingly divorced from the actual—and quite innocuous—meaning of the word. It has instead become about control, and borrows more and more heavily from a business, rather than human service, model. The assumption that we should all, collectively, be striving for more and heightened efficiency in our work as teachers and teacher educators is based on the flawed assumptions that (1) more is always both better and possible, (2) improvement can be indefinitely continuous, and (3) more stringent controls always result in higher quality. None of these are reliable. One of the biggest problems with the race for "accountability," "alignment," and standardization—and, indeed, most forms of measurement and control in work with human beings—is that they are so very fast-moving and require so much maintenance and work that they leave little time for either reflection, very little room for change and adjustment, and are generally mandated and superimposed on often incongruous organic systems with which they may be a poor fit.

A certain degree of viscosity allows ample time to reflect on not just the "what" of high quality teacher preparation (which is often very nicely measured by accountability systems) but also the elusive "why." This includes the concrete question of why certain practices are valued over others, but also the abstract questions of why we do the work of teacher education at all, and why preservice teachers respond as they do. For teacher educators, a more viscous, less efficient programmatic pace might allow for increased opportunities for interrogation. This could be interrogation of our own practices as teacher educators and scholars, removing the feeling one participant described of being constantly responding to licensure demands. It might also include interrogating the ways in which the academy itself may be benefiting from the structures of sex-segregated labor. For example, as touched upon in earlier chapters, teacher educators need time and space to explore the ways in which the teacher education and public schooling machine might benefit from the disenfranchisement, boredom, insecurity, or alienation that drove Kari, Adrienne, and Rachel (and to some extent, Maya as well) from their initial areas of interest.

Conclusion

While my work has focused on beginning to understand the huge numbers of young white women that dominate the primary preservice cadre, it goes without saying that a singular imperative lies in the diversification of the teaching force. However, as Meiners (2002) suggests, white women, who were historically used as colonizing and control agents through the call to teach, seem particularly reluctant to question the "Lady Bountiful" ideal, and in some ways I wonder if teacher educators themselves reinforce a modern day "Lady Bountiful" trope as a barrier to the diversification of the teaching force? Using a more nuanced interpretation of who the wise and foolish virgins are, and what we can learn from them both, this chapter has outlined what I see are prescriptives for positive change. As I indicated in chapter 3, a qualitative, descriptive study can hardly purport to prove which practices in teacher education are effective and which are not. What it can do is offer informed speculation based on the patterns that have emerged in that work.

Chiefly, I speculate that business-as-usual in teacher education is not working. The teacher education machine must slow down enough to see that it may have remained predominantly young, white, female, and middle class because students of color, older students, working class students, and others may not fit the machinery of its furious, whizzing efficiency, geared as it is to fit only one kind of student—and ultimately make only one kind of teacher.

Notes

1. According to AFT, IMPACT is "designed to weed out teachers rather than help them improve." (*Washington Post*, July 24, 2010. Page AOID.)

2. Rhee later said her statement was taken out of context, and that she meant that the abusive teachers constituted a minority of those fired.

3. "A younger woman is prompted by a thousand cultural goads into thinking of herself as a newer and therefore better model. There is in our throwaway culture no suspicion that an individual might improve with age and accumulate desirable characteristics . . . they do not see how much of the hatred of Mrs. Thatcher derives from the fact that she is old and female, or how much of the high-principled rhetoric of the opposition parties makes use of the animus against the aged female" (Greer, 1993, p. 237).

4. And no matter what the rhetoric of self-sacrifice and vocation might be, few teachers may be willing to sacrifice their livelihood to teach those students whom they perceive to be less likely to learn quickly, show rapid improvement on high-stakes tests and have fewer obstructive behavioral problems. This puts teachers in a very difficult situation, as some could be drawn to classrooms dominated by white, middle to upper SES students who speak English and have fewer learning disabilities or behavioral issues (Timmons Flores, 2007). While pundits in favor of merit pay offer the classic arguments about the power of the free market system model and ask, wide-eyed, "Don't you *want* teachers' salaries to increase?" It's just not that simple.

5. Again, R. W. Connell has insisted that there can be no such thing as an "hegemonic" form of femininity. However, as she also agrees, there are forms of femininity that may be more aligned with the products and practices of patriarchy, and for lack of a better term, I use it here to suggest that form of femininity that is at least tacitly accepting of female subordination as part of a natural order.

6. The following brief discussion appeared in an abridged form in a recent *Gender and Education Association* newsletter (August, 2010).

~

Conclusion

Boldness, Be My Friend: Final Thoughts on Self and Story in the Feminized Profession

Boldness be my friend!
Arm me, audacity, from head to foot!

—*Cymbaline*, Scene VI, Act I

While many of the male jobs require skills such as intelligence and decision-making ability, female jobs more often require qualities such as beauty, youth, and/or the desire to serve. In sum, *Seventeen*'s over-arching message to girls about work is that it remains a man's world in which women labor (mostly at being beautiful) as a means to meeting or assisting more powerful men.

—Massoni, 2004, p. 62

The stories we tell can be considered part of our identity kits (Goffman, 1963), as the "stock story" one keeps at the ready may be an aspect of the paraphernalia of one's identity, even though it is not as concrete as many of the other items in the kit. In this way, stories are (1) aids in the problem-solving enterprise involved in figuring out who we are and how we fit into the world; (2) tools in the equally important task of performing that identity for an audience of others; and (3) an impetus for subtle shifts in one's trajectory and ultimately the crafting of a valued identity and moral career. Also, as discussed in chapter 1, the telling and retelling of stories is a way of performing and re-performing roles—which is to say refining one's performance as per audience cues.

At two of the three research sites, preservice teachers and teacher educators negotiated what were often very different perspectives on the nature of teachers' work: the idea of what a teacher does, or should do, and her function in the classroom, and in the culture, were oftentimes both sources of conflict as well as secret agreement. That is to say many teacher educators were in agreement with the preservice population's interpretation of teaching as gendered care work, and used those comfortable ideas as inducements to build relationships and encourage program performance, though they may have maintained a more critical cover story to function in the academy. It's difficult to make a definitive statement based solely on these data.

As Terkel (1972) documented, there is more to contemporary employment than the mere exchange of services for a paycheck. "Work" may be less about the discrete mechanics of what one does than how one feels about occupying a particular vocational role and the subsequent meaning assigned to work. This can be true for many preservice teachers; many do not have a clear picture of the day-to-day realities of teachers' work (and are not troubled by that lack of clarity) but most *do* have a firm understanding of what it means—both to themselves and in the popular culture—to *be* a teacher. Choosing to do work that is historically gendered, iconic, political, and public is further complicated because of way in which people become teachers. Preservice teachers learn from teacher educators at the university or college level, as well as in an apprenticeship fashion from practicing teachers once they reach the student teaching phase. Many in formal licensure programs, such as found at Mountain and Valley, must pass a series of teacher tests which are designed and given by bodies outside of the teacher education program and not always aligned with teacher education curriculum. Finally, the state grants a teaching license. However, when asked about when they become "real teachers" most respondents suggest that these formal indicators have little to do with it. At Mountain and Valley, they are almost always "already teachers" or had been so "all along." The only difference is that now they can do the official work of the teacher in an official capacity. So, who makes teachers? And, if it's not teacher educators, or the state licensure authority, then we must accept that the role-making and role-taking process is where teachers are made, and that for most preservice teachers the working of becoming is first and foremost about the appearance and belief of *being*, rather than the concrete work of *doing*.

In the last chapter I laid out a rationale for resisting hegemony through openly adopting and naming feminized practices—even if these look like institutionalized inefficiency. I acknowledge that this is more than a "modest proposal." But its seeming boldness is intentional.

The reasons for the preponderance of white, middle to upper class, female teachers have been alternately attributed to the effects of civil rights and labor movements leading to other, higher earning and higher status avenues of work for people of color and the working classes (this leaves out why the feminist movement made more women teachers, not less). However still others, like Barbara Holmes (1986, 1989), who suggested over twenty years ago that the other professions are not glutted with people of color, that our universities are not granting degrees in areas of practice to huge numbers of people of color (and, I would argue, working class people)—rather, she suggests, and others agree, it is the fruits of restricted historical educational access combined with increasingly expensive and difficult licensure tests and pathetic attempts at recruiting a diverse student base that is whiting out the teaching cadre and putting all students at a marked disadvantage. For the white women who do dominate the field of preparation, even their diversity—epistemological, gender identity or sexual expression, linguistic, political, and so forth—is being similarly controlled for and weeded out. Preservice teachers (and teacher educators, for that matter) are individuals, but the pressure to become more homogenous is overwhelming. This is a function of the institutional (one possible cost of "proficiency") focus on impression management and ultimately, a pastoral kind of control. It begins with something as simple as the taming of the labile student in reductionist ways—the dress code, which is really about sexuality; the standardized syllabus and the primacy of forms and worksheets that compartmentalize and tabulate the experience of teaching and learning. The hidden curriculum of homogenization, the cult of impression management and perfect performance, and goal displacement derived from obsessive rule-following purges all but the least transgressive from our midst.

There is a connection and mutually reinforcing relationship between dominant group (and in that respect, raced and classed) girl culture and the world of work; this is only amplified in the realm of the feminized professions, and within these, teaching in particular. As Massoni (2004) found, the media outlets for adolescent and immediately postadolescent girls are saturated with messages about work, self, and gender identity. These messages, directed as they are at mostly white girls and women, wholly and completely reinforce the dominance of Mahalik et al.'s (2005) Western feminine norms, including compulsory heterosexuality, but also the idea that men are the primary workers in the world. Complicit in that is the message that for women, a job is never just a job—it is a route to something else; a placeholder for marriage and family, an occupation designed to attract desirable males, and so on. Writes Massoni, in contemporary girl culture, the underlying ideology of work is not about work:

> Superficially, there is some liberatory rhetoric about women's power, positions, and possibilities. Read more closely, however, the real (and enduring) story is about women claiming temporary positions of power until the possibility of hetero attachment supersedes them. The hierarchy of prestige is clear: An entertainment job is more important than a journalist job—but a date trumps them both. In the occupational world of *Seventeen* [or other teen and post-adolescent media], Prince Charming still exists as the ultimate goal. (2004, p. 58)

As so many study participants admitted, they wanted jobs that were compatible with marriage and family, and teaching fit the bill. That they felt that such beliefs were somehow taboo in talking to me—that they admitted these strategies only under their breath—also sends a message about the contradictions inherent in their experience of girl culture. While Massoni found that the presence of liberatory rhetoric about women's power and career identity relatively transient, in the experience of my participants, it served as a carefully constructed "cover story" (Clandinin & Connelly, 1996) that they were reluctant to expose to outsiders. As a former teacher, and someone working in teacher education, for some participants I constituted an insider, and I could be privy to the unmasking of the cover story—which usually was a careful orchestration (Bakhtin, 1981) of teacher education ideologies about teaching as a critical, transformative and activist orientation and career. This is very different than teaching as a pragmatic choice for those who knew that their valued identity hinged, at least in part, on the ability to secure marriage and motherhood while also making a professional life possible. In one way, it's a very smart strategy if you're white, middle class, and heterosexual (opting out is simply not portrayed as a choice in its racist, classist depictions of women of color and working class women). There are very few negative implications in popular girl culture for "opting out"—meaning, educated women leaving career paths to become mothers in the home—so it is a choice that does not significantly compromise (and may even boost) the valued identity and eventual moral career. It may even be compatible with teaching, as the moral career of a primary teacher may include opting out as a desirable coda. However, despite its language, which co-opts the feminist discourse of choice and autonomy (Kuperberg & Stone, 2008), media images of opting out are not without complications and contradictions. For example, the media sources they reviewed were rife with the contradiction that the powerful high-wage-earning woman with high status employment who gives up employment without considering of the loss of income to her family must assume the existence of an unseen, typically male, breadwinner to offset that loss. Additionally, the entire package associated with opting out assumes that all women will and should find almost total fulfillment in motherhood. While 100 percent of my sample of preservice teachers scored very highly in the CFNI "likes children" areas, "liking children" and being at home with children all day every day may not be the same thing. However, for teachers, like for most young, white, middle class women in popular US culture, admitting indifference or even uncertainty about eventual motherhood, is taboo, and calls their valued identities and moral careers into the risk zone. I think back to the Spanish church and its stone women—the Wise and Foolish Virgins, either crippled in their grief or smug in their reward—and I wonder about the ability of either to really imagine a world beyond the bridal party in a culture permeated with that particular reward-and-punishment trope. Asking individuals to assume an identity of "Wise Fool" as I discussed in chapter 8 is asking a lot of a group of people already accustomed to working and living with contradiction.

While Kuperberg and Stone found that the media images included child-centric familial orientations that translate very nicely from the child-centered care and love world of the fantasy classroom, questions still remain about those of us who leave teaching to become teacher educators. The ideologies of selfless love and care, and filial piety to patriarchal institutions, is unchanging, but in leaving the K–12 universe do we lose, potentially, some of the flexibility to have our proverbial (and patriarchal) cake and eat it too? At what point did we give up on the easy segue from caring for others' children to marrying and raising our own? And, if what many suggest, that the scales fell from our eyes and we realized the truth of the "cover story" and left to advance our careers in PhD programs, how is it that we actually perpetuate this girl culture in the predominantly white, middle class universe of preservice teacher development? I know this is a lot of questions—especially at the conclusion of an argument. But so many of us are, even in middle age and beyond, participants in that same girl culture, and that problematic reality is certainly not going anywhere. We have no choice but to attempt to turn hegemony on its ear, to be "Wise Fools" and to act accordingly.

Bibliography

Abramson, L. (2010, June 2). In teacher layoffs, seniority rules. But should it? *National Public Radio*. Retrieved July 10, 2010, from http://www.npr.org/templates/story/story .php?storyId=127373157.

Acker, S. (1995). Gender and teachers' work. *Review of Research in Education, 21,* 99–162.

Anderson, D. S. & Piazza, J. A. (1996): Teaching and learning mathematics in constructivist preservice classrooms. *Action in Teacher Education 18* (2), 51–62.

Anzaldua, G. (1987). *Borderlands/La Frontera: The new Mestiza.* San Francisco: Aunt Lute Books.

Aronson, P. (2003). Feminists or "post-feminists?" Young women's attitudes toward feminism and gender relations. *Gender and Society, 17,* 903–22.

Asakawa, K., Hektner, J., & Schmidt, J. (2000). Envisioning the future. In M. Csikszentmihalyi & B. Schneider, *Becoming adult: How teenagers prepare for the world of work* (pp. 39–64). New York: Basic Books.

Bakhtin, M. M. (1981). *The dialogic imagination: Four essays.* Austin, TX: University of Texas Press.

Banerjee, N. (2008, May 19). Dancing the night away, with a higher purpose. *New York Times.* Retrieved January 5, 2010, from http://www.nytimes.com/2008/05/19/us/19purity .html?_r=1&partner=rssnyt&emc=rss.

Battenhouse, R. (1975). Falstaff as parodist and perhaps holy fool. *PMLA, 90*(1), 32–52.

Bauer, J. M. (1998). Indecent proposals: Teachers in the movies. *College English, 60*(3), 301–17.

Baumgartener, J. (2007, January). Would you pledge your virginity to your father? *Glamour,* p. 6.

Bearman, P. S., & Bruckner, H. (2001). Promising the future: Virginity pledges and first intercourse. *The American Journal of Sociology, 106*(4), 859–912.

Becker. B. (2009, Dec. 5). Troops finding new service as teachers. *The New York Times*, A38.

Beggs, C. S. (2005, March 21). Fashion takes a vow of chastity. *Fox News*. Retrieved March 16, 2010, from http://www.foxnews.com/story/0,2933,150968,00.html.

Beijaard, D., Meijer, P. C., & Verloop, N. (2004). Reconsidering research on teachers' professional identity. *Teaching and Teacher Education, 20*, 107–28.

Bennett, W. S., & Hokenstad, M. C., Jr. (1975). Full-time people workers and conceptions of the "professional." In, Harris, A., Lawn, M. & Prescott, W., (Eds.), *Curriculum Innovation*. New York: Taylor and Francis.

Berliner, D. C. (2000). A personal response to those who bash teacher education. *Journal of Teacher Education 51*, 358–71.

Bersamin, M. M., Walker, S., Waiters, E. D., Fisher, D. A., & Grube, J. W. (2005). Promising to wait: Virginity pledge and adolescent sexual behavior. *Journal of Adolescent Health 36*(5), 428–43.

Boler, M. (1999). *Feeling power: Education and emotions*. New York: Routledge.

Borko, H., Stecher, B., & Kuffner, K. L. (2007). Using artifacts to characterize reform-oriented instruction: The Scoop Notebook and Rating Guide. CSE Technical Report 707. UCLA National Center for Research on Evaluation, Standards and Student Testing.

Borman, K. M. (1991). *The first "real" job: A study of young workers*. Albany: SUNY Press.

Bourdieu, P. (1977). *Reproduction in education, society and culture*. Nice, R. (Trans.). London: Sage.

Boyd, D., Grossman, P. L., Hammerness, K., Lankford, R. H., Loeb, S., McDonald, M. Reininger, M., Ronfeldt, M., & Wyckoff, J. (2008). Surveying the landscape of teacher education in New York City: Constrained variation and the challenge of innovation. *Educational Evaluation and Policy Analysis 30*(4), 319–43.

Brannon, L. (1993). M[other]: Lives on the outside. *Written Communication 10*, 457–65.

Brooks, R. (Director), & Fields, F. (Producer). (1977). *Looking for Mr. Goodbar* [DVD]. US: Paramount Pictures.

Brumberg, J. J. (2002). Introduction. In L. Greenfield, *Girl culture* (p. 5). San Francisco: Chronicle Books.

Bruner, J. S. (1991). *Acts of meaning*. Cambridge, MA: Cambridge University Press.

Bruner, J. S. (1993). Explaining and interpreting: Two ways of using mind. In G. Harman (Ed.), *Conceptions of the human mind: Essays in honor of George A. Miller* (pp. 123–37). Hillsdale, NJ: Lawrence Erlbaum.

Campbell, S. A. (2005). *Ariadne's thread: Pre-service teachers, stories and identities in teacher education*. Unpublished Doctoral Dissertation. University of Colorado at Boulder.

Campbelljones, B. M. (2002). *Against the stream: White men who act in ways to eradicate racism and white privilege and entitlement.* Unpublished doctoral dissertation, Claremont Graduate University: Claremont, CA.

Carpenter, A. (2000). *An ethnographic study of preservice teacher resistance to multiculturalism: Implications for teaching.* New Jersey, ERIC Document Reproduction No. ED 446 044.

Carrington, B., & McPhee, A. (2008). Boys' "underachievement" and the feminization of teaching. *Journal of Education for Teaching 34*(2), 109–20.

Case, K. A., & Hemmings, A. (2005). Distancing strategies: White women preservice teachers and antiracist curriculum. *Urban Education 40*(6), 606–26.

Chalfen, R. (1998). Interpreting family photography as pictorial communication. In J. Prosser (Ed.). *Image-Based Research.* London: Falmer Press.

Chandler, M. A. (2009, July 31). Business is brisk for teacher training alternatives. *The Washington Post,* B25.

Chang, D. B. K. (1989). An abused spouse's self-saving process: A theory of identity transformation. *Social Perspectives 32*(4), 535–50.

Chizhik, E. W. (2003). Reflecting on the challenges of preparing suburban teachers for urban schools. *Education and Urban Society 35*(4), 443–61.

Clandinin, D. J., & Connelly, F. M. (1996). Teachers' professional knowledge landscapes: Teacher stories—stories of teachers, school stories—stories of school. *Educational Researcher 25*(5), 2–14.

Cole, A. L. (1999). Teacher educators and teacher education reform: Individual commitments, institutional realities. *Canadian Journal of Education, 24*(3), 281–95.

Connell, R. W. (1987). *Gender and power.* Palo Alto, CA: Stanford University Press.

Connell, R. W. (1995). *Masculinities.* Cambridge: Polity Press.

Connell, R., & Messerschmidt, J. (2005). Hegemonic masculinity: Rethinking the concept. *Gender & Society 19*(6), 829–59.

Coppola, F. F. (Director/Producer), & Fuchs, F. (Producer). (1996). *Jack* [DVD]. US: Hollywood Pictures.

Cornbleth, C. (2008). *Diversity and the new teacher: Learning from experience in urban schools.* New York: Teachers College Press.

Cortina, R., & San Roman, S. (Eds.) (2006). *Women and Teaching: Global Perspectives on the Feminization of a Profession.* New York: Palgrave Macmillan.

Cresson, J. (Producer), Fryer, R. (Producer), & Neame, R. (Director). (1969). *The prime of Miss Jean Brodie* [DVD]. UK: 20th Century Fox.

Csikzentimihalyi, M., & Schneider, B. (2000). *Becoming adult: How teenagers prepare for the world of work.* New York: Basic Books.

Dahl, R. (1988). *Matilda.* New York: Viking Kestrel.

Dale, M. (2004). Tales in and out of school. In D. L. Liston & J. Garrison (Eds.), *Teaching, learning and loving: Reclaiming passion in educational practice* (pp. 62–81). New York: Routledge Falmer.

Darling-Hammond, L., MacDonald, M. B., Snyder, J. W., Whitford, B. L., Ruscoe, G., & Fickel, L. (2000). *Studies of excellence in teacher education: Preparation at the graduate level.* New York: American Association of Colleges of Teacher Education (AACTE) Publications.

Delamont, S. (2002). *Fieldwork in educational settings: Methods, pitfalls and perspectives.* London: Routledge Falmer.

deMarrais, K. B., & LeCompte, M. D. (1998). *The way schools work: A sociological analysis of education* (2nd ed.). White Plains, NY: Longman Publishers.

De Vito, D. (Director/Producer) (1996). *Matilda* [DVD]. California, USA: Whittier Pictures.

Douglas, S. J. (2010). *Enlightened sexism: The seductive message that feminism's work is done.* New York: Times Books.

Downing, N., & Roush, K. (1985). From passive acceptance to active commitment: A model of feminist identity development for women. *Counseling Psychologist 13,* 695–709.

Drudy, S., Martin, M., Woods, M., & O'Flynn, J. (2005). *Men and the classroom: Gender imbalances in teaching.* New York: Routledge.

Duncan, A. (2009). Teacher Preparation: Reforming the Uncertain Profession— Remarks of Secretary Arne Duncan at Teachers College, Columbia University, October 22, 2009.

Ducharme, E., & Agne, R. (1982). The educational professoriate: A research based perspective. *Journal of Teacher Education 33*(6), 30–36.

Duncan-Andrade, J. (2006). Utilizing cariño in the development of research methodologies. In J. Kincheloe, P. Anderson, K. Rose, D. Griffith & K. Hayes (Eds.), *Urban education: An encyclopedia* (pp. 451–86). Westport, CT: Greenwood Publishing.

Dunkin, M. J., Precians, R. P. & Nettle, E. B. (1994.) Effects of formal teacher education upon student teachers' cognitions regarding teaching. *Teaching & Teacher Education,* 10(4), 395–408.

Dworkin, A. G. (1987). *Teacher burnout in the public schools: Structural causes and consequences for children.* Albany, NY: State University of New York Press.

Ellis, C., & Bochner, A. P. (2000). Autoethnography, personal narrative, reflexivity: Researcher as subject. In N. Denzin and Y. Lincoln (Eds.), *The Handbook of Qualitative Research,* pp. 733–768 (2nd ed.). Thousand Oaks, CA: Sage.

Etzioni, A. (1969). *The semi-professions and their organization: Teachers, nurses, and social workers.* New York: The Free Press.

Fairclough, N. (1995) *Critical discourse analysis. The critical study of language.* New York: Longman.

Faludi, S. (1992). *Backlash: The undeclared war against American women.* New York: Three Rivers Press.

Farber, S. (1969) The prime of Miss Jean Brodie [Review]. *Film Quarterly,* 22(3), 62–63.

Fine, M., Weis, L., Powell, L. C., & Wong, L. M. (Eds.). (1997). *Off white: Readings on race, power and society.* New York: Routledge.

Florio-Ruane, S., & Lensmire,T . J. (1990). Transforming future teachers' ideas about writing instruction. *Journal of Curriculum Studies 22*, 277–89.

Fox News (May 27, 2009). *Rove's report card: Supreme court nominee Sotomayor.* Retrieved June 4, 2010 from http://www.foxnews.com/story/0,2933,522160,00.html.

Fried, R. (1999). *The passionate teacher.* Boston: Beacon Press.

Fuller, M. L. (1992). Teacher education programs and increasing minority school populations: An educational mismatch? In C. A. Grant (Ed.), *Research and multicultural education: From the margins to the mainstream* (pp. 184–200). London: Falmer.

Galman, S. A. C. (2006). Rich white girls: Developing critical identities in teacher education and novice teaching settings. *International Journal of Learning 13*, 3–13.

Galman, S. A. C. (2009a). Doth the lady protest too much? Pre-service teachers, identity and the experience of dissonance as a catalyst for development. *Teaching and Teacher Education 25*(3), 468–81.

Galman, S. (2010) Princesses and passengers: Some thoughts on pre-service elementary teachers and contemporary US girl culture. *Gender and Education Association Newsletter* July, 2010 (4–5).

Galman, S. (2009b). The truthful messenger: Visual methods and representation in qualitative research in education. *Qualitative Research 9*(197), 197–217.

Galman, S., Pica-Smith, C., & Rosenberger, C. (2010). Aggressive and tender navigations: Teacher educators confront whiteness in their practice. *Journal of Teacher Education*, 61 (3), 225–36.

Garner, D. M. (1991). *Eating disorder inventory—2 manual.* Odessa, FL: Psychological Assessment Resources.

Gee, J. (1999). *An introduction to discourse analysis: Theory and method.* New York: Routledge.

Gee, J. P., Hull, G., & Lankshear, C. (1997). *The new work order: Behind the language of the new capitalism.* New York: Westview.

Gibbs, N. (2008, July 17). The pursuit of teen girl purity. *Time Magazine.* Retrieved on June 4, 2010, from http://www.time.com/time/magazine/article/0,9171,1823930,00.html.

Ginsburg, M. (1995). *The politics of educators' work and lives.* New York: Garland.

Glaser, B. G., & Strauss, A. L. (1965). *Awareness of dying.* Chicago: Aldine.

Glazer-Raymo, J. (1991). The fragmented paradigm: Women, tenure and schools of education. In W. G. Tierney (Ed.), *Rethinking Roles and Rewards for the Twenty-First Century*, pp. 169–88. Albany: State University of New York Press.

Glazer-Raymo, J. (2001). *Shattering the myths: Women in academe.* Baltimore: Johns Hopkins University Press.

Goetz, J. P., & LeCompte, M. D. (1978, November). *Data crunching: Techniques for analyzing field note data.* Paper presented at the Conference on Educational Evaluation, American Anthropological Association, Los Angeles, CA.

Goffman, E. (1959). *The presentation of self in everyday life.* Garden City, NY: Doubleday.

Goffman, E. (1963). *Stigma: Notes on the management of spoiled identity*. New York: J. Aronson.

Goffman, E. (1967). *Interaction ritual: Essays on face-to-face behavior*. New York: Doubleday Anchor.

Goffman, E. (1968). *Asylums: Essays on the social situation of mental patients and other inmates*. Harmondsworth: Penguin.

Goodlad, J. (1984). *A place called school: Prospects for the future*. New York: McGraw Hill.

Goodlad, J. (1990). *Teachers for our nation's schools*. San Francisco: Jossey-Bass.

Gordon, T. (1992). Citizens and others: Gender, democracy and education. *International Studies in Sociology of Education*, 2, 43–56.

Grant, C. A., & Gillette, M. (1987). The Holmes Report and minorities in education. *Social Education 51*, 517–21.

Greenfield, L. (2002). *Girl culture*. San Francisco: Chronicle Books.

Greenhouse, S. (Sept. 18, 2009). Recession drives women back to the work force. *The New York Times*, B1.

Greer, G. (1993). *The change: Women, aging and menopause*. New York: Ballantine Books.

Griffin, P. (1998). *Strong women, deep closets—lesbians and homophobia in sport*. Champaign, IL: Human Kinetics.

Griffiths, M. (2006). The feminization of teaching and the practice of teaching: Threat or opportunity. *Educational Theory 56*(4), 387–405.

Grumet, M. R. (1988). *Bitter milk: Women and teaching*. Amherst: University of Massachusetts Press.

Guba, E. G. (1981). Critique for assessing the trustworthiness of naturalistic inquiries. *ERIC/ECTJ Annual Review 29*(2), 75–91.

Hall, D. E. (1996). *Fixing patriarchy: Feminism and mid-Victorian male novelists*. Houndsmills, UK: Macmillan.

Hall, E. J., & Rodriguez, M. S. (2003). The myth of postfeminism. *Gender and Society 17*(6), 878–902.

Haynes, V. S. (2008, March 27). Teachers expect early-retirement offers: Schools could lose hundreds of experienced employees, union president says. *Washington Post*. Retrieved June 3, 2010, from http://www.washingtonpost.com/wp dyn/content/article/2008/03/ 26/AR2008032602948.html.

Hellman, L. (1934). *The children's hour*. New York: Alfred A. Knopf.

Henson, K. D., & Rogers, J. K. (2001). "Why Marcia, you've changed!" Male clerical temporary workers doing masculinity in a feminized profession. *Gender and Society 15*(2), 218–38.

Heshusius, L. (1993). *Methodological concerns around subjectivity: Will we free ourselves from objectivity?* Keynote Address, Qualitative Research in Education Conference, College of Education, University of Georgia, October 6–10.

Hill, M. H. (1998). Teen fathers learn the power of literacy for their children. *Journal of Adolescent and Adult Literacy 42*(3), 196–202.

Hirakata, P. E., & Daniluk, J. C. (2009). Swimming upstream: The experience of academic mothers of young children. *Canadian Journal of Counseling 43*(4), 283–94.

Hoff-Sommers, C. (2000). *The war against boys: How misguided feminism is harming our young men.* New York: Simon and Schuster.

Hoffman, N. (2003). *Woman's "true" profession: Voices from the history of teaching.* Cambridge, MA: Harvard Education Press.

Holland, D. C., & Eisenhart, M. (1990). *Educated in romance: Women, achievement and college culture.* Chicago: University of Chicago Press.

Hollins, E. R., & Guzman, M. T. (2005). Research on preparing teachers for diverse populations. In M. Cochran-Smith & K. M. Zeichner (Eds.). *Studying teacher education: the report of the AERA panel on research and teacher education.* (pp. 477–548) Mahwah, NJ: Erlbaum.

Holloway, D. (2000). *Authoring identity and agency in the arts.* Unpublished doctoral Dissertation. Boulder, CO: University of Colorado at Boulder.

Holmes, B. J. (1986). Do not buy the conventional wisdom: Minority teachers can pass the test. *The Journal of Negro Education 55*(3), 335–46.

Holmes, B. J. (1989). A closer look at the shortage of minority teachers. *Education Week* 29.

hooks, b. (1994). *Outlaw Culture.* New York: Routledge.

Intrator, S. (2000). *Stories of the courage to teach: Honoring the teacher's heart.* San Francisco: Jossey-Bass.

Jackson, J., & O'Callaghan, E. M. (2009). What do we know about glass ceiling effects? A taxonomy and critical review to inform higher education research. *Research in Higher Education 50*(5), 460–82.

Jacobson, J. (2004). A liberal professor fights a label. *The Chronicle of Higher Education 51*(4), A8.

Jong, E. (2003). *Fear of flying.* New York: New American Library.

Judge, H. (1982). *American graduate schools of education: A report to the Ford Foundation.* New York: Ford Foundation Office of Reports.

Judge, H. (1995). The images of teachers. *Oxford Review of Education 21*(3), 253–65.

Kagan, D. M. (1992). Professional growth among preservice and beginning teachers. *Review of Educational Research, 62*(2), 129–69.

Kipling, R. (1999). *The collected poems of Rudyard Kipling.* London: Bibliophile Books.

Klingner, J. K. (2004). Personal communication.

Krasnow, I. (1997). *Surrendering to motherhood: Losing your mind, finding your soul.* New York: Hyperion.

Kuperberg, A., & Stone, P. (2008). The media depiction of women who opt out. *Gender and Society 22*(4), 497–517.

Labaree, D. (2004). The trouble with ed schools. New Haven, CT: Yale University.

Ladson-Billings, G. (1989). A tale of two teachers: Exemplars of successful pedagogy for Black students. Paper presented at the tenth Educational Equality Project Colloquium, "Celebrating diversity: Knowledge, teachers, and teaching," The College Board, May 5, 1989, New York.

Lanier, J., & Little, J. (1986). Research on teacher education. In M. Wittrock, (Ed.), *Handbook of Research on Teaching*. (pp. 527–69). New York: Macmillan.

LeCompte, M. D. (2002). The transformation of ethnographic practice: Past and current challenges. *Qualitative Research (2)*3.

LeCompte, M. D., & Dworkin, A. G. (1991). *Giving up on school: Student dropouts and teacher burnouts*. Newbury Park, CA: Corwin Press.

LeCompte, M. D. & Goetz, J. (1982) Problems of reliability and validity in ethnographic research, *Review of Educational Research*, 52(1), 31–60.

LeCompte, M. D. & Preissle, J. (1993). *Ethnography and qualitative design in educational research*. (2nd ed.) New York: Harcourt Brace.

LeCompte, M. D. & Schensul, J. J. (1999). *Analyzing and Interpreting Ethnographic Data*. In: Schensul, J. J. & LeCompte, M. D., eds. *Ethnographer's Toolkit*, Vol. 5. Walnut Creek, CA: Altamira Press.

LeCompte, M. D., Schensul, J. J., Weeks, M. R. & Singer, M. (1999). Researcher Roles & Research Partnerships. In: Schensul, J. J. & LeCompte, M.D., eds. *Ethnographer's Toolkit*, Vol. 6. Walnut Creek, CA: Altamira Press.

Lewis, T. (1993). Defending children against fairy tales. *The Hudson Review* 46(2), 403–408.

Lincoln, Y. S., & Guba, E. G. (1985). *Naturalistic inquiry*. Beverly Hills, CA: Sage.

Liston, D. P. (1995). Work in teacher education: A current assessment of U.S. teacher education. In N. Shimahara & I. Holowinsky (Eds.), *Teacher education in industrialized nations*. (pp. 87–123). New York: Garland Publishing.

Liston, D. P. (2000). Love and despair in teaching. *Educational Theory* 50(1), 81–102.

Liston, D. P., & Garrison, J. (2004). Introduction. In Liston, D. P. & Garrison, J., (Eds.), *Teaching, learning and loving: Reclaiming passion in educational practice*, (pp. 1–20) New York, London: RoutledgeFalmer.

Lortie, D. (1972). *Schoolteacher: A sociological study*. Chicago: University of Chicago Press.

Luttrell, W. (1993). The teachers, they all had their pets: Concepts of gender, knowledge and power. *Journal of Women in Culture and Society* 18(3), 505–46.

Magolda, P., & Ebben, K. (2007). Students serving Christ: Understanding the role of student subcultures on a college campus. *Anthropology and Education Quarterly* 38(2), 138–58.

Mahalik, J. R., Morray, E. B., Coonerty-Femiano, A., Ludlow, L. H., Slattery, S. M., & Smiler, A. (2005). Development of the conformity to feminine norms inventory. *Sex Roles* 52(7/8), 417–35.

Mannes, M. (1964). *But will it sell?* Philadelphia, PA: Lippincott.

Massoni, K. (2004). Modeling work: Occupational messages in *Seventeen Magazine*. *Gender and Society* 18(1), 47–65.

Mazzei, L. (1997). Inhabited silences in feminist poststructural inquiry. Paper presented at the Annual Meeting of the American Education Research Association. Chicago, Illinois, March 10–15.

McCabe, J. (2005). What's in a label? The relationship between feminist self-identification and 'feminist' attitudes among U.S. women and men. *Gender & Society*, 19(4), 480–505.

McCall, A. L. (1995). Constructing conceptions of multicultural teaching: Preservice teachers' life experiences and teacher education. *Journal of Teacher Education* 46(5), 340–50.

McCullick, B., Belcher, D., Hardin, B., & Hardin, M. (2003). Butches, bullies and buffoons: Images of physical education teachers in the movies. *Sport, Education and Society*, 8, 3–16.

McGurn, W. (2010, July 27). Giving lousy teachers the boot: Michelle Rhee does the once unthinkable in Washington. *Wall Street Journal*. Retrieved August 1, 2010, from http://online.wsj.com/article/SB1000142405274870370090457539147120958 2034.html?mod=googlenews_wsj.

McWilliam, E. (1996). Seductress or schoolmarm: On the improbability of the great female teacher. *Interchange* (27)11, 1–11.

Mead, G. H. (1934). *Mind, self and society: From the standpoint of a social behaviorist*. Chicago: University of Chicago Press.

Meiners, E. R. (2002). Disengaging from the legacy of Lady Bountiful in teacher education classrooms. *Gender and Education* 14(1), 85–94.

Merriam, S. B. (1998). *Qualitative research and case study applications in education*. San Francisco: Jossey-Bass.

Merrigan, T. W., & White, W. N. (2010, April 14). Harvard Business School grapples with gender imbalance: Current and former female faculty members allude to 'unconscious bias' against women at school. *Harvard Crimson*. Retrieved July 2010, from http://www.thecrimson.com/article/2010/4/14/faculty-school-business-women/.

Meyer, S. (2006). *Twilight*. New York: Little, Brown and Company.

Meyers, D. T. (2001). The rush to motherhood: Pronatalist discourse and women's autonomy. *Signs* 26(3), 735–73.

Miles, M. B., & Huberman, A. M. (1994). *An expanded sourcebook: Qualitative data analysis* (2nd ed.). Thousand Oaks, CA: Sage.

Mills, M., Martino, W., & Lingard, B. (2004). Attracting, recruiting and retaining male teachers: Policy issues in the male teacher debate. *British Journal of Sociology of Education* 25(3), 355–69.

Mishler, E. G. (1990). Validation in inquiry-guided research: The role of exemplars in narrative research. *Harvard Educational Review* 60, 415–42.

Montero-Sieburth, M. & Perez, M. (1987). Echar pa'lante, moving onward: The dilemmas and strategies of a bilingual teacher. *Anthropology and Education Quarterly* 18(3), 180–89.

Monzo, L. D., & Rueda, R. S. (2001). Professional roles, caring, and scaffolds: Latino teachers' and paraeducators' interactions with Latino students. *American Journal of Education* 109(4), 438–71.

Morales, R. (2000). Effects of teacher preparation experiences and students' perceptions related to developmentally and culturally appropriate practices. *Action in Teacher Education* 22(2), 67–75.

Munby, H. (1982). The place of teachers' beliefs in research on teacher thinking and decision making, and an alternative methodology. *Instructional Science* 1(1), 201–25.

Munby, H. (1984). A qualitative approach to the study of a teacher's beliefs. *Journal of Research in Science Teaching* 21, 27–38.

Munby, H. (1986). Metaphors in the thinking of teachers: An exploratory study. *Journal of Curriculum Studies* 18, 197–206.

Munby, H. (1987). Metaphor and teachers' knowledge. *Research in the Teaching of English* 21, 377–85.

Nail, P. R., & McGregor, I. (2009). Conservative shifts among liberals and conservatives following 9/11/01. *Social Justice Research* 22(2–3), 231–40.

National Council on Teacher Quality. (2010). *Teacher layoffs: Rethinking last hired, first fired policies.* Washington, DC: National Council on Teacher Quality.

Nespor, J. (1987). The role of beliefs in the practice of teaching. *Journal of Curriculum Studies* 19, 317–28.

Neuhouser, K. (1998). "If I had abandoned my children": Community mobilization and commitment to the identity of mother in northeast Brazil. *Social Forces* 77(1), 331–58.

Noddings, N. (1984). *Caring: A feminine approach to ethics and moral education.* Berkeley: University of California Press.

Noddings, N. (1990). Feminist critiques in the professions. *Review of Research in Education*, 16, 393–424.

Norris, N. (1997). Error, bias and validity in qualitative research. *Education Action Research*, 5(1), 172–76.

Nussbaum, M. C. (1995). *Poetic justice: The literary imagination and public life.* Boston: Beacon Press.

O'Callaghan, E. M. (2009). Unintended consequences: Considering sex-based discrimination in the tenure process. Lecture delivered to the University of Nebraska Women in Educational Leadership Conference, Lincoln, Nebraska, October 10–11.

Okopny, C. (2008). Why Jimmy isn't failing: The myth of the boy crisis. *Feminist Teacher* 18(3), 216–28.

Palmer, P. (1998). *The courage to teach: Exploring the inner landscape of a teacher's life.* San Francisco: Jossey-Bass.

Pang, V. O., & Gibson, R. (2001). Concepts of democracy and citizenship: Views on African-American teachers. *The Social Studies* 92, 260–66.

Pajares, M. (1992). Teachers' beliefs and educational research: Cleaning up a messy construct. *Review of Educational Research* 3, 307–32.

Patton, M. Q. (1987). *How to use qualitative methods in evaluation.* Newbury Park, CA: Sage.

Peshkin, A. (1988). In search of subjectivity—one's own. *Educational Researcher* (*17*)1, 17–21.

Pinnegar, S. (1998). Introduction to methodology. In M. Hamilton (Ed.), *Reconceptualizing teacher education* (pp. 31–33). London: Falmer.

Pohan, C. A. (1996). Preservice teachers' beliefs about diversity: Uncovering factors leading to multicultural responsiveness. *Equity and Excellence in Education* 29(3), 62–69.

Reynolds, E. (2001). Learning the "hard" way: Boys, hegemonic masculinity and the negotiation of learner identities in the primary school. *British Journal of Sociology of Education* 22(3), 369–85.

Ringrose, J. (2007). Successful girls? Complicating post-feminist, neoliberal discourses of educational achievement and gender equality. *Gender and Education* 19(4), 476–489.

Rockwell, N. (1956). *Teacher's surprise* [Painting]. Retrieved from Norman Rockwell Museum online database June 2010, http://www.nrm.org/.

Sadker, D., & Sadker, M. (1994). *Failing at fairness: How America's schools cheat girls.* New York: Scribner.

Saffold, F., & Longwell-Grice, H. (2008). White women preparing to teach in urban schools: Looking for similarity and finding difference. *Issues and Ideas in Public Education* 40(2), 186–209.

Schutz, A. (2004). Rethinking domination and resistance: Challenging postmodernism. *Educational Researcher* 33(1), 15–23.

Seidman, I. (1998). *Interviewing as qualitative research: A guide for researchers in education and the social sciences* (2nd ed.). New York: Teachers College Press.

Seyaki, D. (2003). Aesthetic resistance to commercial influences: The impact of the Eurocentric beauty standard on Black college women. *The Journal of Negro Education* 72(4), 467–77.

Shannon, V. (2010). Equal rights for women? Survey says: Yes, but . . . The *International Herald Tribune.* Retrieved July 8, 2010 from http://www.nytimes.com/2010/07/01/world/01iht-poll.html?ref=thefemalefactor.

Shrecker, E. (2006, February 10). Worse than McCarthy. *The Chronicle of Higher Education* 52(23) B20.

Silver, L. R. (1988). Deference to authority in the feminized professions. *School Library Journal* 24(5), 21–27.

Simpson, R. L., & Simpson, I. H. (1969). Women and bureaucracy in the semi-professions. In A. Etzioni (Ed.), *The Semi-Professions and Their Organization: Teachers, Nurses and Social Workers.* (pp. 196–265) New York: The Free Press.

Skelton, C. (1997). Primary boys and hegemonic masculinities. *British Journal of Sociology of Education* 18(3), 349–69.

Sleeter, C. E. (2008). Preparing white teachers for diverse students. In M. Cochran-Smith, S. Feiman-Nemser, D. J. McIntyre, & K. E. Demers (Eds.), *Handbook of research on teacher education: Enduring questions in changing contexts* (pp. 94–106). New York: Routledge.

Smith, F., Hardman, F., & Higgins, S. (2007). Gender inequality in the primary classroom: Will interactive whiteboards help? *Gender and Education* 19(4), 455–69.

Spanbauer, J. M. (2009). Tenured faculty at colleges and universities in the United States: A de facto private membership club. *Forum on Public Policy Online* (2), 1–26.

Spradley, J. P. (1980). *Participant observation*. Fort Worth, TX: Harcourt.

Strauss, A., & Corbin, J. (1990). *Basics of qualitative research: Grounded theory procedures and techniques*. Newbury Park, CA: Sage.

Surber, J. P. (2010, February 7). Well, naturally we're liberal! *The Chronicle of Higher Education*. Retrieved June 7, 2010, from ProQuest Educational Journals (DOI 1961182061).

Suarez-Orozco, M. M. (2001). Globalization, immigration and education: The research agenda. *Harvard Education Review*, 71(3), 345–65.

Terkel, S. (1974). *Working: People talk about what they do all day and how they feel about what they do*. New York: Pantheon Books.

Timmons Flores, M. (2007). Navigating contradictory communities of practice in learning to teach for social justice. *Anthropology and Education Quarterly*, 38(4), 380–404.

Titus, J. J. (2000). Engaging student resistance to feminism: "How is this stuff going to make us better teachers?" *Gender & Education*, 12(1), 21–37.

Tokarczyk, M. M. (1988). Working class women as teachers. Retrieved from the ERIC Database, ED3024630.

Trotman, J. (2008). *Girls Becoming Teachers: An Historical Analysis of Western Australian Women Teachers, 1911–1940*. Amherst, NY: Cambria Press.

Tyack, D., & Hansot, E. (1988). Silence and policy talk: Historical puzzles about gender and education. *Educational Researcher* 17(3), 33–41.

Valenzuela, A. (1997). Mexican American youth and the politics of caring. In E. Long, (Ed.), *From sociology to cultural studies*, (322–50). London: Blackwell.

Valenzuela, A. (1999). *Subtractive Schooling: U.S.-Mexican Youth and the Politics of Caring*. New York: SUNY Press.

Vare, J. W. (1996). Gendered ideology: Voices of parent and practice in teacher education. *Anthropology and Education Quarterly*,26(3), 251–78.

Weber, S. J. (2005). The pedagogy of shoes: Clothing and the body in self-study. In C. Mitchell, & S. Weber, & K. O'Reilly-Scanlon, (Eds.), *Just who do we think we are: Methodologies for self-study* (pp. 13–21). London: Routledge Falmer.

Weber, S. & Mitchell, C. (1995). *That's funny, you don't look like a teacher! Interrogating images and identity in popular culture*. London: Falmer Press.

Weinstein, C. (1989). Teacher education students' perceptions of teaching. *Journal of Teacher Education* 40(2), 53–60.

Weis, L. (1988). Introduction. In L. Weis, P. Altbach, G. Kelly, H. Petrie, & S. Slaughter (Eds.), *Crisis in Teaching* (pp. 1–14). Albany: SUNY Press.

Whitehead, J. (1993) *The growth of educational knowledge: Creating your own living educational theories*. Bournemouth, UK: Hyde.

Williams, M. (2005). *The woman at the Washington Zoo: Writings on politics, family and fate.* New York: PublicAffairs.

Wolcott, H. F. (1981). Home and away: Personal contrasts in ethnographic style. In D. A. Messerschmidt (Ed.), *Anthropologists at home in North America: Methods and issues in the study of one's own society* (pp. 255–65). New York: Cambridge University Press.

Wolcott, H. (1994). *Transforming qualitative data: Description, analysis and interpretation.* Thousand Oaks, CA: Sage.

Yip, A. K. T. (1997). Attacking the attacker: Gay Christians talk back. *British Journal of Sociology, 48*(1), 113–27.

Zumwalt & Craig (2005). Teachers' characteristics: Research on the demographic profile. In M. Cochran-Smith & K. M. Zeichner (Eds.), *Studying teacher education: The report of the AERA panel on research and teacher education* (pp. 111–56). Mahwah, NJ: Erlbaum.

Index

~

About the Author

Sally Campbell Galman is a professor in the School of Education at the University of Massachusetts at Amherst. She teaches qualitative research methods and data analysis, childhood studies, visual art, and elementary methods courses to undergraduate and graduate students. She completed her PhD at the University of Colorado at Boulder in 2005. Her research interests center around the identity development and gendered experiences of pre-service and novice teachers working in diverse schools, particularly around their cognizance and treatment of the terrain of so-called "women's work," their feminized and/or feminist practices in the classroom and their developing ethical systems. Her research also explores the educative and political work of mothers of any gender, including teachers as cultural and social mothers, especially in cultures and communities where mothering is positioned as a political, even radical, act. She is currently co-chair of the Western Massachusetts Masculinities Working Group and the University of Massachusetts Status of Women Council. Dr. Galman was born in Japan and is a graduate of Punahou School in Honolulu, Hawaii and Grinnell College. Like her mother and grandmother before her, she has spent many years teaching little children. She is a former infant/toddler, preschool, and elementary school teacher, as well as an award-winning cartoonist and visual artist. Dr. Galman lives in rural Western Massachusetts with her partner, Matthew, and their three small children. You can follow her adventures here: blogs.umass.edu/sallyg/

CPSIA information can be obtained at www.ICGtesting.com
Printed in the USA
BVOW060640030412

286696BV00002B/2/P